D1211833

LITERARY MONOGRAPHS • *Volume 4*

LITERARY MONOGRAPHS

Volume 4

EDITED BY
Eric Rothstein

Published for the Department of English by

THE UNIVERSITY OF WISCONSIN PRESS
Madison, Milwaukee, and London 1971

Published 1971
The University of Wisconsin Press
Box 1379, Madison, Wisconsin 53701
The University of Wisconsin Press, Ltd.
27–29 Whitfield Street, London, W.1

First printing

Printed in the United States of America
The Heffernan Press Inc., Worcester, Mass.

ISBN 0–299–05860–3; LC 66–25869

Publication of this volume has been made possible in part by a gift to the University of Wisconsin Foundation from the estate of Beatrice T. Conrad, Davenport, ***Iowa.***

PREFACE

The Department of English of the University of Wisconsin continues with this volume a series of monographs in English and American literature. The series was inaugurated in 1967 to serve scholars whose work might take a form too lengthy for journals but too brief for a separate book.

For future volumes of *Literary Monographs* we invite works of high quality, scholarly or critical, that contribute to English or American literary studies. We welcome any promising contribution, from the United States or from abroad. We welcome not only conventional literary essays but also those involving experimental critical theories and methods whenever they are eloquent and persuasive. And we will be flexible enough to welcome monographs involving comparative literature or comparative aesthetics, so long as they significantly illuminate literature in English.

The editorial board of *Literary Monographs* would like to express its appreciation to the University of Wisconsin Foundation for making possible the publication of this volume through a gift from the estate of Beatrice T. Conrad, Davenport, Iowa.

Eric Rothstein

Madison, Wisconsin
August 1970

NOTES ON SUBMISSIONS

Manuscripts should be from 15,000 to 35,000 words in length. They should be submitted, with return postage and self-addressed envelope enclosed, to

The Editor
Literary Monographs
Department of English
University of Wisconsin
Madison, Wisconsin 53706

Manuscripts should follow the *MLA Style Sheet,* with a few exceptions or amplifications included in the specific instructions given below.

1. Paper should be 16-pound or 20-pound weight bond in normal quarto size; do not use highly glazed paper (sold under such trade names as "Corrasable"). To make satisfactory photocopying possible, the paper should be white and the typewriter ribbon black. Handwritten corrections may be made in pencil or washable ink; avoid ballpoint pen. Leave margins of 1 to 1½ inches on all sides.

2. Manuscripts should be double spaced throughout, including notes and all excerpts, prose or verse. Do not indent prose excerpts, but mark them with a pencil line along the left margin to the full length of the quotation and allow an extra line of space above and below.

3. Brief references should be inserted in the text (see *MLA Style Sheet,* Sec. 13*f*). In notes, first references should be cited in full. Succeeding references to books should use short titles rather than "*op. cit.*"; e.g., Taylor, *Problems,* p. 12. Short references to journal articles should use author's name, journal name, volume, and page; e.g., McKerrow, *RES,* XVI, 117.

As can be seen from this volume, *Literary Monographs* reserves the use of footnotes for information that is needed in order to follow the argument of the text or to understand a system of in-text citation. Endnotes supply documentation, or they may extend or parallel the text discussion. Contributors are requested to organize their manuscripts so that endnotes and footnotes are on separate pages, with separate numbering sequences.

CONTENTS

MYTHOS AND DIANOIA: A DIALECTICAL METHODOLOGY OF LITERARY FORM

Michael McCanles

For the tendency to maintain an existing condition impelleth every change of position.

Giordano Bruno, *On the Infinite Universe and Worlds*

It is my thesis that plot, considered in the Aristotelian manner as the ultimate principle of coherent form to which the other parts of a literary mimesis are subordinated as to their final cause, is generated out of the attempt on the part of the agent of the plot to avoid and deny plot. The logic which controls this generation of plot out of a "refusal" of plot is a dialectic, the forms of which are themselves various corollaries to the principle of noncontradiction. I shall show how the basic principles of this dialectic, characterized by their own abstract, immanent exigencies, illuminate the internal necessities which govern the disposition of the parts of any literary mimesis, insofar as this disposition grows out of a dialectical tension and interplay between the dianoia (or static informing meaning of the whole) of the work, and its mythos, its sequence of parts moving through time. This disposition of parts, its plot, will be seen as generated out of the drive of the agent within the work to achieve a perfect, univocal and "plotless" existence, resulting in the sequence of actions he both initiates and suffers by reason of this drive. The plot of a work is, in short, a dynamic dialectic which results from the attempt to avoid dialectic.

I am indebted for the basic terms of this essay to Northrop Frye's distinction between *mythos* and *dianoia:*

The word narrative or *mythos* conveys the sense of movement caught by the ear, and the word meaning or *dianoia* conveys, or at least preserves, the

> sense of simultaneity caught by the eye. We *listen to* the poem as it moves from beginning to end, but as soon as the whole of it is in our minds at once we "see" what it means. More exactly, this response is not simply to *the* whole *of* it, but to *a* whole *in* it: we have a vision of meaning or *dianoia* whenever any simultaneous apprehension is possible.
>
> The *mythos* is the *dianoia* in movement; the *dianoia* is the *mythos* in stasis. One reason we tend to think of literary symbolism solely in terms of meaning is that we have ordinarily no word for the *moving* body of imagery in a work of literature.[1]

This essay will attempt to extend this relation between static theme and dynamic plot in such a way as to show that not only do they mirror each other, but that they do so primarily *in opposition to* each other.

The disposition of a literary work—a lyric, a narrative, or a play—from the author's point of view is plot as an "action-made." As such, a work's form results from the author's employing and exploiting the partial and univocal divisiveness and discursion of language in the interests of creating a harmonic whole. Frye's description is most suitable to this perspective on the mythos-dianoia relationship. The ultimate principle of a work's organization of its parts, of its mythos or plot, is the informing idea which is, as it were, present everywhere and therefore visible nowhere as itself one of its parts. For the author, the conflicts, ambiguities, tensions which make up the work's plot "co-operate" by coalescing into a total statement of the work's dianoia.

But seen from a viewpoint taken within the work, from within the perspective of the agent, plot is "action-done," and here the relation between mythos and dianoia is reversed. The agent is usually the protagonist of a narrative or a drama, and the speaker or persona of a lyric. From his viewpoint, the mythos he generates—the action of a narrative or drama, the sequence of words in a lyric—results rather from his resistance to the total vision of his situation which is summed up in the dianoia. He struggles with an antagonist, whether this be another agent, the natural world, or the recalcitrant (because divisive and partial) univocality of words and their meanings; his goal is a monistic resolution of his predicament into a static harmony according to his own necessarily partial and incomplete categories of thought and motivation. "And they lived happily ever afterwards" is a rubric which sums up neatly the final escape from plot, from time, from discursion, and from dialectic. The point which I will be making over and over again in different forms is that, within the fiction, the agent finds himself involved in plot precisely because he refuses plot in the interests of this escape, and in doing so he acts and suffers in a mythos, the logic of which is the dianoia of this mythos, a logic which the agent is doomed to enact because he tries to refuse to enact it.

Plot as "action-made" (from the author's and audience's viewpoint) has as its informing principle and as its ultimate theme, the logic of dialectic summed up in the dianoia. Plot as "action-done" (from the agent's viewpoint) has this logic as its informing principle because this logic is refused. The logic of dialectic I shall present here has little to do with Hegel, and much to do with Kenneth Burke, whose work on literary form and dialectic in *The Philosophy of Literary Form* and *The Grammar of Motives* has provided me with some of the seminal insights this essay attempts to explore. The logic of dialectic is first a paradigm for all conflicts, and second a tool for the analysis of the disposition of parts which go to make up a whole. Dialectic occurs, whether within literature or out of it, when men attempt to put an either/or question to a both/and reality. The ultimate source of the question is the radical structure of human thinking governed by the principle of noncontradiction. Enforced with rigid and tyrannical urgency, this principle continually generates antinomies when it comes face-to-face with a world characterized by diversity and change. And when two partisans, both attempting to resolve a common both/and question according to the demands for an either/or answer, proceed to absolutize that part of the question which can be resolved according to noncontradiction, each invites the attack of his correlative opposite, who in turn moves to the attack under the sign of just those elements in the total question which the other had excluded. Since dialectic charts the logic of the actions that agents generate because they desire resolution according to the principle of noncontradiction, it will become clear how authors construct plots by building into their works principles and motivations which have as their goal just such resolutions. In literary works mythos or plot results from a refusal of the dialectic which is the work's dianoia. The dianoia becomes the work's informing principle and its thematic significance, because it names the total logic which comes to govern the plot insofar as that plot results from the agent's attempt, enforced by his partial and univocal view of his total predicament, to deny this dynamic dialectic in the interests of a static resolution.

To test this logic I have chosen examples of the lyric, narrative, and drama from the Renaissance, a period of English literature when the distinctions between these three modes were carefully observed, and which provides us with greatly realized embodiments of all three. As examples of dialectical plot in the lyric I will analyze some poems of John Donne, in narrative Milton's *Paradise Lost,* and in drama Shakespeare's *Macbeth* and Jonson's *Volpone.* In Donne's lyrics we will find the various personae demanding clear, conceptualizable, verbal formulations of human and divine mysteries, and thereby causing the dialectical mythoi of the lyrics precisely because the principle of noncontradiction which underlies these demands cannot be fulfilled except at the expense of paradoxical contradiction. One of the specific issues of *Paradise Lost* is the confrontation between a finite, sinful, discursive intelligence—the narrator—and a divinely ordained reality the intelligibility of which can only be fully realized in a single total and instantaneous intuition. The mythos of *Paradise Lost* is largely the result of this confrontation, and I shall show how the poem's structure manages to incorporate its overriding dianoia through a discursion of marvelously diverse yet reciprocally mirrorlike parts. I will show further how *Paradise Lost* demonstrates the ideal way of coming to terms with the created "sequential" world's embodiment of the Divine "eternal" dianoia primarily through ironic treatments and discountings of inadequate or perverse readings of this embodiment. The main agents of *Macbeth* and *Volpone* generate the plots of these plays by attempting to manipulate situations and other agents, so as to bring them into conformity with an ideal of "plotless" stasis. In the tragedy, Macbeth's attempts to find total peace and security lead to increasingly strenuous and destructive actions, calling ironically down upon him the very counteractions which he had sought to avoid. In the comedy, the plot is made up of the multiple conflicts generated when a number of agents seek to bring one another into perfect subjection to their dreams of a meretriciously defined ideal of power and possession. In all three sets of examples, the logic of dialectic will be shown to be the model of the author's construction of his action, and of the action's coherent structure of mutually reciprocal parts.

I can only hope to suggest the applicability of dialectical logic to other works by showing how it operates in the three main modes of lyric, narrative, and dramatic. The order of my discussion is deliberate. I move from the genre least obviously characterized by dialectical conflict to the one where dialectic is open and palpable. Since my purpose in these three illustrative sections is to demonstrate the essential identity among the dialectical structures in three sharply different genres, I want to call the reader's attention to the peculiarities of this structure first of all in instances where, by the force of incongruity, it stands out in sharpest relief. The *sic-et-non* of the dramatic genre, by which it gathers to itself the meaning of the word *dialectic* in its more traditional sense, I hope thus to illuminate in a new way by juxtaposition with the dialectical structures of the lyric and the narrative, where *sic-et-non* debates operate just as surely, if not as obviously. My specific readings make no special claim to completeness, but since the purpose of this essay is to illustrate a method for interpretation, rather than to exhibit specific interpretations in their own right, I hope that the persuasiveness of this method does not depend wholly on the reader's agreement with these readings. My main purpose in treating specific works is that the reader be moved to test this method in other cases, particularly those quite different from the ones I have chosen.

The essay is in five parts, the middle three of which will deal with the lyric, narrative, and dramatic examples, with the first and fifth introducing the logic of dialectic and its relevance to literary analysis, and some general conclusions respectively.

1. The Dialectic of Mythos and Dianoia

The logic of the dialectic in a plot calls for some realignment of the parts given by Aristotle in the *Poetics*, in such a way that all of them become really versions of each other. R. S. Crane has given us a suggestive interpretation of how four of the parts—plot, character, thought, and diction—are related in the *Poetics:*

> They are distinct parts in the sense of being variable factors in the complex problem of composing works which, when completed, will produce their effects, synthetically, as organic wholes. Hence it is that in the *Poetics* they are treated, not discretely as co-ordinate topics, but hierarchically in a causal sequence of form-matter or end-means relationships in which plot is the most inclusive or architectonic of the four, subsuming all the others as its poetic matter; in which character, while subordinated materially to plot and effect, is similarly a formal or organizing principle with respect to thought and diction; in which thought, while functioning as matter relatively to character, incident, and effect, is the form which immediately controls the choice and arrangement of language in so far as this is employed as a means to imitative rather than ornamental ends; and in which diction, though necessarily

having a form of its own by virtue of its rhythmical, syntactical, and "stylistic" figuration, is the underlying matter which, as significant speech, at once makes possible all the other "parts" and is in turn, mediately or immediately, controlled by them.[2]

Descending from the top, we find plot the final cause of the whole, the entelechy to which character, thought, and diction are subordinated as means to ends. Thus, we can say that the choice of character—his ethical disposition—is dictated by the structure of the plot, his thought in turn dictated by his character, and the verbalization of this thought is likewise dictated by all three in this descending order. We have here a model for selectivity and decorum that would apply to any well-constructed work based on the assumption that the teleology of the whole controls the selection and disposition of its parts.

Dialectical logic does not so much abrogate this notion of teleology as merely translate it so that what is at the top of the hierarchy, the all-inclusive teleology of the work, namely its plot, is in turn made a function of a prior model of order. Though plot is made the summary term of order to which all the rest are subordinated, plot is itself an order—an order of actions—and therefore does not, from the viewpoint of dialectical logic, ground itself. Rather, plot is itself a function of a prior principle of "order-in-general," to which it is subordinated just as character, thought, and diction are subordinated to it. This principle of order-in-general concerns simply but radically the possible dispositions of parts allowed by the very fact that they are parts and therefore divisive and "partial." The various parts of any discourse (the analogue of prime matter in Crane's analysis), namely language, are themselves necessarily divisive insofar as discourse can encompass a complex issue only by breaking it up into separate words. Syntax, the allowable means by which words are joined intelligibly, merely exploits language's divisiveness in order to make up coherent wholes of words mediating the intelligible coherence of the total subject. The discursiveness of language, formally a function of its syntax, stands, as Northrop Frye points out, in a relation to logic which is analogous to the relation of mythos to dianoia:

Let us . . . in spite of history, begin with an association between narrative and grammar, grammar being understood primarily as syntax or getting words in the right (narrative) order, and between logic and meaning, logic being understood primarily as words arranged in a pattern with significance. Grammar is the linguistic aspect of a verbal structure; logic is the "sense" which is the permanent common factor in translation.[3]

But if we extend this rough-and-ready analysis to the other parts which go to make up the plot, for instance character and thought, we find that these parts are likewise disposed according to the "syntax" that the plot itself dictates. And finally, plot equals in this context the total organized whole, a whole in which the separateness and divisiveness of these various parts are exploited to work them up so that they "fit together."

Dialectical logic becomes therefore a kind of "grammar of grammars," the summing-up of the various ways in which parts may possibly be related to wholes. Choosing freely from statements in the *Poetics,* I find that several of them are open to realignment according to the logic of dialectic and the tension between mythos and dianoia which it controls. This central statement is an example:

Tragedy is essentially an imitation not of persons but of action and life, of happiness and misery. All human happiness or misery takes the form of action; the end for which we live is a certain kind of activity, not a quality. Character gives us qualities, but it is in our actions—what we do—that we are happy or the reverse. In a play accordingly they do not act in order to portray the Characters; they include the Characters for the sake of the action. So that it is the action in it, i.e. its Fable or Plot, that is the end and purpose of the tragedy; and the end is everywhere the chief thing.[4]

The teleology of the action in a tragedy is happiness and misery. Considering the plot as an action-made by the writer, he disposes his characters so that they will perform actions the intelligibility of which, as determined by their final cause, is the achievement of happiness. In a tragedy, of course, the ultimate goal of the action-made is rather misery, but this is just the point. From within the perspective of the action-done by the agent himself it is happiness and not misery which is the goal. Aristotle's statement is made from within the perspective of action-made rather than action-done, but it is by the internal requirements of the latter that the author constructs his characters and sets them acting with the achievement of happiness as their goal. My own addition to this would be the observation that the plot which the tragic hero initiates with this goal as its final cause invariably evokes a counteraction against himself which changes him from agent to patient. The logic of this counteraction is ambiguously both opposed to his own overt actions, and also generated by them. This addition to the Aristotelian formulation is summed up by Kenneth Burke's triad of "purpose, passion, perception":

This is the process embodied in tragedy, where the agent's action involves a corresponding passion, and from the sufferance of the passion there arises an understanding of the act, an understanding that transcends the act. The act, in being an assertion, has called forth a counter-assertion in the elements that compose its context. And when the agent is enabled to see in terms of this counter-assertion, he has transcended the state that characterized him at the start.[5]

A further passage from the *Poetics* concerns the distinction between Character and Thought:

Third comes the element of Thought, i.e. the power of saying whatever can be said, or what is appropriate to the occasion. . . . One must not confuse it with Character. Character in a play is that which reveals the moral purpose of the agents, i.e. the sort of thing they seek or avoid, where that is not obvious—hence there is no room for Character in a speech on a purely indifferent subject. Thought, on the other hand, is shown in all they say when proving or disproving some particular point, or enunciating some universal proposition.[6]

Without denying the general truth of this, I would simply point out that, whatever moral tonality a character conveys to the audience, it is his thinking out his situation which determines what he feels is plausible for him to do. How he sizes up a situation moves plots in a certain direction, though it is certainly his moral character which moves him to move a plot at all. My point is not to reverse Crane's assertion that Thought stands to Character as matter to form, but rather to indicate further ramifications of this relation. If that which moves the Character to act is the goal of happiness, then the categories within which this happiness is projected are a function not of his ethical disposition but of the kinds of thoughts he thinks. In terms of action-made, certainly the author will choose thoughts for a character appropriate to his character. But within the perspective of action-done, the specific configuration of his thought processes leads the character to choose a certain kind of action according to his conscious formulation of a certain goal. My point here is to prepare for further analysis wherein the apparent thought structures of a character determine the plot as a kind of debate, wherein various characters cooperate in either harmony or conflict in arguing for their own versions of what ultimate happiness might be.

A final commentary I want to make by way of introduction is on a congeries of texts dealing with the coherence of the plot and the agent's flaw as it contributes to this coherence. At one point Aristotle says that "the story, as an imitation of action," must be "a complete whole, with its several incidents so closely connected that the transposal or withdrawal of any one of them will disjoin and dislocate the whole." Shortly after this, when speaking of the effects of pity and fear, he says that "such incidents have the very greatest effect on the mind when they occur unexpectedly and at the same time in consequence of one another." Finally, he says that the protagonist's change (in a tragedy) from happiness to misery "must lie not in any depravity, but in some great error on his part."[7] From the viewpoint of dialectical logic, let me say at the beginning, the error on the protagonist's part is simultaneously one of the will and one of the intellect. He is moved, no matter what the particular issue may be in any tragedy, by a desire for some sort of absolute, a desire the prelogical and willful conditions of which I will discuss shortly. But once he is so moved, a function of his character, it is in the thought that determines goals and the means of achieving them, his radical presuppositions about the nature of man in his world, that his error occurs. The protagonist moves a plot the successive actions of which are unexpected precisely because his thought has sized up his situation according to a demand for a perfect univocal stasis in his condition, which is always envisioned at the expense of the total requirements and pressures of the human condition. The nemesis that overtakes the protagonist and becomes the object of the anagnorisis or recognition is, as Frye has said, "the recognition of the inevitability of a causal sequence in time."[8] The protagonist commits his error in believing that he can bring all the diversity and change indigenous to the human condition into static conformity with his willed, partial, univocal vision of it. To achieve such would be, by my interpretation, the achievement of happiness. This sequence becomes both inevitable and surprising when it is discovered that the dianoia has always been controlling the consequences of the protagonist's action primarily by reason of his own implicit refusal of this dianoia. Involved in this recognition is the irony that the protagonist suffers the rebound of his actions upon himself precisely because he had erred in denying the fullness of his human predicament which the dianoia embodies in the anagnorisis. In short, the protagonist acts and suffers to the exact degree that he has implicitly denied the truths stated by the dianoia controlling his mythos, and in denying them he is doomed to enact them. Thus, the mythos is generated in a literary work *in opposition to* its dianoia, and the dianoia is relevant to the mythos by reason of that fact. Moving then to the first of Aristotle's statements quoted above, concerning the coherence of parts in a plot, we can see that the whole sequence, that is, the causal relations among the parts (which are unexpected by reason of the protagonist's error), is determined every step of the way "ironically" by the dianoia, the meaning of the work as a whole. It is on the basis of this determination that analysis of the parts of the mythos, in terms of the dialectical logic that the dianoia states, becomes a meaningful and significant procedure in literary criticism.

Therefore, my original assertion that the parts of a literary mimesis as described by Aristotle become realigned so that each becomes a "version" of each other means this: the plot of a work, its total coherence of parts—character, thought, diction, melody, and spectacle—all cooperate in enacting their functions according to the dianoia which informs them. The question "What is the ultimate formal cause of a work's plot?" can only be answered by seeing how all the parts which make up the plot are made by the author to function necessarily as dialectically generating each other, and as therefore all controlled by the same logic. The drive toward univocal stasis would, if fulfilled, be characterless, thoughtless, speechless, melodyless and spectacleless. It would be like the logical state of that archetype of univocal perfection, the "One" in Plato's *Parmenides,* so perfect in its absolute absorption of the finite conditions of space and time into itself, that nothing can be said about it, not even that it exists. The protagonist's drive toward this condition, being necessarily partial, incomplete, and therefore erroneous, involves him in having to act, think, and speak, and in having to confront characters who do likewise. The logic of this confrontation, of the total action which is the plot, informs every part of this plot, because it dictates their mutual and reciprocal functions *vis-à-vis* one another, as each struggles or is used as a means in a struggle to enforce a divisive and partial intention on the others. Speech encounters speech, thought thought, and character character, all divided and contending in the drive toward some absolute. And it is the logic of dialectic which spurs them both to defeat itself and necessarily to enact itself.

The three-part schema which follows gives the essential relations found in all concrete dialectical situations, though these relations are almost never, save in some fully articulated philosophies, found concretely in their purity. The logic of the movement from the first to the second proposition, and from both taken together to the third, is not that of formal, syllogistic implication. Rather, the three propositions are linked together in stating, one by one (they could have been stated in any order: 3, 1, 2 for example), the three essential "moments" of the same dynamic process generated by the attempt to force either/or categories on a both/and reality.

1. A resolution of antinomies is opposition-under-the-sign-of-unity.
2. A conflict of antinomies is unity-under-the-sign-of-opposition.
3. Both resolution and conflict (the subjects of the first two propositions), since they contain the elements of both in a reciprocal dialectical relationship (the hyphenated predicates), are themselves related as mutually cause and effect.

The full significance of the relation between this three-part schema and the concrete reality which it names will only become clear after the necessities underlying each proposition are explained individually. As we will see, the very fact that dialectical logic entails just such rigidity of interrelation among its three moments generates a continually dialectical development in concrete situations. I call these three statements moments because they sum up the three essential steps the critic may go through in establishing the dialectical logic governing a particular mythos. The totality of a literary text—its mythos, dianoia, and the dialectical relations between them—would ideally be perceived in a single intuitive moment, wherein the reader's understanding renders all of these parts at once. In this way, the unity of the whole would be reflected in a unity of a single moment of understanding. Obviously, such an ideal is impossible; critical discourse is just as much bound to the exigencies of sequence as is the literary discourse it discusses. I mean to indicate here that the sequence of these three moments as I have stated them may nevertheless be understood in themselves in any sequential arrangement, because they all mutually imply each other. This is not to say, however, that any one sequence necessarily corresponds to the sequence of the mythos of any given work. In general, I have found it useful to assimilate the unfolding of the mythoi I discuss in the following three chapters to the pattern I have given here. But this was not necessary: one might just as well begin by detailing how the third moment of dialectical logic is rendered in a given lyric, narrative, or play, except that to explain fully that moment one would still have to explain the other two as well. My point here is that these three moments, taken one by one, are each inadequate to render the total dialectical logic in a literary text, because this logic is implicit in all three of its moments at all points in the mythos itself, and because the whole of the mythos is always controlled by its overriding dianoia. The inadequacy is, I suppose, built into the necessarily discursive ways in which we think and speak.

The foundation of this three-part logic is the univocalist demand of the mind which, in aiming at the grasp of the manifold of intuited experience within a calculus of clear and distinct concepts, both causes antinomies and drives toward their solution. I have already given some general notion of what I mean by *univocalism* when speaking about Aristotle's statement that the motive moving a protagonist is towards happiness. The word *univocal* itself refers in formal logic to the extension of a term, such as *man* or *substance,* by which that term stands for or signifies all the singulars which fall under it indifferently and according to the same definition or "intension." That the same term remain univocal in its extension throughout its use in a syllogism or a chain of reasoning is one of the basic criteria of correct reasoning in traditional formal logic. I am using the word *univocalism* to sum up a larger realm of human mental acts, less easily defined and circumscribed. In general, however, the term means a demand of the human mind that the world, in all its change and diversity, its uncertainty and unpredictability, make sense to it according to the principle of noncontradiction. When I speak of a character in a fiction as making a "univocalist demand," I am referring to a desire that the world be somehow totally under the control of the character's will and understanding. Just as the univocal function of terms in formal logic sums up and stands for only those specific notes intended by those terms, and ignores any notes which do not fall under it, so likewise a character motivated by this drive toward univocal control and certitude is moved to bring all the world into orbit around himself. To do this, he must ignore or forcibly destroy all the centrifugal energies of the world which resist this subjection, and in doing so he only calls back upon himself the assault of these energies. This, as I have already indicated, constitutes the formal cause of plot in a literary work. As we shall see, Macbeth and Volpone are such characters, as are Satan in *Paradise Lost* and, in a different fashion, the speakers of Donne's poetry.

The terms for exploring univocalism are more readily found in the history of philosophy than in that of literature. Thus for Plato and Aristotle, the primordial emotion caused when the mind confronts a cosmos of diversity and change which consistently resists its demands for univocal clarity under the sign of noncontradiction, is wonder, the source of all philosophizing. "This sense of wonder is the mark of the philosopher," says Socrates to Theaetetus. "Philosophy indeed has no other origin, and he was a good genealogist who made Iris [philosophy] the daughter of Thaumas [wonder]."[9] The source of this wonder, its consequent ignorance and the desire to escape this ignorance, is the apparent irreconcilability of the mind's either/or questions with the world's both/and "answers." How is it possible that the world we see seems to hold in solution the one and the many, stability and change, appearance and reality without falling into a real chaos mirroring that chaos which threatens thinking when it is asked to grasp contradictories? Because it is just this chaos that the mind feels coming upon it when it does confront such a world and tries to make intelligible sense of it: to grasp this world according to the principle of noncontradiction is to be required to admit to contradiction.

Univocalism is therefore the reaction to wonder and the fear of ignorance which this wonder breeds. More broadly, it names the anxiety that accompanies the feeling of powerlessness when we are confronted with objects and events the causes of which we do not understand. From these two viewpoints, univocalism aims at power, both the "intentional" power granted through the understanding and the potentially real power over the world which accompanies this understanding. Univocalism thus finds its way into the radical causes of plot by way of Bacon's equation of knowledge with power. Univocalism names a motive that defined strictly is intellectual, but more broadly is the desire to make the world conform to the categories of one's own thinking. My main point here, however, is to emphasize the prelogical, preintellectual origins of univocalism. In Aristotle's scheme it falls rather within the area of Character than that of Thought; nevertheless, for both fictive characters and men at large, univocalism reaches its articulation in thought and becomes the logical, as distinct from the moral, motive for a character's actions and indirectly of the actions he suffers.

The three-part schema of dialectical logic I have just outlined attempts to render the radical patterns of dialectical action which result when a character proceeds to act according to univocalist motives. The schema itself, it will be noticed, uses the most general and all-inclusive terms for the elements of that action: resolution and conflict. It attempts to set forth the necessary consequences of univocalist action, consequences that always have a double valence: they result in conflict because the original attempt to univocalize a complex reality causes the agent to suffer the onslaughts of those parts of the reality which he has had forcibly to omit; and they result in resolution because the radical motivation of both sides of a conflict is toward resolution. The dual result of an original attempt to univocalize the world is "monizing" and, another ad hoc coinage for the purposes of terministic symmetry, "atomizing."

Monizing is in general the desire to resolve conflicts; it means univocalizing, as I have defined it so far, though as I shall show, univocalizing results in both monizing and atomizing. Dialectically, monizing results in atomizing to the exact extent that the mind splits a both/and situation into antinomical opposites under the pressure for precise knowledge and perfect control governed by the law of noncontradiction. And again, this same criterion that produces atomizing (conflict, plot) out of monizing likewise in reverse generates monizing again, insofar as it holds up as a goal the resolution of these "atomistic" antinomies. In mimetic terms, this simply means that the immanent *telos* of plot is the resolution that both sides drive toward, but in doing so they come into conflict because both desire total resolution on their own partial terms. By this logic, to win a battle and consolidate one's goals is only to prepare for the next battle, because one cannot indefinitely insist on the absolutism of a partial resolution without sooner or later suffering the attack of those "claims" which have been forcibly excluded in the interest of univocal completeness of control. The "completeness" here is of course ironic: if dialectical logic says nothing else it is this.

The distinction indicated by the phrase "under-the-sign-of" can be rendered as that between overt and covert, and indicates how in general the apparently complete realization of either monizing or atomizing in concrete situations contains implicit in or hidden under it the concomitant potential for turning into its opposite.

Any attempt on the part of the agent of a plot to enforce a univocalist resolution on the world around him must perforce be partial and incomplete. Indeed, we might even go further and say that he attempts a univocalist resolution precisely in order to abrogate those elements in his situation which refuse to be so resolved. Therefore, the agent generates a plot the goal of which is the destruction of whatever cannot be made wholly subject to his will, and insofar as that will is articulated in a set of univocalist categories ruled by noncontradiction, he is committed to suffering attack on the part of other agents, who are vehicles carrying those elements which his partial resolution has denied. The notion that resolution is really a covert opposition is an attempt to state statically a relation which in actual plots exists only dynamically. This first proposition of dialectical logic embodies as dianoia the fact that in mythos protagonist and antagonist are in conflict precisely because they share in divided form the motives and values of a total situation, and that the protagonist's attempt to deny part of them in the interest of static resolution is what invites conflict and kinetic plot.

Unity-under-the-sign-of-opposition refers to the fact that if there is to be genuine conflict there must be a common ground of agreement between the opponents. The second moment of dialectical logic is merely the first seen from the opposite viewpoint. It indicates that the conflict in a plot becomes possible because both sides "agree" on a conmon issue and share a common univocalism in projecting possible resolutions. It means that the claims and counterclaims which constitute a plot, when put together in some sort of harmonious resolution (such as the dianoia might state), form the common ground which both sides stand on, and which therefore allows their meeting head on. The second statement further indicates that the very goal of univocal resolution which generated the conflict in the first place, does in fact drive the conflict forward under the sign of destroying the opponent in the name of unity and resolution. The protagonist and antagonist by this description are in conflict because they attempt to absolutize two correlative and partial sides of the antinomy which is the basis of contention between them.

Finally, the third moment of dialectical logic merely sums up what I have already said: namely that the motives of resolution and conflict are reciprocally causal of each other, because both are generated by the same radical motive, the absolutizing of a single univocal viewpoint. Attempted resolution generates conflict, and conflict has as its goal resolution. The third moment becomes a kind of paradigm for the dianoia of any plot, because it states (statically) the essential terms and the essential relations between them which, when they are embodied in characters whose ways of thinking and acting are governed by the desire for a perfect resolution ("happiness"), necessarily will generate a plot the goal of which is this resolution. In short, the demand for noncontradiction does nothing so much as involve the character in contradiction, and that contradiction is, within dialectical logic, simply another word for plot.

I have already stated that fictive plots are enacted in opposition to the dianoia which informs them. In more concrete terms this means that the author, when he devises his plot and the characters to go with it, must make these characters less knowledgeable than himself about what they are in fact doing. This is of course a truism, so obvious that we tend to forget it. Certainly, no author can make a character who knows more than he does. But my meaning goes beyond this point. It is arguable that Shakespeare after *Hamlet* created tragic heroes all of whom necessarily knew less about either the general tragic nature of the human condition or about their own predicaments than did Hamlet himself. The trouble with Hamlet—and this is hardly a new insight—is that the state of his awareness of the total dianoia controlling his situation in Denmark approximates (or appears to do so) almost that of Shakespeare himself. Result: knowing the full dialectical possibilities of all action, he refuses to act. In *Hamlet* the mythos is really little more than Hamlet's meditation on the dianoia of that mythos. It was Shakespeare's dramatic genius that allowed him to make a play of such a situation. But imagine an Othello who at the beginning of the play is fully aware of the total potentialities of his love for both good and evil, innocence and cynicism. He would not have been temptable by Iago; or to put it another way, Iago could not have been invested by the playwright with that dark awareness which the actual Othello is at first so blithely ignorant of, and which so complements his own that from this complementarity there might arise conflict. A similar example would be an Oedipus who begins the play, rather than ends it, in full possession of the devious ways the decree of the gods and man's free will intertwine, such knowledge as might lead him to suspect himself first (rather than last) of all. The cases of both plays would be radically altered. I venture to say that we would not even have *Othello* and *Oedipus Rex* under such conditions. Or to put the matter in reverse, the prime condition by which plots are generated in both plays is that the protagonists start out necessarily ignorant of the total dianoia that is going to inform their actions.

The dianoia in any plot is, as I have already indicated, present everywhere in that plot but never visible anywhere as a part of it. An exception might be Prospero in *The Tempest*, who controls all the actions that occur, and since these actions occur under the power of a character within the play who "knows all," I might question whether *The Tempest* does in fact really have a plot in the sense I am using the word. In short, for there even to be a plot in which is manifested a total dianoia, the agents in the plot must be ignorant of it. And, in addition, as I will show, they must in some way or other fight against the knowledge which that dianoia embodies.

We must justify this place of dianoia "in" the plot in such a fashion that the literary critic may be aware of just where to look for it. I am going to use here a distinction made by Martin Heidegger in *Being and Time*, that between phenomenon and appearance. " 'Phenomenon' signifies *that which shows itself in itself*, the manifest."[10] Using the example of a symptom of a disease, Heidegger distinguishes phenomenon from appearance while at the same time showing their intimate connection:

> The emergence of such occurrences [symptoms], their showing-themselves, goes together with the Being-present-at-hand of disturbances which do not show themselves. Thus appearance, as the appearance 'of something,' does *not* mean showing-itself; it means rather the announcing itself by [von] something which does not show itself, but which announces itself through something which does show itself. Appearing is a *not-showing-itself*. . . . In spite of the fact that 'appearing' is never a showing-itself in the sense of "phenomenon," appearing is possible only *by reason of a showing-itself* of something. But this showing-itself, which helps to make possible the appearing, is not the appearing itself. Appearing is an *announcing*-itself through something that shows itself.[11]

Heidegger's distinction is important here because it throws light on the logic governing the status of the dialectical structure, the dianoia, within the fiction itself. Its status is that of an appearance which does and can only announce its presence through the phenomena but can never appear "in itself." The basic dialectical logic governing a conflict cannot show itself fully as such in any of the expressed statements of the characters, because the very existence of the conflict presupposes that each partisan has univocalized a both/and situation, and in so doing has marked himself as controlled by, contained within the total logic of his position; as, in other words, unaware of the total dianoia governing and illuminating (for the audience) his situation. Since, as I pointed out before, conflicts arise specifically because both sides, under the pressure of the demand for noncontradiction, attempt to absolutize positions which are partial because they cannot include all of the necessary elements of the complex issue to be resolved, this simply means that for one reason or another both sides ignore the partiality of their positions in order to monize them. In fact, we can even say that they monize them in order to escape the claims of elements in the issue which make for contradictory assymmetry; i.e., they absolutize the partial because it is partial. If both sides do this (indeed, can there even be two sides if they do not do this?), then we can say that their implicit refusal of the total dianoia governing their position is that which allows them to move a plot. For this reason the critic can never expect overt statements of the dialectical logic to appear in the phenomena of the work itself—in speeches and action. It is certainly true that in Shakespeare, for instance, we can find the dianoia stated in partial and ambiguous ways even by the tragic hero himself. But what we do not find, not even in *Hamlet,* is a total statement of the dianoia of that work intended and understood by that character in the largest and deepest fashion that the work as a whole "intends" this dianoia. Therefore the dianoia governing the action can only be looked for as it appears, i.e., announces itself through the phenomena of the specific plot, and this is because the dialectical logic of the dianoia could not even exist-to-be-announced in this fashion were it not buried in the characters' very unawareness of this logic's operating in their conflict. This fact might lead one to suspect that whenever a partisan attempts to give what appears to be an objective analysis of the conflict in which he is engaged, such a statement must by definition be discounted as not naming the ultimate structure of that conflict. A prime example might be Ulysses' famous speech on degree in *Troilus and Cressida,* which is often taken at simple face value as an objective statement about what is wrong with the Greek army. On one level it is certainly that; but the total meaning of the speech within the ironic and debunking context of the play lies in the fact that Ulysses is using the motives and values of "order" in a specific situation where these motives and values are rhetorically directed toward rousing the listeners to further acts which smack of a meretricious pride, honor and disorder. Thus the speech on degree is itself subject to ironic discounting, as are most of the actions and speeches in that play. Ulysses' statements about degree and order are encompassed by, rather than encompassing, the dianoia of the play, a dianoia that is interested rather in the ambiguities in the relations between high and low degrees of value and motivation, than in the mere statement that such exist.

Before going on to more concrete analysis and examples of dialectical logic at work, one final theoretical point must be cleared up. I have already said that the plot in a fiction takes place not only because of the ignorance of the agents of the dianoia controlling their actions, but even in opposition to it. This opposition would, of course, only be implicit on their parts, though for the author's part he would certainly be conscious enough that such is the case (as he hopes the reader or audience will be also). My point here is that dialectical logic can be seen by the literary critic as regulative of the meaning of a work precisely because the action-done in that work embodies this logic by and through rejecting it. For instance, we might take some of the preceding statements about the generation of plot a step farther, and say that plots maintain their drive through a work because the relations between resolution and conflict are in themselves so rigid and unchanging. Since the radical *telos* of the agent of a plot is to grasp and control the world of his experience according to clear univocal categories governed by noncontradiction, and since this *telos* results in the creation of conflicts which the conflicts further seek to resolve, this restless search is continually driven on by the desire to escape the dialectical oscillation between resolution and conflict, with all its built-in flux and uncertainty of resolution-leading-to-conflict and conflict-leading-to-resolution. To state this according to the essential tautology that lurks at the heart of dialectical logic, dialectical mythoi evolve continually according to the logic of dialectic, because it is precisely this logic that keeps mythoi dialectical by driving the characters on to abrogate itself.

An appropriate conclusion to this first part is a dialectical analysis of the story of creation from Genesis, since it is really in the primal and radical "separation" of the finite world from the Creator, a finite world necessarily made up of temporal and spatial parts, that we find the mythical origin of dialectic. Kenneth Burke has with remarkable efficiency fused both the mythical and verbal implications of the Genesis story, by treating the disposition of its parts as if they conformed to the inner necessities involved in writing the "plot" of such a story. Thus God "writes" the world in creating it, much as a literary artist would, nature imitating art in this case. Burke's point is that once one begins with a term, any term, one has already, out of the indefinite variety of choices of organization and disposition of parts available before the choice was made, excluded a large part and limited oneself to the specific options for organization which this term dictates. And if this term is such a central one as God, and a nearly related term such as order, then the possibilities of development from this term are immediately implicit in it. Thus, as Burke says, "All told, 'evil' is implicit in the idea of 'Order' because 'order' is a polar, or dialectical term, implying an idea of 'Disorder.' "[12] Burke's point is that "logologically" (i.e., according to the logic allowed by the univocality of words) the fall of man and of the universe is dialectically implied in the very notion of creation. This position I personally find not so much Manichean as merely illustrating the logic that underlies the pure possibility of a Manichean position's being held. One does not have to hold to the necessity of a fall, to the exact degree that one does not have to hold to the univocalist position that the "logic" of the cosmos is logological. But if one is a univocalist, then in one way or another one will do just that. (I am not saying that Kenneth Burke is a univocalist in the sense in which I am using the term; rather he is an extremely insightful student of what happens when other men act univocally.) Here is Burke's "deduction" of the Fall from the Creation:

> We want to so relate the ideas of Creation, Covenant and Fall that they can be seen to implicate one another inextricably, along with the ideas of Sacrifice and Redemption.
>
> Creation implies authority in the sense of originator, the designer or author of the things created.
>
> Covenant implies authority in the sense of power, sovereignty—the highest or most radical sovereignty in case the Covenant is made by God.
>
> The possibility of a "Fall" is implied in the idea of a Covenant insofar as the idea of a Covenant implies the possibility of its being violated. One does not make a covenant with stones or trees or fire—for such things cannot break agreements or deny commands, since they cannot even understand agreements or commands.
>
> Also, the possibility of a "Fall" is implied in the idea of the Creation, insofar as the Creation was a kind of "divisiveness," since it set up different categories of things which could be variously at odds with one another and which accordingly lack the proto-Edenic simplicity of absolute unity.[13]

From these examples and comments, I draw this conclusion: the total plan of any work, its dianoia, calls for the dividing of this plan into separate parts, which by their dialectical interaction with one another embody, imitate, demonstrate, and so on, the totality of the work embodied implicitly and potentially in each part as they relate to one another in sequence. The result is a conception of the interrelations among parts in which the key term is not harmony, a univocal drive toward "a place for everything and everything in its place"; rather, interrelations are determined by the dialectical logic of action and counteraction, where like causes (i.e., leads to, causes to come next) not only like, but also unlike:

> The two main symbols for the charting of structural relationships would be the sign for "equals" and some such sign as the arrow ("from ——— to ———"). . . . The arrow is obviously required for noting an ambiguous dialectical operation whereby one event calls forth an event, not similar in quality, but compensatory. If we met a sequence, for instance, "murder to night to a vision of peace," here "murder" and "night" might be consistent in quality ("murder equals night") while the third event might be of opposite, or compensatory quality (which would require "night → peace"). . . . . . . The confusion might be approached in another way: A total drama, as the agon, is analytically subdivided into competing principles, of protagonist and antagonist. Their competition sums up to one over-all cooperative act (as the roles of Iago and Othello "dovetail" with each other in order to compose the total progression of the tragedy).[14]

Such a conception of literary form—harking back to my distinction between action-made and action-done—conforms in some of its features to Kant's notion of teleology within the organic whole of the natural world. "An organized product of nature is one in which every part is reciprocally purpose [end] and means."[15] An organized verbal mimesis would be one, then, in which the "conflicts" within the action-done are, from the viewpoint of action-made, "cooperations." Adapting Kant's words, the action-done aims at disrupting the reciprocity of means and ends in the interest of making all possible means be directed univocally to the ends of the agent of the plot. But here content and formal principle organizing this content (dianoia) are seen to be one. Because this drive within the action-done, a function of the concrete characters and motivations, cooperates "in spite of itself" with the action-made, it generates a coherent plot the structure of which is rather a Kantian reciprocity of means and ends, the dianoia. The formal principle of a plot's organization, which is the object of the critic's search, becomes likewise the very principle within the action-done which controls the agent through his own overt attempt to avoid it. The protagonist begins with a purpose and would make other characters means to it, with the result that agent becomes patient, suffering a reversal from projector of means to an end, to a means to a still larger and all-inclusive "end," an end that is ultimately neither his own nor that of his opponents, but the end of the total dianoia which encompasses him, his opponents and the whole fictive world within which he acts.

Before going on, however, I would like to obviate one possible misunderstanding about my use of the term *sequence* in discussing the dialectical dynamism of a plot. The ordinary way of proceeding in reading a lyric or a narrative or watching a play is to begin at the beginning and end at the end, moving between these two points in simple sequential order in time and syntax. But in reading a poem or beholding a play according to the ordinary sequence, the reader finds that not only does what comes first illuminate what comes after, but also vice versa, what comes last illuminates everything that came before. I would argue that there is no one natural way of reading a poem or a narrative: there is only the fact that, by reason of the sequential, one-way-street nature of verbal discourse, we must first proceed through one sequence before we proceed through any other. But that "first" is in priority only in an instrumental, pragmatic sense, but certainly not in any evaluative sense. Rather, the first sequence does itself carry some of the meaning of the work: the fact that in this sequence *this* causes *that* to happen later is obviously important for the meaning; but it is only one of the parts of the total plot of the work, and not that plot itself. Therefore I do not intend the notion of dialectical generation of part out of part to be taken to refer only to a before/after sequence. Part generates part, not simply *vis-à-vis* each other, but rather as both confront partially the whole and they stand in relation to one another only after they stand in this primary one.

2. The Dialectic of the Lyric: John Donne

> In knowing, soul or mind abandons its unity. . . . Our way then takes us beyond knowing; there may be no wandering from unity; . . . out of discussion we call to vision.
>
> Plotinus, *Enneads* VI.9.4

As far as the dialectic of mythos and dianoia is concerned, the lyric can be distinguished from the narrative and dramatic modes.

Whereas the mythoi of the latter move for us (the readers or audience), and move us to grasp the dianoia which is the meaning of the plot, the lyric mode overtly strives rather toward the stasis of simultaneous statement. In this case, we the readers move for it, the lyric's stasis generating the reader's dynamic process of apprehending the dianoia embodied in the frozen motion of a set pattern of words. The gradual accretion of meaning from word to word, sentence to sentence, and stanza to stanza is a discursive plot analogous to that found in narrative and drama. However, the drive toward univocal and static resolution which is the *telos* of plot in these two modes is consummated only at the end of the discursive sequence. In the lyric, that resolution is the whole poem itself, presenting itself as having rendered the whole of its meaning in the whole of its statement. The interaction of part and part in the lyric is therefore subject to dialectical logic, but unlike the narrative and drama, these parts are not dramatically called up in answer to still other statements (unless, of course, the lyric is really a disguised drama, as in Browning). On the contrary, the lyric is the statement of a persona whose final statement is all there before us, overtly presenting itself as univocally resolving the issues into a stasis which is the whole lyric itself. But insofar as the lyric is discursive and composed of parts, the reader can perceive the tensions among these parts as dynamic rather than static, and he may therefore reverse the persona's achieved stasis, causing the parts to react with one another in his understanding of them all over again. The result is therefore a dynamism of reading generated out of a stasis of "resolved" lyric statement, the reader partaking in the lyric's action more than he does in the other two modes. The dianoia of the lyric, then, is the discovered and renewed motion on the reader's part, which stands over against the lyric's overt presentation of itself as univocally final and static. This dialectic between mythos and dianoia is just the reverse of that in narrative and drama, where the dianoia is the total statement of the interrelations between competing parts, parts which themselves exist in the work in a dynamically sequential form.

In dealing with Donne's lyrics, and by extension with the lyrics of other poets, we must keep this distinction in mind. Dialectical logic is present in the lyric according to the same static "three-moment" pattern as it is in narrative or dramatic works. But the presentation of the sequence of a lyric's parts, in being overtly static rather than dynamic, will interact with its dianoia in a fashion which is quite *sui generis*. Donne wrote a letter to Sir Henry Wotton in 1600 accompanying a copy of his early *Paradoxes*, and his remarks call attention to some of the essential points to note in grasping the significance of the sequence in a lyric:

Sir,

Only in obedience I send you some of my paradoxes: I love you and myself and them too well to send them willingly for they carry with them a confession of their lightnes, and your trouble and my shame. But indeed they were made to deceave tyme than her daughter truth: although they have beene written in an age when any thing is strong enough to overthrow her. If they make you to find better reasons against them they do their office: for they are but swaggerers: quiet enough if you resist them. If perchaunce they be pretyly guilt, that is their best for they are not hatcht: they are rather alarums to truth to arme her than enemies: and they have only this advantadg to scape from being caled ill things that they are nothings. Therefore take heed of allowing any of them least you make another.[16]

When we look at the kind of rhetorical address they make to the reader, Donne's point about his *Paradoxes* being "alarums to truth" is immediately apparent. We are simultaneously aware both of their internal (though sophistical) consistency, and of their inconsistency with the reality they purport to describe: they demonstrate the discrepancy between the logic of concepts and the nature of objects in the very attempt to reduce objects to concepts. The persona of these *Paradoxes* is very much like the personae of Donne's more serious love and religious poetry, in that they all strive valiantly to think as if the demand for concept/object correspondence were indeed a fact. On the other hand, the very strictness with which the chain of argument is worked out generates the reader's complementary criticism and recognition of the ultimate inability of the mind to reduce the real wholly to itself. Many have commented on the tendency in Donne's poetry to carry a given idea, metaphor, or assertion to its logical extreme. Donne's purpose in this is to push an argument to the point that its inadequacy for reflecting reality becomes fully recognizable. As such it then becomes an "alarum to truth," as Donne says, and requires the mind of the reader to take a new look not only at the reality but also at its own capabilities for grasping that reality.[17] Here are two excerpts from the first of the prose *Paradoxes*, "A Defence of Womens Inconstancy":

That Women are *Inconstant*, I with any man confesse, but that *Inconstancy* is a bad quality, I against any man will maintaine: For every thing as it is

> one better than another, so is it fuller of *change*; The *Heavens* themselves continually turne, the *Starres* move, the *Moone* changeth; *Fire* whirleth, *Ayre* flyeth, *Water* ebbs and flowes, the face of the *Earth* altereth her lookes, *time* stayes not; the Colour that is most light, will take most dyes: . . .
>
> . . . For as *Philosophy* teacheth us, that *Light things doe alwayes tend upwards,* and *heavy things decline downeward;* Experience teacheth us otherwise, that the disposition of a *Light* Woman, is to fall downe, the nature of Women being contrary to all Art and Nature.[18]

In these passages the comparison between women and natural phenomena omits any differences alongside the univocal similarities, and thereby calls up in the reader an awareness of precisely those differences. One line of argument univocally pursued has generated its dialectical opposite, the realization of some of the ways in which women are not like the elements and falling bodies.

These examples provide a simple case of dialectical "compensation." The reader is called upon to provide the counterargument and thereby to destroy the speaker's simplistic assumption that whatever things can be joined in conceptual similarity are necessarily linked in reality as well. This strategy finds its counterpart in several of Donne's strictly "paradoxical" lyrics, such as "Confined Love" and "The Flea." The dialectical interaction between reader and the persona's argument which we find in the latter poem presents us with a model which even Donne's densest poems follow:

> Marke but this flea, and marke in this,
> How little that which thou deny'st me is;
> Mee it suck'd first, and now sucks thee,
> And in this flea, our two bloods mingled bee;
> Confesse it, this cannot be said
> A sinne, or shame, or losse of maidenhead,
> Yet this enjoyes before it wooe,
> And pamper'd swells with one blood made of two,
> And this, alas, is more than wee would doe.
>
> Oh stay, three lives in one flea spare,
> Where wee almost, nay more then maryed are:
> This flea is you and I, and this
> Our mariage bed, and mariage temple is;
> Though parents grudge, and you, w'are met,
> And cloysterd in these living walls of Jet.
> Though use make thee apt to kill mee,
> Let not to this, selfe murder added bee,
> And sacrilege, three sinnes in killing three.

Cruell and sodaine, hast thou since
Purpled thy naile, in blood of innocence?
In what could this flea guilty bee,
Except in that drop which it suckt from thee?
Yet thou triumph'st, and saist that thou
Find'st not thy selfe, nor mee the weaker now;
'Tis true, then learne how false, feares bee;
Just so much honor, when thou yeeld'st to mee,
Will wast, as this flea's death tooke life from thee.[19]

The rhetorical end of the poem is, of course, seduction, and to that end the facts noted in the first stanza can hardly be denied: in microscopic fashion the blood of both lovers is already mingled inside the flea. The logical twist comes in the second stanza when we ask what interpretation is to be given to this marriage of blood. If marriage means a physical joining of separate bodies, then the flea has joined them in something that is more than marriage, because now there is "one blood made of two." By reducing the concept of marriage to the mingling of blood, the speaker can assert that "this flea is you and I." The lady, like the reader, reacts to the logical conclusion that the flea's death will involve murder, suicide, and sacrilege by simply testing it against the facts. She finds that the argument is meaningless and that she is no "weaker" after having "killed herself" than she was before. Then the speaker pulls off an ingenious equivocation. First he disingenuously insists that the flea was guilty in nothing but "that drop which it suckt from thee," thereby going back on his previous argument which held that that "drop" had in fact married them. Then again, by his own argument throughout the poem, the lady should be dead. That the consequence is palpably untrue in fact should mean that the chain of reasoning is untrue also. Yet that argument that the flea's death should have resulted in her death (but did not) depends precisely upon this chain of reasoning's being true. Either both she and the flea are dead, or she is still living, and if she is then the statement that "this flea is you" is pure fantasy. And if it is, then he has no business attempting to argue logically in the last line that the flea's death has anything to do with her at all. In a word, he tries to have it both ways, and in doing so catches himself in his own logic.

But the destruction of logic by logic in this poem is only part of its wider purpose, which is to display comically the complete independence of the rational argument from the things it is about. The verbal action-done by the speaker corresponds, in Kenneth Burke's triad, to "purpose," and the "passion" he suffers is supplied partly by the lady herself and partly by the reader. Certainly, there is no perception or anagnorisis on the persona's part; but then, as Donne says in his letter to Wotton, such "paradoxes" exist only to be knocked down, they are "quiet if you resist them." Designed, as A. E. Malloch says, "to present one part in a verbal drama,"[20] this kind of lyric plot invites the reader to participate actively in its development. The total dianoia that results from this interaction could be taken as the way in which the persona's attempt to manipulate the lady by logically twisting their situation to that end only succeeds in calling back upon itself the very answer which defeats it.[21]

In "The Flea" the logic of dialectic moves with exemplary simplicity. The speaker's assumption that his own set of terms exhausts the totality of the facts of the case generates the opposite recognition on the part of the reader. But as a matter of fact, the dialectical movement halts right there, namely at the first moment of dialectical logic, the discovery that attempted resolution has been in reality a conflict-under-the-sign-of-unity. The poem does not call us to go on to the second moment, wherein we might realize that both viewpoints (ours and the speaker's) are relevant, and that we are in opposition only because we agree in sundering univocally the totality of the human situation under consideration. Nevertheless, this truncated dialectic contains within it the germs of a much more complex kind of plot to be found in other poems by Donne. In these, wherein Donne's speakers attempt to render in clear concepts the union-plus-separation of lover and lover, there is a dynamic dialectic between speaker and reality, and between both of these and reader, the conclusion of which is an unresolved tension between concept/object correspondence and concept/object split.

In the most acute and extensive analysis of Donne's thought to date, Robert Ellrodt has examined extensively a pattern which occurs continually in a variety of manifestations in his poetry. The center of this pattern is an ideal of reducing human perceptions in time and space to a single moment of intuitive, transdiscursive vision. "Le dépassement perpétuel est une façon de 'transcender' la pure continuité et de tendre toujours vers un instant plus intense, un absolu qui échappe, ou devrait échapper au changement."[22] He quotes a passage from the "Obsequies to the Lord Harrington," which is a touchstone for this pattern throughout his poetry:

> As when an Angell down from heav'n doth flye,
> Our quick thought cannot keepe him company,
> Wee cannot think, now hee is at the Sunne,
> Now through the Moon, now he through th'aire doth run,
> Yet when he's come, we know he did repaire
> To all twixt Heav'n and Earth, Sunne, Moon, and Aire;
> And as this Angell in an instant knowes,
> And yet wee know, this sodaine knowledge growes
> By quick amassing severall formes of things,
> Which he successively to order brings;
> When they, whose slow-pac'd lame thoughts cannot goe
> So fast as hee, thinke that he doth not so;
> Just as a perfect reader doth not dwell,
> On every syllable, nor stay to spell,
> Yet without doubt, hee doth distinctly see
> And lay together every A, and B;
> So, in short liv'd good men, is'not understood
> Each severall vertue, but the compound good;
> For, they all vertues paths in that pace tread,
> As Angells goe, and know, and as men read.[23]

On this passage Ellordt remarks: "On saisit ici sur le vif le lien entre l'intuition de l'instant et la rapidité de l'intelligence, rapidité qui est un trait marquant de l'esprit de Donne. . . ."[24] The "rapidity" which this passage both refers to and evokes in the reader is an attempt to communicate the experience of transdiscursive knowledge through a mode of understanding that is itself only discursive. Donne employs the medieval doctrine of angelic knowledge which held that angels are able to perceive a multitude of singulars through a single species. The movements of angels through the spheres and the movement of the eye and the mind across words also carry the same tenor, namely the assimilation of a discursive series in a glance which only the idea of great rapidity can approximate. Ellrodt's "rapidité de l'intelligence" can refer by extension to demands made by a number of Donne's poems, in calling the reader to approximate an intuitive vision through a rapid alternation between two very close but acutely distinguished dialectical opposites. And as dialectical logic instructs us, we are to suspect that such a demand for intuitive vision will manifest itself quite often in its opposite form—the sundering of a single object of vision into discrete parts. Ellrodt's formulation of this aspect of Donne's poetry is exemplary:

Habituellement, les brusques changements de rythme et de ton dont le poète est coutumier révèlent différentes facettes d'un même état d'esprit, d'un même moment de conscience. Il y a rarement progression temporelle. Le développement dialectique a précisément pour fonction de déguiser de la durée, d'y substituer des relations, des perspectives, des alternatives qui relèvent de l'ordre logique, et, en quelque manière, de la spatialité. On dirait d'un même moment dramatique qui se morcèlerait en moments logiques, se développant à la manière d'un syllogisme ou d'une démonstration qui se décompose en propositions distinctes pour traduire une vérité unique.[25]

Quite often a Donne poem consists of a number of discrete, univocal perceptions of a complex reality, which when laid out in sequence can only render this complexity in paradox. The "plots" of Donne's poetry, as Kenneth Burke has pointed out, would be permutations of dramatic plots, where "his exploitation of *one* metaphor throughout an entire poetic unit was the *equivalent*, in the lyric, for the *plottiness* of drama. It pledged the poet to much *rational business* in the unwinding of the poem's situation."[26] In still other terms the poem stands to the reality it seeks to encompass as the *explicatio*, the "out-folding" into many parts, to the *complicatio* of these parts, all grasped at once in a single vision of unity.

One example in which such an *explicatio* is easily seen is "Loves Infiniteness":

If yet I have not all thy love,
  Deare, I shall never have it all;
I cannot breath one other sigh, to move,
  Nor can intreat one other teare to fall.
All my treasure, which should purchase thee,
  Sighs, teares, and oathes, and letters I have spent,
Yet no more can be due to mee,
  Then at the bargaine made was ment.
If then thy gift of love were partiall,
That some to mee, some should to others fall,
  Deare, I shall never have Thee All.

Or if then thou gav'st mee all,
  All was but All, which thou hadst then,
But if in thy heart, since, there be or shall,
  New love created bee, by other men,
Which have their stocks intire, and can in teares,

In sighs, in oathes, and letters outbid mee,
This new love may beget new feares,
For, this love was not vowed by thee.
And yet it was, thy gift being generall,
The ground, thy heart is mine, what ever shall
Grow there, deare, I should have it all.

Yet I would not have all yet,
Hee that hath all can have no more,
And since my love doth every day admit
New growth, thou shouldst have new rewards in store;
Thou canst not every day give me thy heart,
If thou canst give it, then thou never gav'st it:
Loves riddles are, that though thy heart depart,
It stayes at home, and thou with losing sav'st it:
But wee will have a way more liberall,
Then changing hearts, to joyne them, so wee shall
Be one, and one anothers All.[27]

The speaker's fears in the first two stanzas seem motivated less by real jealousy than by a desire to see just how far he can push an anatomy of his and the woman's love, when this is grounded on an economic model of buying and selling, gain and depletion. The poem concludes that such a model, while demonstrating its own inadequacy, has in the process proved at least its value in leading a mind anxious for a clear conceptualization through and beyond formulations that seek to satisfy this anxiety. The dialectical reversals forced on the speaker in the poem can be summed up in the equivocations on the meaning of "all." On the one hand it refers quantitatively to a certain "amount" of love, with the result that the speaker can ask how it is possible for "all" to refer to the love which the woman gave him at the beginning, as well as to a continuously growing "amount." If "all" refers to the first gift of love then the speaker would prefer not to call it "all," for he also wants the "new rewards in store" which come with increase. On the other hand, "all" refers qualitatively, or at least non-quantitatively, to a continuously expanding totality which is complete at every point of growth. The conceptual problem arises because quantitatively speaking the signification of "all" becomes equivocal at every increase, referring now to one amount, now to a greater, and if this is so then "I shall never have Thee All."

The speaker is working, obliquely and negatively, toward a conception of "all" which is both quantitative and "qualitative," which can grasp the totality of their love union at every particular point of growth (the static completeness of love totally given and received), while allowing the possibility for growth. The best way to approach the poem is to start at the end and work backward, for the last five lines give not so much an answer to "loves riddles," as rather the achieved recognition of why it is such. The answer to the riddle is that the lovers are both "one" and "two": from the viewpoint of duality the heart departs, from that of unity "It stayes at home." Insofar as the lovers are "one" being, there is no place for the language of addition and depletion, because each gives his love to "himself." Their love is both growing and yet always complete because they remain always separate persons, a condition yielding the possibility of ever-closer union by which this union remains the same not despite but because of this growth.

The dialectical plot of the poem is thus generated out of the speaker's attempt to render this paradoxical "fact" in the univocal and therefore partial language of quantification. In this respect the poem moves quite exemplarily along the lines charted by the three-moment sequence of dialectical logic. The speaker begins by saying that his love is entire and complete, and goes on to insist that her love should be complete also. This in turn generates the opposite realization that "Hee that hath all can have no more." Each side of the conflict generates its opposite insofar as both demonstrate themselves as partial views of the unity-plus-separation and completeness-plus-growth of the love union. The bulk of the poem, up to the last five lines, fulfills most clearly the second moment of dialectical logic, because it shows a conflict grounded upon the agreement of both formulations in univocally sundering simple static completeness. The last five lines ask the reader to hold in his mind simultaneously union and separation, for in joining their hearts the lovers will "be one" as well as "one anothers All." I take this puzzling last line as a mimesis of the third moment of dialectic, wherein the lovers are one both as individuals and as lovers: "Be one" suggests the unequivocal meaning of "unity" until we come to "one anothers All," which then takes up the meaning of mutual exchange, and in retrospect emphasizes the first "one" as identifying the lovers as separate individuals. But in fact, the reader is required by the poem at the end to attempt to realize simultaneously what the poem up to that point has set forth in sequence: the interpenetration of union and separation, growth and completeness. "Lovers infiniteness" directs the continuum of his thought, finally, to double back on itself, to affirm as far as possible, contradictories, for contradictory predications (". . . though thy heart depart, / It stayes at home, and thou with losing sav'st it") come closest to rendering the paradoxical fact in a single moment of intuitive vision.

The mythos of this poem—the disposition and sequence of statements about the love union—embodies its paradoxical dianoia in the very act of attempting to adrogate it. The speaker's demand for a clear, univocal conceptualization of the totality of this dianoia has forced him into a sequential plot of statements, each of which is both univocally exclusive of the others, while at the same time they mutually cooperate in rendering the total fact in the very act of breaking it up into partial perspectives. Even the summary moment of intuitive vision at the end, where paradox becomes overt in the poem, differs from the previous part of the plot only in degree, for it renders this vision in those discursive terms which most approximate it while nevertheless remaining discursive and univocal.

So far we have seen Donne's personae standing in two distinguishable relations with the matters of their discourses. In "The Flea" the speaker pushes a single line of argumentation to such a narrow extreme that the reader is invited to reverse this direction with a simple negation. "Loves infiniteness" shows, in Leonard Unger's words, "the process by which the speaker arrives at a consciousness of rival attitudes."[28] The persona answers his own assertions as his mind travels around the matter, recording apparently contradictory aspects. In this latter case we find an archetypal pattern that can be found in lyric poetry of all ages, a pattern whereby the speaker is related to his subject matter in a dynamic fashion most cogently formulated by twentieth-century philosophical phenomenology. In discussing Husserl's distinction between the "noetic" and the "noematic" aspects of our knowing experiences, one of his disciples deals with the latter in such a way as to indicate the term's relevance to my own notion of mythos:

The noema is to be distinguished from the real object. The latter, the tree for instance, as a real thing appears now in this determined manner; but it may offer itself from a different side, at another distance, in a different orientation and aspect; and it does so in fact when the subject goes around it. It shows itself in a multiplicity of perceptions, through all of which the same real tree presents itself; but the "perceived tree as such" varies according to the standpoint, the orientation, the attitude, etc. of the perceiving subject, as when for instance he looks at the tree from above, or at another time perceives it while in the garden. Indeed, a real thing may not present itself as such except by means of a series of perceptions succeeding one another. These perceptions enter into a synthesis of identification with one another, and it is by, and in, this synthesis and the parallel synthesis among the corresponding noemata, that what appears successively constitutes itself, for consciousness, into this real thing which it is, one and identical as opposed to the multiple perceptions and also the multiple noemata.[29]

"Loves infiniteness," as is the case with many of Donne's poems, calls attention to itself as expressly an incomplete, partial noematic continuum, in which is reflected a reality around which no human mind can ever completely walk. This verbal situation invites a similar stance on the reader's part, for whom the "object in itself" is at once the poem and the reality which it points to; more precisely, the object is specifically the "poem-as-pointing," and showing itself as pointing inadequately. The reader is thus called upon to make continual adjustments as he looks through (i.e., by means of) the poem at what the poem is referring to, grasping this reality just as the poem itself does, by a constant realignment of individual statements in relation to one another. The dianoia is in a sense the total reality of which the mythos is the noematic continuum of interrelated perceptions. Like the tree in the passage by Gurwitsch quoted above, the total fact requires just such a continuum, because the speaker's demand for an ideal grasp of it completely in a single moment of vision creates statements which manifest their own partiality at the very moment of pretending to absolute adequacy, and so call for still further statements. The need for further statements announces the operation of dialectical logic through the phenomena of a discourse wherein the speaker overtly wills against dialectic in the name of intuition. Taking the mythos of the poem as a total set of noematic syntheses, we can see that it embodies its dianoia only at the expense of a univocal fragmentation of that dianoia.

But if mythos is generated through an attempt to deny it, what would be the case in which the poem overtly attempted to embody the totality of its dianoia in the phenomena of its discourse? Donne provides us with interesting examples of this case in his religious "La Corona" sonnets. For instance:

> *Salvation to all that will is nigh,*
> That All, which alwayes is All every where,
> Which cannot sinne, and yet all sinnes must beare,

Which cannot die, yet cannot chuse but die,
Loe, Faithfull Virgin, yeelds himselfe to lye
In prison, in thy wombe; and though he there
Can take no sinne, nor thou give, yet he'will weare
Taken from thence, flesh, which deaths force may trie.
Ere by the spheares time was created, thou
Wast in his minde, who is thy Sonne, and Brother,
Whom thou canceiv'st, conceived; yea thou art now
Thy Makers maker, and thy Fathers mother,
Thou'hast light in darke; and shutst in little roome,
Immensity cloysterd in the deare wombe.[30]

This second poem, "Annunciation," from the set of seven is a collocation of paradoxes, all reducible to a continual oscillation between Christ-as-God and Christ-as-man. Rather than enforcing our sense of the mysterious union of opposites in Christ, these paradoxes generate the opposite—the attempt to make them exponible, to break them down. In "Loves infiniteness" the sense of reaching toward a fleeting, intuitive glimpse of the mysterious coalescence of opposites is achieved through an attempt to render this intuition in precise conceptions and language. When overt paradoxical statements do occur, they have been "earned" poetically through the labor of trying to avoid them: they come as a last resort, as it were, and force themselves on the speaker. But here, dialectic does not appear through the phenomena of the poem, but is rather itself the overt and intended significance of the phenomena itself. And the ease with which the paradoxes are presented militates, oddly enough, against precisely what would seem to be their intended effect, namely, an invitation to the reader to transcend discursive thought and to wonder at the mystery of the Incarnation. The actual, though probably not the intended, result is a clear apprehension of how "Thy Makers maker, and thy Fathers mother" is easily broken down into alternating predications grounded on Christ-as-God and Christ-as-man. Thus, in a curious sense, the dialectic between dianoia and mythos remains, but works in a reverse manner to that already outlined. Rather than opt for a univocal ideal of perfect static intuition of the mystery of the Incarnation, the speaker attempts to render it overtly in language which communicates precisely its incommunicability. Supposedly, then, mythos and dianoia reflect each other simply. But such in fact is not the case. If the poem only succeeds in making the reader aware of just how this mystery can be broken down into discrete predications grounded on discrete concepts, then the actual dianoia of the poem is rather a dissolving of mystery than its enhancement.

I realize that Donne's poetry is preeminently open to the kind of dialectical analysis I have made it exemplary of, and it might well appear that this fact would limit the universality which I have claimed for this approach. Before I close this section I want to examine a poem which operates quite differently from those of Donne, though written at about the same time: Ralegh's "The Nymph's Reply to the Shepherd." This poem allows me to test the operation of dialectical logic in a lyric that is itself overtly presented as a corrective to still another lyric's presumed partial and univocal view of its subject. Marlowe's "Passionate Shepherd to His Love" and Ralegh's "Reply" are usually taken, together with Donne's "The Bait," as forming a single debate. However, though I am interested in Ralegh's poem for its own sake, it is interesting to note that in the context of the debate situation in which it is overtly placed, it shows itself clearly taking an inadvertently partial stance, such as I have argued that all lyrics implicitly take. In this respect, all lyrics are in some way or other "replies" to a variety of other statements, whether they are made by some situation in the poet's life, some portion of the history of the race or nature, or, for that matter, poems by other poets. This reply aspect of the lyric, summed up with such neatness in Ralegh's poem, is another way of formulating my essential point about the dialectic of the lyric: the fact that the lyric necessarily embodies one answer chosen from (presumably) several ones possible on a given matter, and as such announces its own univocal partiality through the phenomena of its overtly projected completeness. As I will show, the reader is moved to uncover a countermovement which announces itself as buried in the movement of the speaker's argument, and realizing the dialectical interrelation of both movements, he encounters rather an enhancement of the richness of the poem's embodied emotion, than, as in "The Flea," an unravelling or discounting of it.

> If all the world and love were young,
> And truth in every Shepherd's tongue,
> These pretty pleasures might me move,
> To live with thee and be thy love.
>
> Time drives the flocks from field to fold,
> When Rivers rage and Rocks grow cold,

And Philomel becometh dumb,
The rest complains of cares to come.

The flowers do fade, and wanton fields,
To wayward winter reckoning yields,
A honey tongue, a heart of gall,
Is fancy's spring, but sorrow's fall.

Thy gowns, thy shoes, thy beds of Roses,
Thy cap, thy kirtle, and thy posies
Soon break, soon wither, soon forgotten;
In folly ripe, in reason rotten.

Thy belt of straw and Ivy buds,
Thy Coral clasps and Amber studs,
All these in me no means can move,
To come to thee, and be thy love.

But could youth last, and love still breed,
Had joys no date, nor age no need,
Then these delights my mind might move,
To live with thee, and be thy love.[31]

Marlowe's shepherd had projected an ideal pastoral landscape which implicitly ignored the fact of time, and what the shepherd ignored, Ralegh's nymph consciously supplies, and supplies in such a way as to call attention to her taking a stand on the fact of time and the whole of human existence as it "really is." The nymph is proposing a corrective by stating the fullness of the dianoia controlling shepherds, nymphs, and all that "The valleys, groves, hills, and fields, / Woods, or steepy mountain yields."

We might, with only partial symmetry, sum up the emotional coordinates that set off the nymph's reply against the shepherd's invitation as those of "disillusionment" vs. "yearning." Certainly, both emotions are always to some extent present in many versions of the golden age, for both emotions imply each other. It is, nevertheless, this mutual implication of both attitudes which the nymph's reply seeks to deny, and in the process of denying only succeeds in affirming. Marlowe's poem, in its careful importation of civilized trappings into the pastoral landscape, seeks to abrogate the ambivalent emotion the denizen of history feels when contemplating a region projected dialectically as the opposite of his own bondage to time and decay. The birds that sing madrigals, the embroidered kirtle, the buckles of gold, coral clasps, and amber studs: these are conflated with the usual items of pastoral existence, so as to achieve the purity (and univocality) of a vision momentarily cut loose from just those claims urged so inexorably by Ralegh's poem. So, to that extent, Marlowe's poem is not characterized by yearning at all: for a single intuitive instant the vision is realized.

But the nymph's reply considers each item in a point-by-point refutation, held rigidly to matching stanzas, and indicates the double potentiality for both beauty and decay inherent in them. Where the shepherd achieves, verbally at least, a realization of vision, the nymph reinterprets his statement as only yearning for this realization, and against this yearning her overt argument asserts simple disillusionment. This disillusionment is carried in the poem by the repetition of a single argument, which is summed up in "fancy's spring, but sorrow's fall" and "In folly ripe, in reason rotten." The mythos of the nymph's reply consists entirely of transforming symbols of yearning into symbols of disillusionment: "ripeness" which turns "rotten" under the presssure of "reason." And this transformation is the heart of the poem's dialectical action. Quite simply, in opting for disillusionment at the expense of yearning, the poem announces the speaker's yearning in the very act of renouncing it. The "If" that opens the poem, and is implicitly carried through it to the "could" in the first line of the last stanza, says that "if" the pastoral world which the shepherd promises could in fact be realized in the timelessness which it implies, then such an invitation might well prove irresistible. And insofar as the speaker shows herself as moving firmly away from an ideal of pastoral timelessness, she announces herself as dialectically attached to it. Dialectically, the poem attempts to project a resolution of the conflict between yearning and disillusionment; in turn, this apparent resolution betrays itself as in fact hiding a real conflict, unresolved and unresolvable because the partial terms of this resolution necessarily imply the yearning which has supposedly been finally escaped. And the third moment of dialectical logic in the poem—its delicate conflation of yearning and disillusionment in mutual reciprocity of tension and harmony—is the substance of the reader's perception of the poem's dianoia. As action-done the mythos of the poem achieves a complexity of emotion through the attempt on the speaker's part to achieve the emotional simplicity of resolution. But as action-made, Ralegh's poem renders as its dianoia the coexistence of yearning for the great, good place and the disillusionment which is both the cause and consequence of this yearning, that has been through history one of the main manifestations of the human drive toward a timeless, "plotless" existence, itself the fountainhead of dialectic.

3. The Dialectic of Narrative: Milton's "Paradise Lost"

Whereas the plot of the lyric is generated in opposition to the divisiveness, partiality, and univocality of language, the plot of the narrative arises out of the action of the narrative's agent as it conflicts with and evokes the counteractions of other agents. And while the dialectical logic of the lyric unfolds in the conflict among the various partial verbalizings of a total fact, in the narrative this conflict is embodied in the cooperation among the various agents, who in verbalizing (i.e., both speaking and acting) one part of the narrative's dianoia act out this dianoia through their mutual conflict.

However, the narrative has one point in common with the lyric, one which definitively sets it off from the drama. Like the lyric, it is speech spoken by a persona, the overt or implied speaker of the narrative itself. The narrator may share in the action of the narrative in a variety of possible ways, as Wayne Booth has pointed out, and therefore is involved in the dialectic of the narrative just as the agents of the narrative are themselves.[32] The narrator stands in a double analogy, on the one hand imitating the author himself in manipulating an action-made, and on the other being part of the action-done. This double function facilitates a number of variations on the narrator's participation in the action, because his para-authorial stance enables him to act as if he were in complete control over the action-made, whereas in fact he is also potentially subject to irony insofar as he is part of the action-done. In this respect, his para-authorial control has a teleology dialectically similar to that of the main character, in that both aim at or assume total control over the matter of their respective actions and thereby invite counteractions. Within the narration, this counteraction is embodied in other characters, and for the narrator himself, it may be supplied by the reader himself, once he is prepared to stand off and view the narrator as himself part of the action-done. The result may thus be a multiplying of the mythos-dianoia dialectic. The narrator as the maker of the action possesses the dianoia of that action in roughly the same way the agent within the narrative believes he also possesses his actions' meaning. But in turn, the narrator's assumption of this dianoia can very well be itself incomplete, becoming thereby part of the overall mythos and subject to the larger dianoia intended by the author himself.

The main use of *Paradise Lost* here lies in the fact that the poem's subject gives us the radical myth and paradigm for all plots: Satan, Adam, and Eve attempt to become "like" God, a state which within the terms used in this essay would be the archetype of all the motives which generate plot in any work. Further, as Kenneth Burke has pointed out, the fact of creation itself is the radical foundation of the "divisiveness" in the time/space world which we know, and Milton in it has given us a myth through which the very existence of dialectic, the logic of divisiveness and conflict, is "explained" at its source. Finally, the fact that the narrator participates in the poem's dialectic allows him to take on some of the archetypal characteristics of all possible narrators of all possible plots. This last point I can only hope to suggest rather than prove, and this is true to a lesser extent of all my assertions about the poem's meaning. Since the main purpose of this essay is not so much to interpret works representative of the lyric, narrative, and dramatic genres as rather to exhibit the usefulness of a specific methodology, I do not pretend to completeness in the interpretations. *Paradise Lost* is the largest and most complicated work I will discuss here, and what follows is not so much a total interpretation of the whole poem, as a skeleton outline of how such an interpretation might proceed along lines suggested by dialectical logic.[33]

The "plottiness" of the poem is the necessary concomitant of the fact of creation. The "division" from God which occurs when he creates beings "other" than Himself, contains within itself the potentiality not only of "harmony-through-division," but also of "disharmony-through-division." Milton proposes to show how the ultimate harmony, the eschatological vision of God as "All in All" (III.341), is moved toward and becomes possible through the discursion which is time and human history.[34] The overarching Providential pattern which the poem attempts to justify to men is shown as both the dianoia of the poem, and by extension the dianoia of history. The dianoia contains within itself, stated statically, the essential contradiction which the temporal progress of the poem lays out in dialectical sequence. Though the kernel of this pattern is the "fortunate fall," I shall indicate that the poem's mythos enacts versions of this pattern which take it far beyond any of the limited interpretations given to it by Augustine and other Church

Fathers.[35] As Milton treats it, this dianoia contains within itself the dual potentiality for either eternal damnation (Satan) or salvation (Adam and Eve). The mystery of this dianoia, which is also the mystery of God's Providence, is laid out in an *explicatio* but never totally exhausted by this means; and it is fully manifested as such when we realize that the Providential plan contains within itself, as one of the prime conditions of its own fulfillment, the existence of any attempt to thwart it. In strict keeping with the logic of dialectic, the dianoia of the poem determines the plot of the epic primarily through the attempts of the main agents to thwart it, and in this respect the dialectic by which dianoia generates mythos by means of the the latter's attempt to abrogate dianoia finds its perfect model in *Paradise Lost.*

It would seem that had Satan, Adam, and Eve remained obedient to God, this would also have fulfilled God's Providence. We as fallen creatures can have at best only a negative idea of what that "plot" would have been like. That there is division and movement in Heaven and unfallen nature, Milton quite definitely indicates.[36] It is not as if the alternative to the plot that fallen creatures must enact was a simply static existence (like that of the ineffable One in Plato's *Parmenides*). What Milton is proposing is the notion that the dianoia which is God's Providence is fulfilled whether creatures attempt to abrogate this dianoia or not. The ultimate tragic feelings that the poem generates in the reader leave him, as they leave Adam in Book XII, "full of doubt" whether to repent of the sin of the fall or to "rejoice / Much more, that much more good thereof shall spring" (XII.469ff.). The dianoia has been justified by the narrator to the extent that the reader now recognizes the mystery of the dialectical logic by which the freedom of the creatures either to fall or not "cooperates" in either case with that dianoia. The concept of the fortunate fall is relevant here, because it sets up various options by which the freedom to fall and to make one's fall either fortunate or unfortunate derive from an eternal and fixed economy of Divine action, in which any possibility is a fulfillment of it.

Adam and Eve make their fall fortunate, but Satan does not. The difference between the two cases, as Milton indicates respectively in Books X and IV, lies in the acquiescence in or refusal to acquiesce in the fact that the violation of God's ordination of place is likewise a violation of one's own freedom of will. The freedom of all three has thus the dual potentiality of either willing itself or willing against itself.

Satan binds himself to his own projected self-image of liberated heroic conqueror and to the consequent enslavement to his followers' opinions of himself (IV.81ff.); whereas the freedom which was the condition of Adam's fall likewise allows him to understand how he himself is responsible for that fall through an abuse of that freedom (x.746ff.). In either case, the free choice to recognize one's responsibility for the fall or not to recognize it leads to bringing good out of evil, because the choice of good over evil, both for Adam and Eve and for their progeny, derives from that same freedom which allows them to reject the good. And that freedom is itself "determined" by God:

> for so
> I form'd them free, and free they must remain,
> Till they enthrall themselves: I else must change
> Thir nature, and revoke the high Decree
> Unchangeable, Eternal, which ordain'd
> Their freedom: they themselves ordain'd thir fall.
> (III.123–128)

The pattern of relation between mythos and dianoia here is quite similar to that in *Oedipus Rex*, where the hero's very attempt to thwart the oracle causes him to leave Corinth to seek out unknowingly his doom. That play presents us with the teasing and ultimately mysterious paradox that, in running from the oracle, Oedipus exhibits himself as simultaneously believing in it and not believing in it. For, had he believed it unequivocally, he would have known that he could not escape it, and the fact that he did believe in its possibility is shown precisely in his attempting to flee it. Likewise in *Paradise Lost*, the dianoia of God's Providence fulfills itself because its very structure, in the dual potentialities paradoxically implied in the fortunate fall, contains within itself a margin of "allowance" by which either road leads to the same conclusion.

Dialectically, the poem's mythos could be laid out in this fashion. The first moment of dialectical logic illuminates the ambiguous states of the unfallen angels in Heaven and of unfallen man and nature. The harmony which exhibits itself as the poem progresses as a "conflict-under-the-sign-of-resolution" is the very divisiveness I have already mentioned, inherent in the notion of creation itself. As Satan says in preparing his angels for revolt, "Orders and Degrees / Jar not with liberty, but well consist" (v.792–793), and the harmony-amid-division finds its unfallen archetype in the perfect mirroring of the Father in the Son "Substantially express'd" (III.140). One of Milton's main devices for rendering a benign harmony-amid-division is the cohesive love that binds all unfallen creatures to one another through recognizing in themselves their own reflection as ultimately that of God. But the conflict which lurks covertly beneath this resolution is merely this mirroring turned upside down: the narcissistic mirroring of Satan in Sin and Death, Eve's temptation and ultimate fall to worshiping herself, and Hell's perverted attempt to mirror heaven. The very act of creation itself creates the condition that may potentially turn harmony into disharmony and creation back into chaos. That creatures, angels, and men, free agents in their own right, must, in being "other" than God, "choose" nevertheless harmonious division over disharmonious division is of course one of the poem's main points.

This first moment, however, leads necessarily into the second moment, a "resolution-under-the-sign-of-conflict," by means I have already partly dealt with. That the attempt to thwart this harmony-amid-division occurs within the circumscribing boundaries of Providence, rather than outside it, is another of the poem's main points. The farthest reach of the poem's attempt to "justify the ways of God to men" (I.26) is the elucidation of the dialectical economy of these ways. For if the conditions of the creation of free agents create the possibility of conflict, they likewise create the possibilities of resolution of that conflict. The freedom to fall, and the further freedom to make this fall either fortunate or unfortunate are always in the poem the same freedom. Satan's choice of acting against the dianoia of creation brings him ironically into complete enslavement to God, not simply through the external agency of God's force, but through the original impulse to become as God, which motivated his fall in the first place. Satan remains from the very beginning dialectically tied to God in opposition, so that he affirms his complete lack of freedom to perform any actions other than those that in one way or another acknowledge God as his conqueror. Satan's dialectical attachment to God extends so far that he condemns himself even to enacting a parody of the Providential pattern:

> If then his Providence
> Out of our evil seek to bring forth good,
> Our labor must be to pervert that end,
> And out of good still find means of evil;
>
> (I.162–165)

Likewise, Adam and Eve's fall took place under the overt sign of perverted mirroring, Eve yielding to the serpent's temptation to narcissism, and Adam in turn yielding to his image in her:

> So forcible within my heart I feel
> The Bond of Nature draw me to my own,
> My own in thee, for what thou art is mine;
> Our State cannot be sever'd, we are one,
> One Flesh, to lose thee were to lose myself.
>
> (IX.955–959)

The theme of mirror images in the poem is only one out of many vehicles Milton uses to test and demonstrate the dialectically opposite conditions of fallen and unfallen creaturehood. That Adam is created "Hee for God only, shee for God in him" (IV.299) sets up the proper ordering of mirror images. Adam is left with the choice of properly valuing his own image insofar as it is the mirror of God's image, or in reverse, of idolatrously worshiping God's image in himself as his own. The movement upwards from Eve to Adam and God is perverted at the fall, where Eve worships her own image and Adam worships his God-given image in her. When Satan first sees the pair and notes that he "could love" them, "so lively shines / In them Divine resemblance" (IV.363–364), only to go on and almost imperceptibly turn this potential love to hate, we grasp the dialectically dual potentialities of man's beauties and desirability as reflector of the Divine.

The second moment of the dialectical logic in the poem grows therefore out of the first moment, and the fact that this second moment of overt conflict also contains the covert possibility of renewed harmony is illuminated in the third moment. Harmony and conflict have already been seen to be mutually causal and reciprocal in that the division which is the concomitant of created harmony implies likewise the possibility of disharmony. The resolution that makes the fall fortunate is negated by Satan's insistence on remaining frozen in the second moment of dialectical logic, whereby his conflict with God generates a dialectical harmony with Him, a harmony which in his pride he must eternally negate, and in negating find himself eternally the instrument of God's Providence. In the case of Adam and Eve, however, the reciprocity of conflict and resolution, which has operated malignly in their fall, now operates benignly in their repentance.

The nature of this repentance is of course bound up with the nature of the fall, and I must pursue this a little further to indicate in more detail the dialectical logic operating in it. Milton gives the key both to the temptation and to the way it might have been resisted in the narrator's exhortation to Adam and Eve, that they "know to know no more" (IV.775). The sense of this exhortation is filled out through Raphael's narratives, during which the lines separating allowed from forbidden knowledge are drawn fine but firmly. If we look forward to the dialogue between Eve and the serpent and ask where it was that she started to go wrong, we discover it when she begins herself to "reason" about God's command to abstain from the forbidden fruit in a manner like the serpent's. The command itself is treated throughout the poem as a purely arbitrary one, whereby Adam and Eve are asked to obey it simply because it is a commandment. Milton expounds this aspect of the command more directly in *De doctrina christiana* when he comments upon a "covenant of works" which God made with Adam:

No works whatever are required of Adam; a particular act only is forbidden. It was necessary that something should be forbidden or commanded as a test of fidelity, and that an act in its own nature indifferent, in order that man's obedience might be thereby manifested. For since it was the disposition of man to do what was right, as being naturally good and holy, it was not necessary that he should be bound by the obligation of a covenant to perform that to which he was of himself inclined; nor would he have given any proof of obedience by the performance of works to which he was led by a natural impulse, independently of the divine command. Not to mention, that no command, whether proceeding from God or from a magistrate, can properly be called a covenant, even where rewards and punishments are attached to it; but rather an exercise of jurisdiction.[37]

If the command itself required only unquestioning obedience to a sanction which, by reason of its very intention, could have nothing clearly rational about it, the question then arises as to just exactly how Adam's and Eve's reason was brought into play. When Eve early in the temptation says to the serpent that "our Reason is our Law" (IX. 654), she is ambiguously stating the faculty both through which she is to be seduced, and by which she might have yet stood unfallen.

The essence of the warning to "know to know no more," as the facts of the temptation and fall inform us, was that Eve was to reason to reason's limitations. When the serpent, using a chain of reasoning itself fallacious (arguing, for instance, that "Your fear itself of Death removes the fear" [IX.702]), proceeds to "prove" to Eve that God's command is unreasonable, the narrator is asking the reader to recognize two closely related facts. First, that the serpent is quite correct in pointing out this unreasonableness; and second, that reason, precisely because erected in the prelapsarian state, contains within itself the seeds of its own hubris. The moment Eve begins to accept reason as the test of the viability of the command ("our Reason is our Law") she is on the way to falling. Her reason would appear to fail, in other words, to the exact extent that she fails to reason to reason's limits, to "know to know no more." The repetition of the word *know* here indicates the precise difficulty involved, for it would seem that the narrator would have us understand that the highest and ultimate act of reason itself is the recognition of its own limitation. But to know to know no more is to call upon an active faculty actively to limit its own activity. Thus the delicate balance between reason upright and reason so upright as to go beyond its own capacity is with a precise poise struck. The final act of reasoning, in other words, is to recognize the infinite transcendence of God in His ineffable will. Making reason her law without qualification, Eve falls.

Dialectically, then, we find the erected state of Adam and Eve before the fall simultaneously both their strength and their weakness. Theirs of course is a relative perfection, not absolute, and the critics, both those who have argued that they are fallen already before Book IX and those who find it impossible to believe that such perfect creatures can in fact fall, miss the dialectically poised balance of the dual potentialities of the state of innocence as the narrator portrays them. In seeking to achieve a state of absolute perfection, they set in motion a dialectical counteraction that had indeed been promised them had they refused to obey, but not in the form in which they actually experience it:

> Soon found thir Eyes how op'n'd, and thir minds
> How dark'n'd; innocence, that as a veil
> Had shadow'd them from knowing ill, was gone,
> Just confidence, and native righteousness,
> And honor from about them, naked left
> To guilty shame: hee cover'd, but his Robe
> Uncover'd more.
>
> (IX.1053–1059)

In attempting univocally to rise they have fallen, and in attempting to thwart Providence they find themselves condemned to fulfill it, but with the all-important proviso that allows them, also as part of that

Providence, to fulfill it by making their fall either fortunate or unfortunate. The copenetration of freedom and determinism in the poem, of mythos and dianoia, is exemplary, because Milton with remarkable insight has lighted on a dianoia that allows both the maximum freedom to the mythos and at the same time controls it rigidly by its own built-in dialectical logic.

The poem enacts the dual potentialities of this logic, however, in still another way, one by which the narrator, and through the narrator the reader, are both brought into the poem's action. The narrator is himself both a fallen creature and an aspirant to divine knowledge, as the great invocations to Books I, III, and VII indicate. The invocation to Book III opens in this manner:

> Hail holy Light, offspring of Heav'n first-born,
> Or of th' Eternal Coeternal beam
> May I express thee unblam'd? since God is Light,
> And never but in unapproached Light
> Dwelt from Eternity, dwelt then in thee,
> Bright effluence of bright essence increate.
> Or hear'st thou rather pure Ethereal stream,
> Whose Fountain who shall tell?
>
> (III.1–8)

The alternatives the narrator offers by which God's light may be expressed, themselves act out the issue facing the narrator. The problem is one of correct "names," of correct language to express the "unapproached Light," and he finds it necessary to posit either an identification of this Light with the Father, or a sequential procession of it from "heav'n first-born." The problem is not "in" God but in human language and thought, which must proceed univocally by either identifications or separations. Here as elsewhere in a variety of ways the Miltonic narrator employs what at first glance appears to be a liability so that it becomes functional in the poem as an asset, namely the fact that as fallen man he is mortally unable to render events occurring before the time/space continuum of fallen human history in the discursion of human language. In aspiring to "the highth of this great Argument," in intending "to soar / Above th' *Aonian* Mount, while [he] pursues / Things unattempted yet in Prose or Rhyme" (I.24, 14–16), the narrator is potentially in danger of repeating the sin of Satan and Adam and Eve. The invocation of the heavenly muse is itself a conventional ploy that has its significance elsewhere than in the conventional notion that the human spirit is in need of divine inspiration. As the precondition of this inspiration, the narrator must himself enact the fortunate fall and realize that he can be raised and supported only after he admits and acquiesces in the fact that as fallen creature he is low and dark:

> So much the rather thou Celestial Light
> Shine inward, and the mind through all her powers
> Irradiate, there plant eyes, all mist from thence
> Purge and disperse, that I may see and tell
> Of things invisible to mortal sight.
>
> (III.51–55)

As regards the narrator's own position in relation to the story he tells, the effort is toward employing the discursion and frailty of human language resulting from the fall as itself a means of purifying this language of its fallenness. That such is impossible in any complete fashion is of course obvious. But as Stanley Fish has pointed out, the reader himself is periodically brought "into" the poem to purge the language of its fallenness by recognizing his own tendency to respond to this fallenness, a recognition that prepares him also to make his own the exigencies of a fortunate fall.[38]

The narrator must carefully inoculate the language he uses to mediate the prelapsarian state of nature and man against the possibility of the reader's attributing to this state any of the malign possibilities inherent in this language. He accomplishes this in general by granting to Paradise the potentialities for a fall while carefully defining them with dialectical acuteness as only potentialities for a fall. The four main streams of Paradise which after, as the narrator says, they "fell / Down" (IV.230–231) are sent "wand-ring" (234) "With mazy error" (239), the nakedness of the couple, the "enormous bliss" (V.297) of Paradise itself contain, as the overtones of the words themselves contain, the potentiality for malign transformation. As a more extended example, we have our first sight of Eve:

> Shee as a veil down to the slender waist
> Her unadorned golden tresses wore
> Dishevell'd, but in wanton ringlets wav'd
> As the Vine curls her tendrils, which impli'd
> Subjection, but requir'd with gentle sway,
> And by her yielded, by him best receiv'd,
> Yielded with coy submission, modest pride,
> And sweet reluctant amorous delay.
>
> (IV.304–311)

If Eve in her "wanton" nakedness calls forth a prurient reaction from the reader, the whole poem calls forth likewise the recognition that such a reaction is due to the reader's own postlapsarian sinfulness, and if he is to participate in the poem's intended meaning he must strive to discount the prurience which the language equivocally conveys.

However, to discount too completely is to miss Milton's meaning. Dialectically, the total logic of the language describing unfallen Paradise can be graphed in a pattern parallel to that characterizing the fortunate fall theme as a whole. The possibly malign and prurient meanings the language may have for us identifies that language as our own, forming the harmony of the first moment. The consequent discounting of these malign meanings which the reader is invited to make correspond to the rest of this moment, whereby we realize that whatever wantonness we perceive, it is not to be projected onto the unfallen pair. But if Adam and Eve's innocence, being their weakness as well as their strength in the face of temptation, may likewise allow the realization of this wantonness and prurience, then the dialectic moves into the second moment. The separation or conflict between fallen reader and unfallen couple masks the possibility of a fateful unity and identification. Thus Eve's "wanton ringlets" and "sweet amorous delay" are ironic types of her lust and her separation from Adam, two events connected with her fall. The discounted fallen meanings are reinstated equivocally. The third moment would then state overtly this dialectical reciprocity which the language forces on the reader's attention.

I have used the word *inoculate* deliberately, it being the medical version of the fortunate fall. The narrator's language is endowed with enough of the disease of fallenness as to allow it to be then discounted in order to mediate the vision of an unfallen paradise to the reader with some degree of purity and safety. That it must, of necessity, be so inoculated is of course due to the stance shared by the reader with the narrator on the hither side of Paradise. In this fashion I hope to convey something of the remarkable resourcefulness with which Milton has brought his narrator's own fallen liabilities to operate as assets in the poem's total plot.

A second reality, if anything even more remote from verbalization, is Heaven and the nature of a God's-eye view of creation. God is first seen Himself seeing:

> Now had th' Almighty Father from above,
> From the pure Empyrean where he sits
> High Thron'd above all highth, bent down his eye,
> His own works and their works at once to view:
>
> (III.56–59)

The intuitive, transdiscursive nature of this Divine Vision is made clear enough by Raphael to Adam:

> So spake th' Almighty, and to what he spake
> His Word, the Filial Godhead, gave effect.
> Immediate are the Acts of God, more swift
> Than time or motion, but to human ears
> Cannot without procéss of speech be told,
> So told as earthly notion can receive.
>
> (VII.174–179)

The precise angle by which the narrator's vision diverges from God's is extremely important in the poem, because, to the extent the narrator attempts to render the poem's events in terms of the overarching dianoia which controls them, he is likewise aspiring to the Divine Vision. He is repeatedly inoculated against the potential pride of this aspiration in the three invocations to Books I, III, and VII. But once this fact is assimilated, nothing less than the radical condition of the epic as verbal discourse becomes the issue. The already large and growing scholarship on *Paradise Lost* which deals with the voluminous internal parallelism, both direct and ironic, with which the poem abounds, suggests Milton's method for dealing with the necessary fact of the poem's discursiveness. Satan's and Hell's various parody mirrorings of God, the Son's total reflection of God's Word and glory, and Adam and Eve's poised state between, all achieve in the reader's total vision of the poem something approximating (but in only approximating, falling infinitely short of) the instantaneous vision of God, in which past, present, and future, and all the parallels which these will present to the discursive mind of historical man, are grasped in an eternal moment of total intuition. Any particular moment of the poem is liable to exfoliate before the reader's eye meanings, direct and oblique, Divine and Satanic, which link it with still other meanings. The poem's very discursiveness enacts its total dianoia only in progressive parts. But in being "partial" they are arranged by the fallen but purified narrator so that they cooperate in their very divisiveness in rendering that total dianoia, through mirrorings that convey to the reader simultaneously separation and identification as reciprocal functions of each other. One example will have to suffice. When Eve tells of the first moments of her creation in Book IV, we have already seen two other versions of self-communion which parallel her incipient narcissism. The first was the idolatrous and incestuous generation of Sin out of Satan, and Death from them both; the second was the Son as mirror reflection of the Father. When Eve speaks of momentarily preferring her own self to Adam, we suddenly become aware of the malign possibilities lurking in that God-given Divine reflection that she sees in the pool. That she is to love her own image in Adam insofar as he is in turn the reflection of God, rather than incestuously in herself, is not a caveat that the reader is allowed to place against her incipient narcissism; on the contrary, that narcissism flows as surely from her natural love of the Divine image as does her love for Adam. Such is the awful freedom that is both their strength and potential weakness. The identification of the three incidents drives the reader to recognize their essential differences. Eve's narcissism is, of course, the moot point, standing halfway between God and Satan. In the first moment of dialectical logic, we recognize that the harmony of the three incidents conceals divergences of various moral import. But in recognizing this we are further reminded that the impulse of Eve's love may follow either the Divine or the Satanic pattern: resolution-under-the-sign-of-conflict. And the third moment, wherein we see the first two moments coalescing dialectically in the poem's language and meaning, is the closest the reader ever comes (though there are many other points in the poem where a similar vision is evoked) to the instantaneous Divine vision of all the poem's materials gathered together within its dianoia.

The poem's own form of discursive narration enacts the dianoia of its informing vision by making those very attempts to thwart that vision which arise through the fallenness of the narrator's language turn back and serve it. The multiple parallelism in the poem causes it to turn inward centripetally on itself in a self-mirroring which is rife with potentialities for both the Divine and the Satanic. That the malign forms of these potentialities are ultimately exorcised by the narrator is due to his having acquiesced in the discursiveness and fallenness of his own language, thereby allowing the self-mirroring of the poem's structure to be inoculated against Satanic narcissism. I might suggest that this inoculation in fact begins the poem: the heroic rhetoric of the first two books, long praised as the height of

Milton's epic style, is in fact a parody of the kind of epic *Paradise Lost* would have been had Satan been the author. Off and on in these opening books we come across lines which could have either the Miltonic or Satanic narrator as the speaker, with ironic contrasts arising by reason of that fact. A small example is the narrator's comments after Belial's speech in Book II:

> Thus *Belial* with words cloth'd in reason's garb
> Counsell'd ignoble ease, and peaceful sloth,
> Not peace: and after him thus *Mammon* spake.
>
> (II.226–228)

We might ask ourselves from whose viewpoint would "ignoble ease" and "peaceful sloth" be reprehensible? Certainly not the Miltonic narrator's, for the criticism in these lines implies an ideal of heroic action in the name of none other than Satanic rebellion. A more extended passage in Book I describes the gathering of the demonic army before its leader. The long comparison of human armies pejoratively to this archetypal army is primarily addressed to the human reader, and the effect intended by the Satanic narrator is neatly undercut when it is placed within the larger context of the Miltonic narrator's rhetoric:

> For never since created man,
> Met such imbodied force, as nam'd with these
> Could merit more than that small infantry
> Warr'd on by Cranes: though all the Giant brood
> Of *Phlegra* with th' Heroic Race were join'd
> That fought at *Thebes* and *Ilium,* on each side
> Mixt with auxiliar Gods; and what resounds
> In Fable or *Romance* of *Uther's* Son
> Begirt with *British* and *Armoric* Knights;
> And all who since, Baptiz'd or Infidel
> Jousted in *Aspramont* or *Montalban,*
> *Damasco,* or *Marocco,* or *Trebisond,*
> Or whom *Biserta* sent from *Afric* shore
> When *Charlemain* with all his *Peerage* fell
> By *Fontarabbia.* Thus far these beyond
> Compare of mortal prowess, yet observ'd
> Thir dread commander: he above the rest
> In shape and gesture proudly eminent
> Stood like a Tow'r; his form had yet not lost
> All her Original brightness, nor appear'd

> Less than Arch-Angel ruin'd, and th' excess
> Of Glory obscur'd:
>
> (I.573–594)

From the Satanic viewpoint this catalogue of fabled knights and armies is intended simply to impress the human reader with how far the army of fallen angels surpasses even these, and in surpassing them they "yet observ'd / Thir dread commander." It is the rhetoric of egoistic self-aggrandizement, a show of strength calculated to awe the beholder; nor is absent long the expected parody of God, who in Book III is described in this fashion:

> Fountain of Light, thyself invisible
> Amidst the glorious brightness where thou sit'st
> Thron'd inaccessible, but when thou shad'st
> The full blaze of thy beams, and through a cloud
> Drawn round about thee like a radiant Shrine,
> Dark with excessive bright thy skirts appear, . . .
>
> (III.375–380)

This Satan mimics in language which before our eyes is already on the way to becoming self-parody—the satiric instrument of the Miltonic narrator—in "th' excess / Of Glory obscur'd," self-parody then suddenly transformed into a debunking comparison with the following lines: "As when the Sun new ris'n / Looks through the Horizontal misty Air / Shorn of his Beams, or from behind the Moon / In dim Eclipse disastrous twilight sheds" (I.594–597).

I shall not develop this point further, but only go on to point out what seems its primary purpose in the poem's total plot. As both Miltonic narrator and Satan soar upwards toward Heaven at the end of Book II, we receive a remarkable effect by reading straight past the book division:

> Or in the emptier waste, resembling Air,
> [Satan] Weighs his spread wings, at leisure to behold
> Far off th' Empyreal Heav'n, extended wide
> In circuit, undetermin'd square or round,
> With Opal Tow'rs and Battlements adorn'd
> Of living Sapphire, once his native Seat;
> And fast by hanging in a golden Chain
> This pendant world, in bigness as a Star
> Of smallest Magnitude close by the Moon.
> Thither full fraught with mischievous revenge,
> Accurst, and in a cursed hour he hies.

> Hail holy Light, offspring of Heav'n first-born,
> Or of th' Eternal Coeternal beam
> May I express thee unblam'd? . . .
>
> (II.1045–1055–III.1–3)

Who speaks these last three lines? The Miltonic narrator, surely, or so at least we may determine as the invocation to Book III proceeds. But the momentary effect is that of Satan seeing the light of Heaven and praising it, just as he momentarily praises God's image in Adam and Eve. This effect calls attention to the fact that the Miltonic narrator's voice has now earned the right to be unequivocally separated from the Satanic voice only after its potentialities for turning into the malign rhetoric of Satan have been allowed and enacted in the previous two books. It is one of Milton's most daring strokes that he open *Paradise Lost* with statements of the poem's ultimate values which show these values and Heaven itself mirrored parodically in an upside-down fashion. Likewise, the language of the Miltonic narrator can justify itself as ready to proceed to tell (and in telling, enact) the dianoia of God's Providence only after parodies of it in the rhetoric of false heroism have been allowed and the language itself inoculated against them. As I have indicated before, the logic of dialectic by which harmonies are really conflicts-under-the-sign-of-resolution is exploited by Milton in his defining the distance which separates the Divine from the Satanic by first joining the two "positions" in parodic and mirror-like identification.

I hope I have by now shown *Paradise Lost* to be in some respects an archetypal narrative. In a very real sense narration itself is one of the poem's main subjects, manifested both in the fable of creation and the fall, and in the narrator's own struggle to achieve the appropriate narrative stance and process. The mythos of the poem is generated in opposition to the poem's dianoia and thereby embodies this dianoia in a fashion that makes this generation and embodiment the poem's main subject. The act of creation, the freedom to fall or not to fall, and the further freedom to make a fall fortunate or unfortunate, all of these take place under the rigid determinism of Divine Providence; and to choose to cooperate with the dianoia of this Providence or not to cooperate with it, is still to cooperate with it. The nature of this dianoia in *Paradise Lost,* and this is true of all three modes that I examine in this essay, becomes manifest only through the mythos as it lays out the dianoia's parts in discursive fashion. That Providence, as Milton sees it, contains as part of the conditions for its fulfillment the free attempts to thwart it, comes through to the reader only through a plot in which such turns out to be the case. The ultimate, paradoxical coexistence of all "parts" of the Providential scheme, seen in their total coalescence statically, which is the poem's dianoia, can only be "stated" for the fallen reader in discursive terms. Perhaps this is true of the dianoia of any complex mythos: that the critic's attempt to state the dianoia in any other way than the author stated it in the mythos of his work, must necessarily fall short of completeness and integrity. Therefore, just as, from a biblical point of view, the fall of man set in motion the action of Providence throughout all of human history, so likewise *Paradise Lost* as a narrative poem imitates its subject in this way, too: that God's Providence can only be manifested to fallen readers through a discursive mythos whose very existence in opposition to its dianoia, carries the ultimate message that this opposition in reality entails dialectically only an ultimate harmony.

4. The Dialectic of Drama: "Volpone" and "Macbeth"

For the chain of causes cannot by any force be loosed or broken, nor can nature be commanded except by being obeyed. And so those twin objects, *human knowledge* and *human power*, do really meet in one; and it is from ignorance of causes that operation fails.

Bacon, *Preface to the Great Instauration*

The dialectic of mythos and dianoia in the comic mode is already implicit in Henri Bergson's contention that the comic arises when mechanical, automatic, and rigid actions are performed within and against a societal context governed by "tension" and "elasticity."[39] It is also implicit in "the movement from *pistis* to *gnosis*, from a society controlled by habit, ritual bondage, arbitrary law and the older characters to a society controlled by youth and pragmatic freedom" which Northrop Frye takes to be one of the main patterns of comedy.[40] However, when Frye goes on to say that "comedy regularly illustrates a victory of arbitrary plot over consistency of character," I will have at least to modify.[41] As his later comments indicate, Frye is viewing comedy primarily as action-made, the decorum of which is governed by the conventions of the comic genre. From that viewpoint, comic characters are made to suffer the absurd complications of situations which arise primarily because they are absurd, and that is what comedy is all about. I would want to modify this statement in the direction of the action-done and note that the arbitrariness of the plot is somehow a result of the equally arbitrary consistency of the comic characters themselves. As such, the comic plot can be seen both as resulting from the comic character's mechanical and rigid intentions, and as causing him to suffer the return upon himself of the actions flowing from these intentions according to a mechanistic, Hobbesian calculus of action-reaction, bound-rebound.

The Hobbesian "ideal" society is that which the comic character acting according to Bergson's "rigidity" projects and attempts to act in terms of. In it every person moves with determined automatism in a straight line until deflected by an equally automatic movement on the part of another similarly motivated character. However, Hobbes provides us equally with the recognition and reversal that befalls such a character, when he shows how such univocal, single-directional motion must necessarily collide with another force, with the first character's intentions thwarted accordingly. Jonsonian comedy, with its plethora of rigidly motivated characters, provides a whole series of variations on this basic Hobbesian comic plot. The "humors" characters of the early comedies, Morose in *Epicoene,* Sir Epicure Mammon, Tribulation Wholesome, and Kastril in *The Alchemist,* Zeal-Of-The-Land Busy in *Bartholomew Fair,* not to mention the characters in *Volpone* which I will take up later in more detail: all of these characters are motivated by rigid, univocal purposes which project and imply a society of mechanical monomania as the ideal context in which to realize their desires. Whether they are thwarted by the more flexible Lovewits and Truewits, or by characters of their own ilk like Volpone and Mosca, they come to suffer themselves the reflex of their intentions and actions, because they are constitutionally unable to take into account the demands of flexibility and common sense which Jonson's dianoias press in upon them. They move encumbered by the blinders of their own obsessions and cannot see beyond the unidimensional thrusts of their understanding of themselves and of the world around them. In ignoring the dialectical possibilities of their actions, motivated by either guile or folly, they are required to abide the rigors of dialectical logic, and suffer as "comic saviors" for the audience if not for themselves. The dianoia of such a plot inevitably posits some norm of flexibility and awareness of multiple possibilities, and, where embodied in such a character as Truewit in *Epicoene,* this awareness invades the plot itself and moves it directly. It gives the Truewit type a broader view of the field, and allows him the freedom to manipulate the rigid characters by impelling them forward, driven by their own blind momentum.

In *Volpone* Jonson gives us malign versions of "Truewit" in Volpone and Mosca, characters whose putative total awareness of the rigidities of folly allows them greater freedom to play the gods of their victims' weak function. Volpone and Mosca are Truewits gone sour, corrupted moralists whose involvement in the very vices they flay lay them equally open to a dialectical comeuppance. The freedom of the Jonsonian man of wit is here perverted as the freedom of disguise and deceit, and it differs only in degree from the bumbling role-playing of the legacy-hunters. As a result, the plot of *Volpone* gives us a number of characters who continually cooperate with one another in mutual deception, a cooperation that progresses through the force of its own increasing entanglement to the final unravelling, wherein each character likewise cooperates in the others' unmasking. Dialectically, the logic of this progression is pristinely symmetrical and uncluttered.

The real subject of the play is not money, but power. Though Corbaccio, Corvino, and Voltore ostensibly plot for Volpone's money, the delight with which Volpone and Mosca gull them shows in its exuberance and single-mindedness a motivation that transcends mere avarice. When in Act v Volpone decides to spring the trap on the legacy-hunters and will everything to Mosca, it is the sight of their faces when they hear this news that Volpone intends to enjoy (v.ii.83–87).[42] And in the next scene, he cannot resist disguising himself again to follow them into the street and torment them by asking questions about their supposed inheritances. Mosca, who waxes eloquent in a famous soliloquy on the subject, epitomizes the sheer *jeux d'esprit* in his own and his master's knavery:

> But your fine, elegant rascal, that can rise
> And stoop, almost together, like an arrow;
> Shoot through the air as nimbly as a star;
> Turn short as doth a swallow; and be here,
> And there, and here, and yonder, all at once;
> Present to any humor, all occasion;
> And change a visor swifter than a thought,
> This is the creature had the art born with him;
> Toils not to learn it, but doth practice it

> Out of most excellent nature: and such sparks
> Are the true parasites, others but their zanies.
>
> (III.i.23–33)

For Mosca and Volpone the joy of power over the gulls for its own sake, rather than simply for the treasure they can bilk them of, provides the true spice of their pursuits. In this respect, they translate the true, underlying motivations of the legacy-hunters. These use, crudely enough, the power yielded by disguised emotions and intentions to obtain Volpone's money. But they are vulnerable to Volpone and Mosca precisely because their simple avarice does not allow them that freedom granted to the manipulators by their sharpened awareness of the true joy and power achievable in the pursuit of money. Being only avaricious, they are open to attack from those who are cynically aware that mere avarice masks a deeper, more demoniac play for sheer power.

But if Mosca and Volpone chase this power with voracious appetite, they are themselves vulnerable to unmasking, if only because the cunning vision of the manipulator of power masks a similar blindness to the partialities of his own reading of the situation. In summing up the credulity of the legacy-hunters in the first court scene (Act IV) Mosca is ironically commenting as well on a blindness in himself and his master:

> *Volpone:* That yet to me 's the strangest; how th'ast borne it!
> That these, being so divided 'mongst themselves,
> Should not scent somewhat, or in me or thee,
> Or doubt their own side.
> *Mosca:* True, they will not see't.
> Too much light blinds 'em, I think. Each of 'em
> Is so possessed and stuffed with his own hopes
> That anything unto the contrary,
> Never so true, or never so apparent,
> Never so palpable, they will resist it—
> *Volpone:* Like a temptation of the devil.
>
> (V.ii.19–28)

The blindness here is of course the motivating force of the play's mythos, which has as its final goal as action-made the unsealing of this blindness to the full light of the play's dianoia—the copenetration of action and reaction which every character seeks to escape, thereby assuring the conclusion that he must fall victim to it.

The conviction of all the players of the game, that if they are cunning enough the line is a straight and sure one between their intentions and the fulfillments of these intentions, this fulfills the first moment of dialectical logic. This resolution, partial and univocal, is unmasked as a covert conflict when the line of the gull's action is deflected as it enters a field of countermovements which his original intention had not taken into account. The second moment indicates that each of the intriguers generates his own appropriate confidence man, who preys upon him under the same motives and values which had powered himself. Volpone gulls the legacy-hunters, is in turn trapped by Mosca, who is in turn unmasked when Volpone in disguise is compelled to drop his disguise under the counterattack spearheaded by the disappointed Voltore. Thus whatever opposition there is between the intriguers is manifested as a covert unity-under-the-sign-of-opposition. The third moment iluminates the interconnections between these first two moments, in pointing out that the prematurely and univocally conceived resolutions (each character's complacent belief in the viability of his intrigue) only opens him up to the opposition of another intriguer. The play's mythos moves through the generation of opposition out of resolution; and that resolution which opposition in turn generates is the final goal toward which the mythos moves, the final unmasking and sentencing of all the malefactors. By this logic, then, every plot and counterplot in the play cooperates in moving inadvertently toward this unmasking under the overt impulse on the part of all to maintain their masks to the last.

The disposition of the parts of the plot, and of the various subthemes which the plot periodically throws up for our contemplation and laughter, can now be seen as rigidly controlled not by the play's dianoia directly, but by the attempts of the characters to deny this dianoia. From this viewpoint, those most obsessed with power—Volpone and Mosca—are those most enslaved. The word *parasite*, and the recurrent images of bestial preying which run throughout the play, carry a theme on the level of diction which is also reflected in plot and character. Every character attempts through disguise and deceit to get "one-up" on some other character, but to that extent he is tied to his victim in a posture of overt (as well as covert and real) subservience. Mosca is not the only parasite in the play: Corbaccio, Corvino, and Voltore are parasites of Volpone as well; and most revealingly, Volpone is a parasite also, battening on the legacy-hunters in an Iago-like fashion, and dependent upon them for his sense of power. Volpone's univocal ideal would be a never-ending series of gulls, perennial victims on whom he could exercise his ingenuity. But the anagnorisis must come, sooner or later, and Volpone must spring the trap. Once it is sprung in Act v, and the legacy-hunters turned away finally, he has no choice but to pursue them again, like Tamburlaine who must continually search for new kingdoms to conquer. In these respects, then, each character is reciprocally master and slave, power-holder and power-seeker. And as I have already indicated, the cooperation which characterizes their mutual deceptions becomes by the dialectical logic governing their actions a cooperation in unmasking, as disguise and counterdisguise turns at the end into unmasking and counterunmasking.

A theme related to that of disguise, as well as to that of power, is that of fantasy. I have already referred to this theme in Mosca's comments on the blindness of the legacy-hunters, where their enslavement to fantasy—the substitution of images embodying wish-fulfillment for a straight-on vision of the real—leads to their undoing. Volpone and Mosca tease them on and are always more than helped by the veil of private fantasy that descends between their feverish avarice and the real world. Fantasy is always linked with expectation, as Mosca makes clear: all characters (in the discussion so far I am implicitly omitting allusion to Bonario and Celia) live in the future, expecting the fruition of their present intrigues. It is this expectation that drives Voltore, Corbaccio, and Corvino to invest present goods in a future return when Volpone dies. But the most egregious example of fantasy run wild is Volpone's feverish wooing of Celia:

> The heads of parrots, tongues of nightingales,
> The brains of peacocks, and of estriches
> Shall be our food, and, could we get the phoenix,
> Though nature lost her kind, she were our dish. . . .
> Thy baths shall be the juice of July-flowers,
> Spirit of roses, and of violets,
> The milk of unicorns, and panthers' breath
> Gathered in bags and mixed with Cretan wines.
> Our drink shall be preparèd gold and amber,
> Which we will take until my roof whirl round
> With the vertigo; and my dwarf shall dance,
> My eunuch sing, my fool make up the antic.
> Whilst we, in changèd shapes, act Ovid's tales,
> Thou like Europa now, and I like Jove,

> Then I like Mars, and thou like Erycine;
> So of the rest, till we have quite run through,
> And wearied all the fables of the gods.
>
> (III.vii.202–205, 213–225)

This is perverted fantasy, a metamorphosing power that transforms the dead metal of gold into the airy regions of refined hedonism. This conversion upwards of gold into refined pleasures is, of course, matched by the conversion downwards of human realities and values into the bestial. The theme of fantasy supports the disguise theme, in giving the moral valence of the attempts to hide avarice, lust, unnaturalness, and deceit under the masks of truth, sincerity, and morality. Thus most of the characters are disguised before others because they are really disguised for themselves, caught up in the mental fantasies which beckon them always on toward the ideal and perfect voluptuousness, only to be unmasked at the play's end to disclose the debased motives which these fantasies both disguised and were in turn generated by.

The characters of the main plot are vulnerable to others' disguises because they are themselves disguised. In the subplot Sir Politic Wouldbe enacts a parallel folly in reverse, and is subject to comic unmasking by Peregrine precisely because he believes everyone is disguised. His passion for state matters and espionage reduces the intriguers' pretenses to absurdity, not a little in the fashion of contemporary cinematic spoofs of spy thrillers.

A final point should be made about the instrument of comic resolution, the Venetian law court. The court is the final audience before which the characters act out their moral posturings. All of them attempt to confuse and gull a legal morality which can take only appearances into consideration; and in a sense the law and moral posturing imply each other, a point made hilariously if grimly when, in Act IV, the unnaturalness of Corbaccio and Corvino is allowed to triumph totally, if temporarily, over the virtue of Bonario and Celia. The court can judge the play's characters correctly only after all their disguises have been stripped off, and all appear as they really are. Obviously the court itself is quite passive in these matters, the first triumph of disguise and its later defeat being brought about mainly through the intrigues of the maskers themselves. My point is that the court represents the appropriate audience for the players of roles, because it embodies the ideals of justice and honesty which all of them most fulsomely dramatize themselves as abiding by. We might even go so far as to say that such intrigues as *Volpone* affords could not be possible if there were not some societal standard of decent behavior for each intriguer to mimic before the others. This, added to the fact that society as represented by the court can of necessity judge only by appearances, dramatizes both the strengths and weaknesses such societal norms must admit to. The legacy-hunters obviously assume that Volpone must leave his money to each of them in justice because of the humane concern they have shown for him. They accordingly strike the appropriate stances of this concern. When they first appeal to the court, society's representative, for justice and succeed only in perverting it, they are implicitly undermining the moral frame which makes possible their own pretenses, a fact which appears overtly in the second court scene. Nevertheless, deceit will out if only the court (and society) will be patient. For Voltore is motivated to unmask Mosca in court only because Mosca has sprung the trap, thereby demonstrating to Voltore how his own disguise had been penetrated. That Voltore should appeal to a representative of society's demand for honesty—the court—is appropriate precisely because it is honesty which he as well as the rest has been mimicking up to this point. The court can expect the disguises to be thrown off sooner or later, if only because the intriguers can be depended to unmask each other once the game is out in the open. And just as the intriguers mimicked honesty the first time, they will the second time call for justice with proportional vehemence precisely because justice, or rather its appearance, is what they have been exploiting against one another all the time. Therefore the court's subjection to appearances proves its ultimate strength as well as its weakness.

The unmasking of all the intriguers before the eyes of the Avocatori is thus the final cause of the play's action, insofar as it is informed by its overarching dianoia. As I have already indicated, all the intriguers cooperate toward this conclusion in being subject to a dialectical logic that governs both intrigue and counterintrigue. When, finally, Voltore arrives to call for justice on Mosca, and Volpone is coerced into dropping his disguise through fear of whipping because he has insulted his now respectable parasite, all the intriguers are confronted with the real and true embodiment of those social norms with which they have been deceitfully defrauding each other throughout the play. To call for justice for the other is to call for it likewise for oneself, and of course justice here means that each one gets what he deserves. That is, he gets what he has been covertly asking for all along, however much it may come to him through a dialectical logic he would thwart if he could, but in the end must accept perforce because he ironically calls for it. Thus, with a supreme irony, a legal morality based on appearances wins out after all.

Of all the examples I will take in this essay, the comic plot of *Volpone* illustrates perhaps most obviously the logic of dialectic's dictating the disposition of parts in a plot. The essence of such a plot is purpose motivated by a univocal reading of the possibilities of action. When agent becomes patient and suffers the return of his action upon himself, it is, as I have suggested, by a structure of action and reaction almost mechanical in its operation. The mechanicalness is in turn made possible by the deliberate limits Jonson works within, in drawing his characters, their ethical motives, and the thoughts which they articulate. The rigidity which Bergson finds as the essence of comic characterization thus allows not so much a perfectly symmetrical dialectic as rather a parody of dialectic, at least when we compare this dialectic with the immensely more dense logics operating in *Paradise Lost* and *Macbeth.* The comic vision, perhaps more than any other, coerces and forms its materials into postures of rigid and mechanical confrontation. Its archetypal dianoia, if one can speak of such a thing, is, however, unlike that of the lyric and tragedy, being concerned with reestablishing a conception of reason, rather than with criticizing it. Lyric aims at a transrational moment of intuition (however it may use rational business to achieve this). *Paradise Lost* likewise aims at such a transcendent, although the density of that transcendent's significance is necessarily developed at greater length, if only because the dimensions of the form itself allow greater development of the obstacles to such transcendence. Further, as I shall show in *Macbeth,* the tragic mode leads the beholder, as it does the tragic hero himself, through and beyond dialectic to the gates of mystery, where rational categories can only confound themselves. But in comedy, whether narrative or dramatic, and nowhere is this more true than for Jonson, the dianoia of the comic mythos recalls us to reason's best and abiding forms, by portraying its own possible perversions in a rigorously and highly artificial dialectic, wherein the rigidities of reason are allowed full rein to gallop to their insane conclusions, thereby inoculating itself against them in a catharsis of laughter similar to that of tragedy, though obviously different from it in emotional quality.

> No individual thing, which is entirely different from our own natures, can help or check our power of activity, and absolutely nothing can do us good or harm, unless it has something in common with our nature.
>
> Spinoza, *Ethics,* Part IV. Proposition XXIX

Whereas the end or goal of comedy is a reassertion of the rational categories which the comic plot had reduced to the absurdity of rigid and mechanical movement and countermovement, the end of tragic dialectic is a transcendence of these categories in an awareness of something like mystery. The logic of plot in *Macbeth* is itself intelligible enough, almost terrifyingly so; but this clarity serves only to bring us with greater force up against a question which dialectic rather points to and manifests than explains. This question probes at the very radical roots of being as opposed to nonbeing, of good as opposed to evil, specifically when the tragic dialectic demonstrates that these opposites mutually imply each other and cause each other. Like the dialectic of the lyric, but unlike that of narrative and comedy, tragic dialectic is enacted to demonstrate both its interior necessity and also the necessity of its annihilation before realities of human potentiality which such dialectic can only render in contradictions and conflicts, but never wholly exhaust. Comedy calls for a return to reason through and by means of reason's perversion; tragedy calls for a recognition of human realities beyond reason which yet can only be mediated to human understanding through reason and therefore through conflict and destruction. I say destruction, because the univocalist rational categories which motivate the tragic hero move him to act toward a goal wherein the equivocations and ambiguities of the plot's dialectic must necessarily be resolved into noncontradiction. But this resolution comes about almost invariably through the destruction of those motives, values, and human realities which stand in its way, a conclusion all the more tightly logical because the persons and values destroyed come into the path of the blind onrush of noncontradiction (fate) mainly through their own volition, and they push the button that sets the machine in operation.

The plot of *Macbeth* from the murder of Duncan until the end shows us the tragic hero attempting to keep the crown of Scotland in perfect static security, and being driven continually to acts of increasing heinousness in order to achieve this security. Because Macbeth's only goal, once the crown is on his head, is a changeless, plotless state, this play is an ideal paradigm for illustrating the generation of mythos in opposition to dianoia. The "restless ecstasy" (III.ii.22) which Macbeth suffers in his bed, trying to sleep, is quite clearly presented to us as a function of his intense desire for rest and peace, a desire so intense that it drives him dialectically into feverish activity to counter and destroy anyone and everyone whom he might suspect of plotting against this peace.[43] Words and images connoting fear and consequent desire for security resound through the last three acts with thudding insistency. In plotting first against Banquo, Macbeth soliloquizes:

> To be thus is nothing,
> But to be safely thus. Our fears in Banquo
> Stick deep; and in his royalty of nature
> Reigns that which would be fear'd. 'Tis much he dares;
> And, to that dauntless temper of his mind,
> He hath a wisdom that doth guide his valour
> To act in safety.
>
> (III.i.48–54)

Macbeth may well envy Banquo his ability to guide his own actions with safety, but it is not this in him which motivates his murder. Nor, for that matter, is it simply the sisters' prophecy that Banquo's progeny shall rule Scotland, but rather Macbeth's realization that the assassination of Duncan has yielded himself nothing except a torturing conscience:

> For Banquo's issue have I fil'd my mind;
> For them the gracious Duncan have I murder'd;
> Put rancours in the vessel of my peace
> Only for them; and mine eternal jewel
> Given to the common enemy of man,
> To make them kings, the seed of Banquo kings!
>
> (III.i.65–70)

Clearly Macbeth is moved less by dynastic considerations here than by the thought of inner pain suffered for no fruitful purpose. When he attempts to have Fleance killed, we realize that he can gain nothing by it, except more remorse. Rather, his fear of Banquo is one with his fear of Macduff, Malcolm, of noises in the night, and of fearful dreams, a fear generated by a conscience which in him is so far from deadened that it demonstrates its lively abhorrence of Macbeth's crimes through the very energy with which it drives Macbeth on to further crimes.

Here we find the center of the dialectical logic in the play. It is Macbeth's extremely active conscience which both reacts violently to his crimes, and in doing so sets up such a fear of retribution that Macbeth is driven on to commit still more murders in order to quiet this fear.[44] In short, the force of good in him is also the cause of his evil. Critical viewpoints which find Macbeth unequivocally evil throughout the play, or perfecting his evil as he moves toward his final confrontation with Macduff, are certainly correct, but they often neglect the complicated inner dialectic of his morality which grounds this evil. To bring my point into the sharpest focus, I would say that Macbeth would not and could not have become so much the monster of blood and treachery we see in the play's latter half, were he not continually, not simply at the play's beginning, a man whose primary motives for action issue from an appetite for the good in him which he only with great difficulty crushes by the play's end. Menteith's commentary on Macbeth sums up neatly this intestinal struggle of good motives generating their equal and opposite perversions:

> Who then shall blame
> His pester'd senses to recoil and start,
> When all that is within him does condemn
> Itself for being there?
>
> (v.ii.22–25)

Quite clearly, Macbeth becomes paranoid because of his guilty conscience; but a guilty conscience is, by traditional Christian moral standards, still a good conscience. Were Macbeth completely without conscience, if he could completely wipe out all feeling for the good with the murder of Duncan (as his wife tries unsuccessfully to do), then he would not be driven to kill more men—and also, we would have no plot and no play.

The fair/foul equivocation which opens the play offers the reader and viewer a statement that is eminently available to being filled out by a wide variety of particulars. For Macbeth himself, however, this equivocation works to set in conflict within him two opposite and mutually contradictory standards of motivation and action in which the terms are related in a simply inverted fashion. After he has received (equivocal) proof of the weird sisters' ability to predict the future, Macbeth's imagination is caught irrevocably by two pictures, superimposed upon each other as it were: the picture of himself as King of Scotland, and of the murder he may have to commit to become king:

> *Macbeth:* Two truths are told,
> As happy prologues to the swelling act
> Of the imperial theme.—I thank you gentlemen.
> [*Aside*] This supernatural soliciting
> Cannot be ill, cannot be good. If ill,
> Why hath it given me earnest of success,
> Commencing in a truth? I'm thane of Cawdor.
> If good, why do I yield to that suggestion
> Whose horrid image doth unfix my hair
> And make my seated heart knock at my ribs,
> Against the use of nature? Present fears
> Are less than horrible imaginings.
> My thought, whose murder yet is but fantastical,
> Shakes so my single state of man that function
> Is smother'd in surmise, and nothing is
> But what is not.
>
> (I.iii.127–142)

The "good" and "ill" here are implicitly measured against two competing standards, and what is "fair" for the one is "foul" for the other and vice versa. The "good" of the crown equals the "ill" of murder, while in turn Macbeth's conscience finds that what is "good" by its standards is "ill" by the standards of vaulting ambition. This equivocation is, once laid out in this fashion, easily understood, and if this were all, then Macbeth is presented with a clear choice: either do the murder and get the crown, or not. To opt for the first is simply to go against conscience and settle for what is foul for conscience primarily because it is fair for ambition. To have decided on these terms would have made Macbeth's first murder quite unequivocal morally: he would have known just exactly where he stood.

But what puzzles him and horrifies him is a fact which he recognizes so clearly that he can state it with precision at the exact moment of reacting to it: Why does he "yield" to an image of murder at the very moment when he beholds it in his imagination with such horror? Quite clearly, he is fascinated with what repels him. I am going to supply an answer which is grounded on every suggestion of the whole text of the play except that of direct statement, namely, that the horror of the image of murder which catches Macbeth up is precisely that horror which a tender conscience could be counted on to supply. Macbeth's active imagination, so often noted, is always most deft in presenting to his inner eye sights of murder and darkness. Like his wife in Act II, Macbeth periodically throughout attempts to coach the powers of darkness to be with him, or rather more accurately, to bring himself to line up with them. But these invocations, like Lady Macbeth's "Come, you spirits" speech, are clearly the felt necessities of a man who has not yet in fact reached the state of permanent and serene evil, a state in which conscience and imagination perversely pricked by conscience have been deadened. And it is problematic whether he reaches this state even by the end of the play. But my point here is to note the equivocal attraction/repulsion which horrifies him at the first thought of Duncan's murder. Once having allowed himself to be caught by the idea of the crown, and almost simultaneously by the murder he will have to commit in order to achieve it, Macbeth's conscience actively solicits the crime in the very act of making him appalled at its heinousness. It is a truism in *Macbeth* criticism that Macbeth's conscience is in a sense created by the murder of Duncan, that is, both by the thought of it before and the recollection of it after. This is true, but it does not go far enough. We must further realize exactly how his conscience creates in him a state of restless uncertainty which in turn craves peace. Of course, this peace could be reached simply by not killing Duncan. But Macbeth's conscience—and I mean by this word the combined force of his fears, his fantasy, and his strong sense of good/evil—will not let him rest in peace precisely because of its immediate and overwhelming representation to Macbeth of the evil he is so ambiguously attracted to. In fact, the ambiguity of this attraction is created by his reaction against the crime his conscience represents to him.

It is this inner equivocation that horrifies him. As such, the choice is not between the norms of fair/foul created by a sensitive conscience and those of fair/foul implied by murder for political ambition. Given the dialectical interaction within his conscience, to choose conscience is to choose that which equivocally draws him on to his ambition precisely by setting it squarely in his fantasy's eye through the very force of its violent reaction. This is why a murder which "yet is but fantastical, / Shakes so my single state of man," namely that he finds himself dialectically attracted to the murder by reason of the very motives which would ordinarily be expected to repel him from it. Well may he conclude, "nothing is / But what is not."

This discussion leads me to say that Macbeth kills Duncan ultimately neither for the crown, nor even because he is somehow attracted to the evil of the deed—though certainly these factors provide the phenomenal manifestations and symptoms of the reason. Rather, the reason is the desire for peace and quiet, the peace and quiet of a conscience which does not solicit evil in the very act of reacting violently to it. In short, Macbeth wants to still his conscience; and through the convolved logic of the play, it is this goal that motivates his actions throughout the play.

But to still his conscience is to still the voice of good in him, as well as the voice of evil. And to do this is to achieve a kind of static and absolute nonfeeling, a state similar to that recorded with such dreariness in the "Tomorrow" speech. The plot of the drama is generated by the protagonist's rejection of the plot's dianoia, namely, the fact that the human conscience contains within itself the dual potentiality for both good and evil, and in so containing this dual potentiality implies likewise the dialectical logic by which the good and evil may at once both fight against each other and dialectically cause each other. The dianoia of the play thus holds in static formulation the terms of conflict which the mythos sets forth in dialectically causal sequence. In attempting to still his conscience, we the beholders note, as he himself does, that he is required to commit more and more murders out of the fear of retribution which his conscience creates. And in doing so, conscience is further exacerbated to motivate still more murders. He refuses the dianoia of the play in the sense that he refuses either to rest in the repentance which his conscience calls him to, or to rest in a state of mindless, imaginationless, and conscienceless evil. As he himself says,

> I am in blood
> Stepp'd in so far that, should I wade no more,
> Returning were as tedious as go o'er.
>
> (III.iv.136–138)

Seeking rest from his conscience precisely through acts which exacerbate it, he makes himself all the more restless, and seeking an end to the need for murder, he continues to kill.

The outer action of the play obviously parallels Macbeth's inner dialectic, and Macbeth succeeds only in generating against him a coalescence of counterforces by those very actions which were intended overtly to quash such a possibility. Therefore, according to the three-moment logic of dialectic, the plot of *Macbeth* can be rendered in this fashion: (1) The murder of Duncan holds up an illusory resolution of stilling the solicitings of conscience, which resolution turns out to equal a conflict-under-the-sign-of-resolution; that is, the looked-for resolution yields really the covertly dual potentialities of his conscience now (as the result of the murder) in open opposition to each other. That is, the good in his conscience makes him fear retribution, a fear that Macbeth projects outward as a fear of Malcolm, Macduff, and Banquo, and in turn drives him to further murders. That Macbeth is quite aware of this possibility even before the murder is made clear to us:

> *Macbeth:* If it were done when 'tis done, then 'twere well
> It were done quickly. If the assassination
> Could trammel up the consequence, and catch
> With his surcease success; that but this blow
> Might be the be-all and the end-all here,
> But here, upon this bank and shoal of time,
> We'd jump the life to come. But in these cases
> We still have judgement here, that we but teach
> Bloody instructions, which, being taught, return
> To plague th' inventor. This even-handed justice
> Commends th' ingredients of our poison'd chalice
> To our own lips.
>
> (I.vii.1–12)

The fate which moves Macbeth, if he is indeed moved against his will by any power, is implicit in this very recognition. We have a kind of "flight forward," an attempt to escape the fear of the deed by doing the deed. But once a "fair" conscience has driven him to perform a "foul" murder, the reaction begins, and this aspect of the plot is noted in the second moment. (2) The dialectical causality by which conscience leads to murder and murder exacerbates conscience is generated because both fair and foul have a common ground, namely Macbeth's sensitive conscience. (3) Taking the first moments together, we find that the attempted resolution into peace and security, the goal of the first moment, generates further conflict, a conflict which manifests nothing so much as the basic fact that the two opposing sides are dialectically reciprocal. Therefore, the third moment of dialectical logic sums up the copenetration of the first two moments: desire for resolution leads to open conflict (both within Macbeth and consequently in the outer action), and open conflict is carried on (the plot) under the drive for resolution.

Macbeth's drive for security is the motive behind his second resort to the witches, who as before gratify him by telling him what he wants to hear. What they say concerning Birnam wood and man not born of woman equivocates to Macbeth's ear, because it presents him with several possible interpretations from which he chooses the one most conducive to his desire for security. The result of this choice is an added equivocation, namely that Macbeth is allowed to take for objective assurance a cause of security which is in reality only a projection of his own desires. In this case Macbeth's strong powers of imaginative projection work quite differently than in such cases as the dagger and Banquo's ghost, where he sees what he fears precisely because he fears it. Here, he sees what he desires precisely because he desires it. The upshot of the witches' equivocal assurances is a Macbeth allowed a specious confidence to develop his potentialities for evil to their uttermost. Whether or not Shakespeare was in fact responsible for Hecate's speech in Act III.v, whoever wrote it had grasped perfectly the ambiguities of the security theme in the play:[45]

> He shall spurn fate, scorn death, and bear
> His hopes 'bove wisdom, grace, and fear;
> And, you all know, security
> Is mortals' chiefest enemy.
>
> (III.v.30–33)

"Security" is Macbeth's "enemy" in various ways, some of which I have already dealt with. Security from an ambiguous conscience, I have already suggested, is the original force setting off the action of the plot with Duncan's murder; and the good and evil potentialities of Macbeth's conscience issue continually in fears which drive him on to additional murders. "Security" is in this tragedy a cognate of univocalism, and it is obvious that Macbeth's desire for it determines his actions in the play and the play's plot.

But security in the last act has an additional significance. If we look at Macbeth's words after Macduff tells him that he "was from his mother's womb / Untimely ripp'd" (v.viii.15–16), we see Macbeth with all his props pulled out from beneath him. "I'll not fight with thee," he says to Macduff. Up to this point, and throughout the play, Macbeth has been the prisoner of his conscience and of the imagination which this conscience has guided. He continued to equivocate with this conscience, or it with him, and as long as the vicious circle of this dialectic continued he could rest secure in neither a fair conscience nor foul murder. But in his last moments, fighting desperately without hope, Macbeth achieves his first and only moment of freedom: he becomes that "so much more the man" which his wife had berated him with in Act I, a supra-human creature capable of mindless and conscienceless evil. But if he becomes more than a man by losing his fear and his desire for security, then likewise he fulfills his own previous notion of manhood: "I dare do all that may become a man; / Who dares do more is none" (I.vii.46–47). At the play's end, Macbeth has himself literally reached both his own death and the final goal of all his action's teleology, the final security of mindless, amoral endeavor, devoid of conscience and fear and imagination:

> I will not yield,
> To kiss the ground before young Malcolm's feet
> And to be baited with the rabble's curse.
> Though Birnam wood be come to Dunsinane,
> And thou oppos'd, being of no woman born,
> Yet I will try the last. Before my body
> I throw my warlike shield. Lay on, Macduff,
> And damn'd be him that first cries, "Hold, enough!"
> (V.viii.27–34)

The equivocation in Macbeth, and the dialectic in the plot he generates, are both finished (if not resolved in the dialectical sense) when he achieves a final equivocation, a state of the supra-human, freed from all human fears and limitations, but only at the expense of becoming less than human, an unnatural creature, a monster.

This is the point of mystery to which the dialectic in the play has been leading us. The mysterious copenetration of good and evil potentialities within the same conscience of the tragic hero is dramatized to us mainly through a mythos in which the two opposites are set in mutual enmity as separate parts: words set against words, thought against thought, and character against character. But the frightful and awe-inspiring discovery, to paraphrase Bradley, that Macbeth's goodness and Macbeth's evil derive from the same moral center and the same moral imperative: this is a tragic truth which we may understand rationally, may even explain discursively (as I am doing here), but never envision whole and absolutely. Dialectical logic, as a means of examining the play, allows us to see that the fate which determines Macbeth, and the freedom by which he chooses his fate, spring from the same source and are nothing more than two facets of the same reality. Fate in tragedy equals the logic of dialectic itself, a rigid set of relations between conflict and resolution. Freedom in tragedy equals the hero's choice of following either the fair or the foul. And fate and freedom copenetrate because the hero can choose only within the logic of dialectic, for this logic controls all the possible relations of union or enmity the hero can be involved in; and yet, by the same logic, the hero remains free within the wide variety of choices the logic of dialectic allows him. His dilemma is that he cannot not choose. And to choose this rather than that, to attempt to pursue this line of univocal, partial action rather than that, condemns him to suffer the consequences of dialectical logic in any case. As Milton has God say in *Paradise Lost*, man is "determined" to be free.

So far, I have been considering two parts out of Aristotle's six, character and thought. My main point has been to show how the moral imperatives grounded in Macbeth's "character," and the logical equivocations with which he articulates the ambiguities of these moral imperatives, become the formal causes of the action-done, both as regards the internal action in Macbeth's own mind, and the external results of action and counteraction. To conclude, I want to indicate some of the ways in which dialectical logic also determines diction and spectacle, melody not being in any dominant sense present in the play, except perhaps in the witches' songs and incantations.

The large number of verbal repetitions and parallels to the fair/foul equivocation theme make this play as integrated on the level of diction as anything else Shakespeare wrote. Leaving aside the more obvious and famous examples in the first act, one has still ample opportunity in this single act alone to watch the formal design which this dianoia imposes on the play in a wide variety of fashions. When asked by Malcolm to give news of the fight between Macbeth and Macdonwald, the Captain says: "Doubtful it stood, / As two spent swimmers that do cling together / And choke their art" (I.ii.7–9). This repeats a favorite theme of Shakespeare's, the ways in which strength encumbers itself through its own energies, and certainly foreshadows the dual potentiality of Macbeth's own strength of conscience; as does also the Captain's further comment: "So from that spring whence comfort seem'd to come / Discomfort swells" (I.ii.27–28). In the first case, Macbeth's encounter with Macdonwald is described in a metaphor drawn from two swimmers who are attempting to help each other, and in doing so find themselves at enmity with their own safety. When the Captain immediately after this says "The merciless Macdonwald— / Worthy to be a rebel, for to that / The multiplying villanies of nature / Do swarm upon him" (I.ii.9–12), we recognize Macbeth here, the Macbeth not of the beginning but of the end of the play. Macbeth is thus identified, via the swimmers metaphor, with Macdonwald, in the sense that he is trying to "help" him in the midst of an overtly intended tenor wherein he is locked in an embrace of enmity with the rebel. The moral energy of Macbeth on the side of the good is manifested in the ferocity with which "he unseam'd him from the nave to th' chaps" (I.ii.22), a ferocity boding ill for himself when he becomes himself the rebel, not only to the king but to his own conscience. But the second, comfort/discomfort equivocation serves no immediate function in the plot, and shows the dianoia of play spilling over even into the accidentals of its business.

A further equivocation, ambiguously identifying Macbeth with another rebel, this time the Thane of Cawdor, occurs shortly after. Ross describes this encounter:

> Bellona's bridegroom, lapp'd in proof,
> Confronted him with self-comparisons,
> Point against point, rebellious arm 'gainst arm,
> Curbing his lavish spirit; . . .
>
> (I.ii.54–57)

Metaphor again proves a foreshadowing of reality, both in making Macbeth the husband of the goddess of war, and more ingeniously through the equivocal and dialectical significance of Ross's language for combat, "self-comparisons," "point against point," and "rebellious arm 'gainst arm." Having been previously branded "traitor," we become aware of still another equivocal attribution of Cawdor when Duncan tells Ross to go "And with his former title greet Macbeth" (I.ii.65). Both of these verbal actions are far from ornamental, since they set in relief a large potentiality for violent action in the name of order and hierarchy on Macbeth's part, and so prepares for the reversal in which this violence is unleashed against the king himself.

A further example of the play's diction enacting the play's dialectic occurs in Angus's speculations on the precise nature of Cawdor's aid to the Norwegians:

> Whether he was combin'd
> With those of Norway, or did line the rebel
> With hidden help and vantage, or that with both
> He labour'd in his country's wreck, I know not; . . .
>
> (I.iii.111–114)

The dramatic significance of this passage is quite small. The whole speech is in answer to Macbeth's query concerning the title of Thane of Cawdor's being given him when he believes the rebel still to be alive. And when Angus answers "Who was the thane lives yet; / But under heavy judgement bears that life / Which he deserves to lose" (I.iii.109–111), the immediate purpose has been served. We have no choice but to regard the additional speculation as the author's attempt to invest the play's language continually with syntactical and logical structures that reflect the play's overriding dianoia. *Macbeth* becomes a play wherein, quite literally, no language is possible which does not, whether a given character intends it or not, mirror the tragic logic which governs it. The question of Cawdor's aid to the enemy is couched as a disjunction between open and secret complicity, and with the dialectical causality of Macbeth's conscience in mind, we are recalled to the fact that this conscience can be said to aid Macbeth's evil either openly, in its overt reaction against it, or secretly, through its driving Macbeth on to more murders in the name of security.

A final example, similar to the ambiguous language for combat in Ross's speech, is Lady Macbeth's first words to Duncan:

> All our service
> In every point twice done and then done double
> Were poor and single business to contend
> Against those honours deep and broad wherewith
> Your Majesty loads our house.
>
> (I.vi.14–18)

Some of this recalls the Captain's narrative of Macbeth's and Banquo's fight with the Norwegians:

> If I say sooth, I must report they were
> As cannons overcharg'd with double cracks; so they
> Doubly redoubled strokes upon the foe.
>
> (I.ii.36–38)

The ambiguous direction of these "strokes" in Lady Macbeth's speech, however, is indicated by the equivocation in the phrase "contend / Against," where the overt meaning of deserve fades in our anticipation of the murder into the covert one of fight with.

The spectacle, that is, the overt action on the stage can likewise be seen as subject to and arranged in accordance with the play's dianoia. The most obvious examples are the witches and Banquo's ghost, the first of which are seen by the audience and Banquo independently of Macbeth, and the second seen by Macbeth alone. Much has been said concerning the dramatic and ontological status of the witches, and I do not want to enter into that debate here, except briefly and most indirectly. In addition to the fact that the witches' speeches are equivocal in themselves, in that they offer statements about the future which Macbeth himself causes to come true through his own free agency (in the case of the first predictions), or interprets amiss through projecting his own wishes (as in the second ones), the witches' very presence on the stage is itself a fact that is intended to convey the dramatic effect of equivocation. Those who find the witches "real" and those who find them merely a projection of Macbeth's own thoughts are both right, and it seems to me that this equivocal fact itself is overtly intended in the play. They do seem to say to Macbeth his own inner thoughts, and at the same time they also seem to bring to his sight and imagination new visions to meditate upon. Their function in this respect is to call attention to Macbeth's own tendency to desire the performance of acts which he both actively cooperates in and yet stands apart from. There are several instances of this tendency in the play, and one well-known example can suffice:

> *Macbeth:* Stars, hide your fires;
> Let not light see my black and deep desires;
> The eye wink at the hand; yet let that be
> Which the eye fears, when it is done, to see.
>
> (I.iv.50–53)

The witches come across simultaneously (and equivocally) as both active, external agents determining future actions in some way, and as projections of Macbeth's own personal intentions. This fact holds true, though with differences, for the second predictions as well as the first. In the second instance, we might take the Birnam wood and man not born of woman prophecies as Macbeth's projection of ideal impossibilities behind which to shield himself against attack. Therefore the appearance of the witches on the stage, strange and unnatural creatures as they are, speaking Macbeth's own mind equivocally to him, signals to us a parallel in the play's spectacle to Macbeth's continuous desire both not to "play false" and yet "wrongly win" (I.v.22–23). Macbeth would be both detached from the crimes he commits, letting them result from some external agency, and yet actively assuring the conclusion that the crimes do in fact take place.

In the case of Banquo's ghost, Shakespeare lets us see for once an example of "these terrible dreams / That shake us nightly" (III.ii.18–19), though again there is something equivocal about the apparition. Macbeth sees the ghost but no one else can, except of course the audience, for the ghost, unlike the dagger, has a place in the play's material properties. Macbeth has previously lamented the fact that Banquo has not yet appeared at the banquet, knowing of course that he has already caused his murder. What the audience sees in the scene is a dramatization of the fact that Macbeth's fantasies are "real" enough, although not with that palpable reality which would allow them to be seen by others. We are, of course, by this made more ready to accept the fact that Macbeth is subject to still another equivocation, this time between reality and his own projected fantasy. The same sort of equivocation occurs in his interpretation of the witches' second prophecies. This scene fills out still another potentiality of the play's dianoia, in that it shows us Macbeth as again willing to have the result (Banquo's death) but also as suffering the guilt that attends it, a further twist of the dialectical rack his own conscience has placed him on. For this guilt continually projects onto external agents of retribution the attacks which his conscience makes internally upon him.

The final battle scene, as in other similar cases in Shakespeare's plays, renders the internal dialectic into overtly physical terms. If Macbeth has suffered from internal combats up to Act V, he is now to suffer the external manifestation of this combat which the logic of the first has inexorably generated. By this point in the play, the intricate and intimate mutual copenetration of good motives and evil motives is ready to be resolved into final polarization of evil tyrant versus righteous revengers. Like Macdonwald in Act I, "The multiplying villanies of nature / Do swarm upon" Macbeth, he becomes the sink in which all the evil of the play is finally gathered, and the equivocal force for good which has up to this point been so entangled in Macbeth's own evil, is now released and freed to gather to the side of Malcolm and Macduff. When Macbeth confronts Macduff at the end he faces the objective, physical embodiment of his own conscience, now almost wholly deadened in himself. The logical contradiction of his own conscience cannot continue, by the very force of its own self-destructiveness, indefinitely. The univocalism and tyranny of the law of noncontradiction that grounds dialectic likewise becomes the necessity by which this dialectic is ended and the original terms of conflict are all destroyed. What throughout the play have been the mutually causal and supportive forces of good and evil, become at the play's end totally polarized, and we are faced with one of the high points of Shakespeare's tragic vision, made manifest in one way or another in all his tragedies. This point is where we come to recognize that the force of the good in the *Macbeth* universe can only unequivocally and with assurance be allowed to conquer after it has suffered all the attacks upon itself that it itself is capable of generating. To borrow from the disease imagery in which Shakespeare embodies this theme so often throughout his plays, health becomes possible safely only after the force of the disease has spent itself.

5. A Dialectical Methodology of Literary Form

A method is a technique for answering questions; a methodology is (for lack of a better word) the acquired wisdom of knowing what questions to ask. If this distinction is allowed to stand at least provisionally, it should be clear that the answers one arrives at about literary structures are only as valid as the methodology, conscious or implied, which generates the questions. It has been one of my working hypotheses in this essay that one's methodology is founded on, and is just as complete and useful in proportion to, one's ability to arrive at certain general characteristics that govern all verbal structures, no matter of what sort.

By methodology I do not mean necessarily a system of basic questions which all literature always and everywhere raises. Rather, I mean something more limited, and perhaps more provisional. One may ask all kinds of questions of a literary text, some of which will show in the answering of them that they are more practically relevant than others. Attempts to decide what are relevant questions to be pursued always involve a prior analysis of just what are the parts which constitute literary discourse. Thus both Wellek and Warren's *Theory of Literature* and Frye's *Anatomy of Criticism* seek to establish these parts as a prolegomenon to the generation of questions to be asked. Wherever one may stand on these and similar methodologies, most would agree that some methodology or other is always implied in any critic's practical pursuit of critical questions. In general, most critical studies of particular texts simply start with a certain question, leaving the question whether this question is a significant or a relevant one unanswered, and even unperceived. Of course, it is one of the frustrations as well as excitements of literary study that one man's relevance is another's foolishness. But the theme of relevant questions itself, that is, of literary methodology, is always present in critical discourse, whether it is stated as such overtly or not. However, one criterion for judging a methodology with which I think none would disagree would be whether it generates questions that apply in some way to all literary discourse, and apply in such a way as to illuminate some of the essential ways this discourse makes its meaning. The logic of dialectic I have outlined and exemplified here can pretend, I believe, to some such general applicability; which is not to say that I claim for it completeness as a methodology of all possible methods-in-general. Perhaps no such methodology, such as was aimed at for instance by scientists in the post-Bacon era of science, is possible for literature, the data itself appearing at the present stage of the history of criticism to be to a large extent recalcitrant to total subsumption under universal "laws." In any case, the ultimate test of any methodology is the practical illumination which methods generated by it bring to individual texts. To those familiar with recent criticism of Donne, Milton, Jonson, and Shakespeare, it should be obvious that I have not departed in any radical direction in my individual interpretations. But this has been intended to help rather than hinder my case; for my efforts in the previous three sections of this essay have been primarily toward translating more-or-less accepted insights into a new grammar and logic. And I have not wanted this translation hindered by advancing readings which would require a large amount of discussion for their own sakes. Rather than seeking to answer questions about these texts, I have sought to raise new kinds of questions to ask.

Having begun with Aristotle's ever-useful division of parts in a verbal mimesis, I have attempted to grasp at the radical formal principles which make possible the coalescence of these parts, no matter what the genre of literature involved. But in claiming so much, it may appear that I have overreached myself. After all, something which applies to "everything" cannot apply to anything with much cogency. And granting dialectic's universal applicability to all the major genres of literature, we may wonder whether it does not so cancel the boundaries among them as to make tragedy dialectically interchangeable with comedy, and a lyric by Blake not essentially different from a novel by Tolstoy. Any attempt to establish a radical paradigm for asking questions about literature runs the risk of being so general as to be practically useless: critics and readers, having done obeisance to it, may well continue to criticize and read as if it did not exist.

But if I am correct that one's questions (and the answers to them), in short one's method, is only as good as one's methodology, then simply succeeding in causing critics and readers to reexamine their fundamental presuppositions about literature can always do some good. However, the methodology I have outlined here has a practical usefulness that goes beyond the merely theoretical and hortatory. I would like to treat briefly the two objections suggested in the last paragraph; namely, that the logic of dialectic is too general to be useful in analyzing individual works, and that it blurs the boundaries between literary genres. The heart of my answer to both objections lies in the fact that dialectic as a regulative principle, standing over a wide variety of literary phenomena, controls and constitutes the uniqueness of each literary work according to the same logic which allows it a general position of applicability to all of them.

This problem is one of methodology rather than method, because it concerns questions about how various methods may work, rather than about how any one method can yield specific answers to specific questions. It concerns, as it were, a method of methods. The logic of dialectic may appear at first similar to any other thesis that informs and in turn is supported by a collection of data. The thesis/data relationship in most cases is a univocal one, whereby the generalization which is the thesis applies to the data insofar as these data all share some common notes. As such, the thesis calls attention to similarities and remains on principle incapable of explaining diversity. It is quite something else to propound a transcendent general thesis which extends equally to all particulars, while connoting the principle which makes intelligible their uniqueness and differences. Such a thesis is the dialectical logic I have outlined here.

My point here is that the logic of dialectic is not only univocally regulative of a wide variety of literary texts, but also immanently constitutive of them as well; and it is each precisely because it is the other. It is regulative of these texts because the very fixity of the relations between resolution and conflict which it defines is what determines the structure of their parts, no matter what in particular these parts might be. On the other hand, individual literary texts are constituted dialectically because their *telos,* which is to escape from dialectic toward a univocal resolution of antinomies under the pressure of noncontradiction, only involves them in more dialectic. Finally, on the basis of the fact that dialectical logic is both regulative and constitutive of concrete situations, we discover that it is also regulative because constitutive, and vice versa. Thus: dialectical logic is regulative of every literary text because constitutive of it, insofar as every text contains at least implicitly the essential three moments given in overt formulaic fashion in the three-part statement. As such, this statement stands over regulatively all specific situations as giving the "chord" (all notes struck simultaneously) of which the dynamism of the mythos is the "arpeggio" (the notes struck in sequence).[46] And again: dialectical logic is constitutive of each text because regulative of it, insofar as the *telos* of each text is the resolving of dialectical antinomies in the attempt to escape this regulation.

The possibilities for filling out the three-part statement of dialectical logic are as numerous as there are actual lyrics, narratives, comedies, and tragedies, both in existence and in possibility. Naming as it does the radical relations that must hold between parts and wholes, as well as the dynamism that these relations generate, the logic of dialectic creates the possibility of endless variation, variation all the more diverse precisely because of the rigidity of these relations in themselves, and not despite it. It seems to me, therefore, that dialectic escapes the objection of being too impractically universal to the exact degree that it escapes the usual univocalist model of thesis/data relation which this objection assumes. On the contrary, it applies universally because all literary texts, insofar as they are wholes made up of parts, embody it in seeking to escape it. And the dynamism in concrete cases, which it names the logic of, does nothing so much as guarantee well-nigh infinite diversity, rather than the reverse.

A similar answer can be given to the objection that a dialectical methodology overrides the distinctions between literary genres, although something in addition needs to be said on this score, and in doing so I hope to indicate some of the practical ways such a methodology may generate specific critical methods. I can only admit the fact that dialectical logic applies indifferently to all genres; this has been in fact one of my primary points. But I have also indicated at various times the different concrete ends dialectic reaches in the cases of Donne's lyrics, Milton's epic, and Jonson's and Shakespeare's plays respectively. I have asserted without much discussion, for instance, that lyric and tragedy display the univocalist categories of reason governed by noncontradiction as somehow inadequate to exhaust the human experiences they mediate. Comedy, on the other hand, aims at the reassertion of reason unperverted by the rigid mechanicalness characteristic of it when noncontradiction operates tyrannically in the organic forms of human life. Narrative, finally, is capable of asserting both of these points, as the modern novel has demonstrated in swallowing much of the rhetoric and purposes of the other three genres. Northrop Frye in *Anatomy of Criticism* has achieved a viable classification of the properties peculiar to the various genres, and it is not to my purpose here to go over that ground again. However, it should be clear that any attempt to deal with the real differences in the ways dialectical logic operates in the different genres would have to start with their peculiar properties and work towards dialectic, rather than the other way around, as I have done here.

I cannot therefore refute this objection, but I can on the other hand wonder aloud as to its relevance. The genre critics—the Chicago school, for instance—are very much concerned with differentiating the functions of individual genres according to the different ends toward which they aim. One cannot disagree with their endeavors, because the history of literature presents a continuing spectacle of the rise, fall, and metamorphosis of genres (and of the conception of genre itself) under the pressure of many forces, economic, social, and political, as well as literary. Insofar as literature serves certain ends required of it by the society in which it is written, it will and has developed different ends and the means of achieving them. In short,

I do not want to question the critical and historical necessity of taking generic distinctions into account.

It seems to me quite possible, however, that the logic of dialectic could be made to subserve these distinctions rather than abrogate them. Though my main purpose in choosing examples from different genres was to demonstrate how dialectical logic is common to all of them, I have nevertheless implicitly established the different ways it operates in them almost by the way. I would urge, furthermore, that no matter how precisely the lines between lyric and dramatic, for instance, are drawn, the critic in doing so has already presupposed some universal principle of form and order of which these genres are in their own ways species. I am aware that a lurking monism has been discovered underneath the Chicago critics' cult of critical pluralism, and I do not want to reopen that battle. My own contribution to this very real issue is to urge the logic of dialectic as a principle which by its very internal principles creates diversity rather than uniformity, dynamism rather than stasis; and as such, dialectic may well prove itself a principle of the diversity of genres as well as of their similarity.

I would certainly agree that different critical methods are required by different genres: the kind of questions one asks of a poem by Shelley must perforce be different from those used to analyze a novel by Fielding. But if the logic of dialectic is a methodology rather than a method, it must also show itself fecund enough to generate practical methods for individual cases. Concrete examples of critical method I have already given, and I think it is possible to go even further in suggesting, in at least a general way, the kinds of questions a dialectical methodology generates and how these might be answered.

1. The distinction between action-made and action-done, dictated as the necessary correlative to that between mythos and dianoia, calls upon the critic to be aware of the differences between the goals of a literary work as an example of its genre (action-made), and the goals of the mythos of that work (action-done); for example, the goal of tragedy as action-done is happiness, while its goal as action-made is misery. The question that arises from this distinction concerns the always "ironically" dialectical relation between the work's dianoia as action-made and its mythos as action-done. The critic may then go on to ask of an individual work how the agent of the mythos is determined in actions he initiates by his implicit conflict with the dianoia of that work. The analysis of theme by this method is thus rigorously

correlated with the analysis of form, inasmuch as the latter is dialectically determined as the sequential *explicatio* of the terms which the theme sums up statically in an implicative manner.

2. The analysis of formal structure, as shown so often and so brilliantly by Kenneth Burke, proceeds on the assumption that part relates to part not simply by likenesses but by unlikenesses, by compensation and not simply by complementarity. The parts of a literary work, measured against the totality of the issue dealt with and summed up in the dianoia, are thus seen to be dynamically related as cooperating-in-conflict in their attempt to encompass the whole in necessarily partial and univocal terms. Part thus generates another part as compensation for its partiality. Whereas the new criticism queries a poem concerning the ways its parts cooperate in making a whole, a dialectical method proceeds in the opposite direction, examining the parts as partial fragments of a given totality. Thus the former critical method begins its close reading with an examination of parts, and moves from a mechanistic model to an organismic one, whereby the parts are functions of the whole. But dialectical logic indicates that parts are generated mechanistically in opposition to the organic dianoia of the whole, and succeed in embodying this dianoia "despite themselves." The metaphor I am assuming is one drawn from the neoplatonism of Nicholas of Cusa, wherein the divisiveness of material creation is the *explicatio* of God, Who contains all of these parts within Himself as a *complicatio.* The parts of a poem, therefore, are in tension with, rather than cooperating with, the totality of the poem, a totality which they succeed in embodying through the dialectical interrelations among themselves. On the basis of such a method, the critic might do well to question the disposition of a literary text according to the ways the parts are in conflict with each other, and to seek out cooperation as a function of this conflict.

3. In the realm of literary history, dialectical method suggests that different works may be related to one another in a way analogous to that by which the parts of each one are related internally. Though the history of literature does not proceed according to the statement/response dialectic of the history of philosophy, a similar kind of relation might be looked for. Works which deal with the same general issue, say the notion of power in the works of Wyatt, Marlowe, Bacon, and Milton, might all be seen as dialectically interrelated to the degree that each author takes up a partial viewpoint on power, leaving it to

another to "take up the slack" by putting forward the viable aspects of power which the first for one reason or another ignored. Thus Marlowe's *Doctor Faustus* and Bacon's *New Organon* take in some respects opposite views of power; but both could be related dialectically insofar as both "divide up" the total collection of statements about power available to them as part of Renaissance culture, each carrying off what the other ignores. This is a large issue which I will deal with in another work; but I want to emphasize that a reexamination of the possible forms of literary history requires, within a dialectical methodology, an equal weight thrown on the internal critical analysis of individual works. I am suggesting that dialectical logic controls not only the internal structures of individual works, but their external historical relations as well, and it does the second because it does the first.

4. The dialectical method, as exemplified it in my concrete interpretations, suggests certain things about the ways literary works operate rhetorically on their audiences. Just as the relation between mythos and dianoia is always to some extent ironic, so likewise the agent who perceives this irony is the reader or beholder himself. I have been suggesting that the reader is called upon to recognize something of the dialectical logic which controls and is exemplified by the plot of a work: if the dianoia is always a specific example of dialectical logic, then for the reader to perceive the work's meaning is for him to perceive this dianoia. The address which the work makes to its reader necessarily requires a certain amount of logical distance; distance because the reader is invited by the author to perceive the total logic governing a plot's movement which the agent himself cannot perceive; and logical in the sense that the reader is invited to become aware of a wider variety of cause/effect relations than any character within the fiction perceives. This situation is most clearly seen in the case of Donne's lyrics, but I believe the same is true in the other works I have examined. The emotional tonality of this logical distance certainly differs in all three cases, the tragedy calling for a provisional involvement in Macbeth's fate that Jonson certainly does not ask for. But in either case, it is the logic of the plot which the audience perceives, and which articulates for him the intelligible ground of the emotional reaction he is to experience.

5. Finally, following Murray Krieger's almost paradoxical assertion that a literary text, to the extent that it is internally organized and distinct from the existential life of history around it, succeeds in re-

flecting that life precisely by being such,[47] I would like to suggest some implications of dialectical method for this relation. Any work must perforce be partial in its reflection of the total actual and potential forms of human existence, even such works as the *Divine Comedy, War and Peace,* and *Finnegans Wake* which make the pretense in their sheer bulk and inclusiveness to giving a representative anecdote of this existence. The tendency in modern criticism to isolate the work from existential reference which Krieger seeks to abrogate, and which is I feel partly the result of critics' awareness of literature's inability to mirror the totality of human life, is itself a kind of univocalism analogous to the univocalisms I have examined here. As Northrop Frye points out, the whole of literature exists "in its own universe, no longer a commentary on life or reality, but containing life and reality in a system of verbal relationships."[48] Literature as a "whole," as distinguished from any individual literary work, thus imitates the universe of human experience not by reflecting the total content of that experience, but rather by reflecting a perceived total form in that experience. Literature's own universe of discourse is in its own right autonomous, obeying its own immanent laws. But both Krieger and Frye might well agree on this, that it is precisely this autonomy, which grants literature its own immanent structure, that enables it to refer centrifugally outside of itself to that other, likewise autonomous and broader universe of human history and experience. What dialectic adds is this: Every individual work engages and comments on this experience primarily by being in tension with it, by attempting and always failing to reduce it to the univocal and partial terms of its own categories. Just as the dianoia of a work is always larger and more encompassing than any single part of its mythos, so likewise that dianoia is in itself partial and univocal in comparison with the total number of potential statements that can be made about the human condition. There is, however, one aspect of the dianoia of any work which makes it universal and assimilable to the dianoia of any other work, and that is its dialectical structure. I shall take the plunge and assert my point directly. The contents of dialectical structures available for individual works are well-nigh infinite in their diversity; but the "ur-myth" of all these contents remains always the same: the internal structure of dialectical logic itself as given in the three-part statement of it. Therefore each work engages the existential, not through the content of its dianoia, which always remains partial, but through the form of that dianoia, which is logically the same for all works. Each work struggles to embody some part of human experience, but the truth of this embodiment is achieved not through but despite its struggle toward universal validity. The mythos of the work renders its dianoia through its attempt to avoid it, by reducing dialectical possibilities to univocal and partial absolutism. And by extension, the dianoia of the work embodies the truly universal form of dialectical logic through its attempt to reduce this form to this or that particular content. Thus mythos generates dianoia, and dianoia in turn states the "ur-myth" of dialectical logic, and both do so through their reductive attempts to circumscribe this logic and make it a function of their own individual, and therefore partial, viewpoints on the universe of human experience at large.

Acknowledgments

I am indebted to Marquette University for grants and a half-time Summer Faculty Fellowship which subsidized the research for this study.

THE ROMANCE OF GENTILITY: DEFOE'S HEROES AND HEROINES

James Walton

I

"The gentleman, indeed!" replied the pettifogger: "a pretty gentleman truly! Why he's the bastard of a fellow who was hanged for horse-stealing. He was dropped at Squire Allworthy's door, where one of the servants found him in a box so full of rain-water that he would certainly have been drowned had he not been reserved for another fate."[1]

The pettifogger in Book VIII of *Tom Jones* is repeating the bigoted prophecy, made by the members of Allworthy's household at the beginning of Book III, that the protagonist was "born to be hanged." His version of Tom's origin is at once a product of his malicious fancy and an unconscious parody of the childhood of the mythic hero. The hero's origin is unknown, his parents presumed low. At his separation from them he is "set upon the waters." He is ultimately taken up by some exalted figure who helps him to realize his destiny. The lawyer's false prediction of Tom's end is bound up with a mistake about his origin. Accordingly, the happier view of the hero's prospects is made to depend on the vindication not only of his moral character but of his birth. Jones must prove to be Allworthy, a true heir of the benevolent squire (and the child of a lady and gentleman), in order to frustrate the prediction of those members of the respectable community who gain superstitious assurance about their own futures from the conviction that in our origins we shall find our ends.

For all the celebrated intricacy of the *Tom Jones* plot, the novel ultimately derives its unity and its narrative appeal from this simple motif, this survival of the "higher" mimetic forms, the theme of the child exile. The most conspicuous link between myth, romance, and the novel, this theme must be transmuted in two ways in order to satisfy the demands of the new form. First, it must be made to emerge from the refractory subject matter which was the novel's stock-in-trade, "social actuality." Gentility, money, and position become the outward manifestations of those spiritual gifts which the hero seeks to realize in the world. Second, it must be expressed in a way consistent with the novel's emphasis on private or inward experience. It is more important as a fact of the hero's mind than of his ancestry. Fielding satisfies the first condition, but in a very detached way. His "fine old moralism," in Henry James's phrase, was rather insensitive to the spiritual value of money, if not to that of birth and breeding. As for the second condition, it is generally agreed that Fielding rejected it in deference to traditional modes of imitation belonging to his dramatic and journalistic career. Tom Jones, said James, "has so much 'life' that it amounts, for the effect of comedy and the application of satire, almost to his having a mind."[2]

What James is responding to, perhaps, is that Tom Jones's mind, presented largely through parodic soliloquies and set speeches, is intended to have an entirely representative significance. In the famous "rutting" episode, for example, his noble impulses toward Sophia are rendered according to the conventions of pastoral romance. This makes them the impulses of a whole civilization. And the sequel, his leap into the bushes with Molly Seagrim, demonstrates an effect of our common fall. He is Chaunticleer flying down from the beam. Finally, Fielding relates the hero's nobler impulses toward Moll to a still more general order of nature by comparing him, in an epic simile, to a stag protecting its mate.[3]

The motif of the lost birthright, of course, also engages universal sympathy, but what this motif implies—that the hero's nature is higher than the world recognizes it to be—is not allowed to become part of Tom's inner life. To give such intimation of quality to a "low" character would have made Fielding guilty of the bathos he attacks in the opening pages of *Joseph Andrews:* Pamela assuming the role of *belle inconnue,* Cibber posing as divine child. In this respect the history of the novel proceeds more from *Pamela* and "bathos" than from Fielding and satire. Novels with a clearly defined central figure use the child-exile motif, either as situation or metaphor, in order to objectify the hero's self-consciousness. In such cases the motif serves as the basis for a subjective reordering of the world. A romantic note struck in the early pages of *Oliver Twist* reminds us of the preciousness and limitlessness of that selfhood which the world threatens to destroy:

> Wrapped in the blanket which had hitherto formed his only covering, he might have been the child of a nobleman or a beggar. . . . But now that he was enveloped in the old calico robes which had grown yellow in the same service, he was badged and ticketed, and fell into his place at once—a parish child—the orphan of a workhouse.[4]

As the threat to Oliver deepens, he gains an ambiguous consciousness of it by means with which Fielding could have nothing to do, "a drowsy state, between sleeping and waking" when "a mortal knows just enough of what his mind is doing, to form some glimmering conception of its mighty powers." Oliver, we are told, is "precisely in this condition" when he sees Fagin draw from a trapdoor a collection of "magnificent" booty. He speaks to it as if it were the reincarnation of the thieves who had stolen it and gone mutely to the gallows. Then he turns his attention to an object more obscure and valuable, "so small that it lay in the palm of his hand. There seemed to be some very minute inscription on it; for the Jew laid it flat upon the table, and shading it with his hand, pored over it, long and earnestly. At length he put it down, as if despairing of success."[5] Later another locket will be flung by Monks through a trapdoor into the swirling river in an effort to destroy Oliver's identity. But we know that he can never be fully disposed of or possessed. He belongs to a different order of reality; his origin and destiny differ from those of the other characters in the novel. Yet Dickens consistently defines his intimations of this as a part of our common experience. The world elsewhere is pastoral:

> The memories which peaceful country scenes call up, are not of this world, nor of its thoughts and hopes. Their gentle influence may teach us how to weave fresh garlands for the graves of those we loved: may purify our thoughts, and bear down before it old enmity and hatred; but beneath all this, there lingers, in the least reflective mind, a vague and half-formed consciousness of having held such feelings long before, in some remote and distant time, which calls up solemn thoughts of distant times to come.[6]

The romance of *Oliver Twist* establishes the hero's uniqueness as the source of his appeal to common experience. Its realism requires that the pastoral world in which he finally takes his place be an English suburb and that the legacy he recovers be money and position.

Such dualism is implicit in the title of *Lord Jim*, for in the first paragraph Conrad "makes us see" his hero at once as water clerk and son of God—and this double vision remains with us throughout the novel. But the world gives Jim a third definition, that of "gentleman." It is given as a concession, not to his background, but to the effect of self-exaltation on his personality, and Jim, conscious of the redeeming power of this word, clings to it after his disgrace. "I am," he tells Marlow, "I am—a gentleman, too."[7]

The word's power, as Conrad is aware, is the result of its evolution from a mark of class in a fixed and orderly system to a reward for merit in a Protestant and individualistic society. Jim's background is humble and, it would seem, evangelical:

> Originally he came from a parsonage. Many commanders of fine merchant-ships come from these abodes of piety and peace. Jim's father possessed such certain knowledge of the Unknowable as made for the righteousness of people in cottages without disturbing the ease of mind of those whom an unerring Providence enables to live in mansions.[8]

Under pressures economic and romantic, his "vocation for the sea declared itself," and his triumphant sense of personal election is revealed among the drab, indifferent, and alien images of industrial England:

> His station was the fore-top, and often from there he looked down, with the contempt of a man destined to shine in the midst of dangers, at the peaceful multitude of roofs cut in two by the brown tide of the stream, while scattered on the outskirts of the surrounding plain the factory chimneys rose perpendicular against a grimy sky.[9]

The passage suggests little difference between what is "given" with respect to class, religion, and motive in *Lord Jim* and in Defoe's fictional worlds. Conrad, whose knowledge of the Anglo-Saxon Protestant mind came as much from books as from experience, discovered in the self-centered idealism of that mind and in what he called its "insatiable imagination for conquest" a romantic principle around which to organize his realistic novels.

As a literary form the novel becomes more atavistic the more it advances. Its most elaborate and self-conscious innovation consists in merging ironically with romance. The hero is a Protestant in a Catholic country, a dreamer called Porter, and King, and Everybody, and his history is defined by a sentence of eternal exile and return:

A way a lone a last a loved a long the riverrun, past Eve and Adam's, from swerve of shore to bend of bay, brings us by a commodius vicus of recirculation back to Howth Castle and Environs.[10]

This, despite their apparently exclusive concern for authenticity, is the pattern of Defoe's narratives. The best known of his exiles is Moll Flanders, a ward of the parish, a felon's daughter, who instinctively claims for herself a higher nature, which she tries to define in wordly terms. But she is not the only one whose birth was but a sleep and a forgetting.

II

Captain Singleton was a stolen child, and his attempt to recall his "Pedigree" is as vivid and fragmentary as a dream:

If I may believe the Woman, whom I was taught to call Mother, I was a little Boy, of about two Years old, very well dress'd, had a Nursery Maid to tend me, who took me out on a fine Summer's Evening into the Fields towards *Islington*, . . . a little Girl being with her. . . . The Maid . . . meets with a Fellow, her Sweet-heart . . . ; he carries her into a Publick-House . . . and while they were toying in the House, the Girl plays about with me in her Hand in the Garden. . . .

At this Juncture comes by one of those sort of People who, it seems, made it their Business to Spirit away little Children. . . .

The Woman pretending to take me up in her Arms and kiss me, and play with me . . . at last . . . bids [the Girl] go back to the Maid, and tell her . . . that a Gentlewoman had taken a Fancy to the Child, and was kissing of it, but she should not be frighted . . . and so while the Girl went, she carries me quite away.[11]

The boy is "disposed of to a Beggar-Woman that wanted a pretty little Child to set out her Case" (2), then to a gypsy, who, like the gypsy guardians in Moll's ill-remembered past, reinforces the sense of mystery in his origins. Finally having been brought to a town that, "whatever its Name was, must not be far off from the Sea Side" (3), he is taken up by the master of a ship who calls him "his own Boy" and carries him across the sea to Newfoundland. Bob Singleton is not spared the child-hero's fate of falling into the hands of a quite different father-surrogate—a cruel oppressor. After the death of the shipmaster, he is enslaved by a Portuguese lieutenant who embodies all the "abandoned Vileness" of his race. Though Singleton is still in a "State of Original Wickedness," he acquires among the Portuguese intimations of his own higher nature: "They were so brutishly wicked, so base and perfidious, not only to Strangers, but to one another; so meanly submissive when subjected; so insolent, or barbarous and tyrannical when superiour, that I thought there was something in them that shock'd my very Nature" (8). While plotting desperately to kill his Master, he is ironically implicated in a plot to murder the Captain (who has been relatively kind to him), and is abandoned with the conspirators to the mercy of "Canniballs" and "Wild Beasts" on the African coast.

Here the personal history seems to degenerate into travelogue, but Singleton continues to play a role typical of the Defoe hero, whose singular qualities are always recognized by his superiors and whose "nature" compels him to assume authority among his peers. His unaccountable brilliance at diplomacy and military strategy—distinctly aristocratic skills—wins him the title of Captain Bob. A "Black Prince" recognizes his preeminence, and an educated gunner among the Portuguese becomes his Silenus, for

> finding me eager to understand and learn, he laid the Foundation of a general Knowledge of things in my Mind. . . .
>
> In especial Manner, he filled my Head with aspiring Thoughts . . . convincing me, that nothing could qualify me for great Undertakings, but a Degree of Learning superior to what was usual in the Race of Seamen. . . . He was always flattering me with my Capacity to learn. . . . (68–69)

Although Bob implores him to become their "Seignior Capitanio," or "General," the gunner, insisting in effect upon the distinction between shaman and hero, says "you must be our Leader, for all the Success of this Enterprize is owing to you" (69).

These are essentially the terms in which Bob later defers to the Quaker William Walters, who combines the roles of leader and wise man and converts the hero from amoral flamboyance to spiritual moderation, from self-destructiveness to security. Bob's character has been derived from the debased form of romance which Defoe probably knew best—rogue biography. However great his debt to the genre, Defoe was always careful, as Michael Shinagel has shown, to correct its implicit values from the standpoint of middle-class dissent.[12] This might also be said of his relation to "high" romance. The middle-class analogue to noble birth is gentility, which the Defoe hero acquires, says Mr. Shinagel, through education, money, "a settled way of life," and repentance (which requires leisure).[13] Under the management of Quaker William, Bob Singleton acquires that conviction of sin which is a sign of election; he converts his pirate's booty into merchandise which is honestly bartered; he finds William's needy sister a worthy object of his penitential charity; and, returning with a fortune to the country from which he had been exiled since early childhood, he marries the woman (to redeem, in effect, his investment) and declares himself "much more happy than I deserve" (335).

The conclusion is a triumph of Defoe's equivocal bourgeois ethic, but neither he nor his protagonist ever fully rejects that absolute or ideal conception of the self which exists independently of class and ethos, is unaltered by one's condition, conduct, or "natural depravity," and is expressed in romantic metaphors. Robinson Crusoe's reckless aspiration beyond the "middle way of life" is explained and partly vindicated by his meditations on the island where he has been shipwrecked:

> I was king and lord of all this country indefeasibly, and had a right of possession; and, if I could convey it, I might have had it in inheritance, as compleatly as any Lord of a Mannor in England.[14]

Singleton, having instinctively "taken State upon [him]self" before a native prince, contemplates in a similar spirit the land to which he has been condemned:

> if I had but a Ship of 20 Guns, and a Sloop, and both well Manned, I would not desire a better Place in the World to make my self as rich as a King. (44)

Before he can achieve this ambition, he must lead a savage life in a savage land. In the midst of his sordid career as thief, extortionist, and murderer—and at the point of his deepest penetration into Africa—he finds an Englishman who is, like himself, a kidnap victim. Having been captured by one native tribe, he found refuge and has lived for many years with another. Naked, covered with hair and black scales, he "appeared to be a Gentleman . . . in spight of all the Disadvantages of his miserable Circumstance" (148). Like Bob's tutor, he is a "Scholar and a Mathematician," and the hero's encounter with him, like those with the scholarly gunner and the Black Prince, serves as a reminder to Defoe's readers that true quality is perceptible beneath the most unprepossessing surface.

Yet the author of *Moll Flanders, Colonel Jacque,* and *Roxana* also put great stock in the trappings of quality. While the Defoe hero tends to define himself romantically or subjectively as a prince in rogue's disguise, he cannot escape realistic or objective definition as a mere rogue who must disguise himself as a prince in order to pass for one. Moreover, he might become what he pretends to be. After a period of meditation and prosperity in Venice, Captain Singleton returns to England, as one returning from a romantic quest, with a treasure and a new identity as a mysterious traveler, an Armenian (or "Grecian") merchant-prince.

Defoe significantly emphasizes his hero's refusal to consider such a homecoming until he can validly regard England as his home, that is, until he is provided with someone to whom he might return. His choice of disguises, paradoxically, might reflect this desire to define his origin. In its racial aspect, it faintly recalls Bob's childhood passage with the gypsy whom he had called "Mother." And the specific object of his return, the poor widow whom he marries and regards as his "Protect'ress," is reminiscent of a still earlier "mother," the beggar-woman in need of "a pretty little Child to set out her Case." Thus his homecoming takes the form of a metaphorical reunion with his earliest remembered guardians and a transformation of his own conscious beginnings.

But the mnemonic return is even more complete than that. By establishing a poor woman in a country house and coming across the sea in princely garb to make her his "Protect'ress," Singleton has united the remembered with the unremembered past, has recovered something of that pastoral summer when as a child "very well dress'd" he was abruptly separated from his origin and launched upon a restless, violent, nostalgic quest for his ideal self.

III

The preface to *Colonel Jacque* might have served as well for *Oliver Twist*:

Here's Room for just and copious Observations, on the Blessing, and Advantages of a sober and well govern'd Education, and the Ruin of so many Thousands of Youths of all Kinds, in this Nation, for want of it; also how much publick Schools, and Charities might be improv'd to prevent the

Destruction of so many unhappy Children, as, in this Town, are every Year Bred up for the Gallows.

The miserable Condition of unhappy Children, many of whose natural Tempers are docible, and would lead them to learn the best Things rather than the worst, is truly deplorable, and is abundantly seen in the History of this Man's Childhood; where, though Circumstances form'd him by Necessity to be a Thief, a strange Rectitude of Principles remain'd with him, and made him early abhor the worst Part of his Trade, and at last wholly leave it off.[15]

Defoe was hardly more able than Dickens to make his hero an example of the corruptive effects of the charity system. Dickens is lyric and mystical—his debt to Wordsworth is clear—in defining the original blessedness which protects Oliver. Defoe translates the myth into the language of formal realism. "I had a strange original Notion," says Jack, "of my being a Gentleman" (60).

His notion is the less strange for being based on his actual parentage: "My original may be as high as any Bodies for ought I know . . . my Mother was a Gentlewoman . . . my Father was a Man of Quality, and [my Nurse] had a good peice of Money given her to take me off his Hands" (3). Besides the money, Jack's father gives the nurse a piece of advice to pass on to the boy, that "she should always take care to bid me *remember, that I was a Gentleman* . . . [for] sometime or other the very hint would inspire me with Thoughts suitable to my Birth, and . . . I would certainly act like a Gentleman, if I believed myself to be so" (3).

Jack's identically named foster brothers seem to embody the antithetical traits appropriate to such a bastard of quality. Captain Jack is an "original Rogue," a Noah Claypole to the hero's Oliver. Coarse, brutal, "of a Carman-like Breed," he "would do the foulest and most villainous Things, even by his own Inclination" (5–6). The Colonel does somewhat less villainous things, always out of necessity rather than inclination, but he persists (out of necessity, it would seem) until he is able to pass for a Parisian gentleman; and this is the material difference between him and his plebeian brother. The fate of Captain Jack, a strikingly puritanical creation, was foreseen during his childhood: "every Body said he had the very look of a Rogue, and would come to be Hang'd" (9). The Colonel's latent quality, though he is a beggar and a shoeblack, is also perceptible: "I remember, the People would say of me, that Boy has a good Face; if he was wash'd, and well dress'd, he would be a good pretty Boy. . . . I wonder what the Rogues Father and Mother was" (7).

The Captain takes upon his head all the evils endemic to the condition of the three brothers. After the other two have become accomplished thieves, they go to Bridewell to watch their brother being flogged. In a later episode, it seems for a time that the roles have been reversed: Colonel Jack is arrested for crimes committed by the Captain. But when the mistake is discovered, the hero, though guilty of comparable felonies, is told by the Justice that he was "born to better Things," that "he was sorry I should fall into such a Misfortune as this, which he hop'd however would be no Dishonour to me, since I was so handsomely acquitted" (80). When they flee England together, the Colonel lives by his brother's thefts, and after they are separated, the scapegoat is hanged in London and the hero flourishes in Paris.

Major Jack is the illegitimate son of an officer of the guards, and his native qualities lead the hero to feel that, given his own genteel paternity, the military vocation is the natural one for him. The Major has "some thing of a Gentleman in him": "native Principles of Gallantry," "a good share of Wit," "a true Manly Courage" (6). He is Colonel Jack's companion in the famous scene at the boiling cook's where the two boys in their first suits of clothes regale themselves on boiled beef and delight in being addressed as "Gentlemen." He also leads the Colonel to become apprenticed to a "Thief of Quality," who succeeds him as the hero's mentor.

Defoe is apparently unwilling to include the gallant Major in his subsequent indictment of the gentleman-thieves with whom Jack becomes involved. This is the inevitable point in rogue narrative by Defoe at which cavalier "virtues" begin to be censured from a Puritan point of view. From this point, the process of identifying the spurious appearance of quality as he strives to regain his birthright becomes the substance of Jack's adventure. Always driven by his "strange Original Notion," Jack is seduced by the invitation of his new master, Will, to join a "brave Gang . . . where . . . we shall all be Gentlemen" (59). Impressed by the facility and daring of this gang, he quickly learns that their corresponding vices are cruelty and cynicism. The amusing conflict between Jack's idea of a Gentleman and Will's is revealing, for it not only opposes aesthetic and moral criteria, but definable social fact and indefinable inner conviction:

his Gentleman was nothing more nor less than . . . a Villain of a higher Degree than a Pick-pocket; and one that might do something more Wicked, and better Entituling him to the Gallows, than could be done in our way: But my Gentleman that I had my Eye upon, was another thing quite, tho' I cou'd not really tell how the describe it neither. (62)

Jack had first acquired the name Colonel by insisting on his preeminence among his foster brothers. Like Moll Flanders, he is certain of his natural claim to gentility without knowing precisely what gentility is. This certainty is the secular analogue to the Calvinist's inner light, and like its spiritual counterpart, it strives to manifest itself in the garish light of day. For the perceptive, Jack's true quality may shine through beggar's rags, but in a world which runs on false appearances, the authentic gentleman must often masquerade as one in order to receive justice. This is the lesson of the boiling cook who feeds Jack's self-esteem, of a second-hand clothier who rebuffs him because of his rags, and of a glass merchant whom Jack overhears scolding a fashionable customer for bad language: ". . . it is not like a Gentleman to swear," says the merchant, " 'tis enough for my black Wretches that Work there at the Furnace, or for these ragged nak'd black Guard Boys, *pointing at me* . . . but for a Man of Breeding, Sir, . . . a Gentleman! it ought to be look'd upon as below them" (61). (italics mine) The didactic purpose of the episode is to show that a beggar can be a gentleman if he observes certain decorums. But Jack's role in the merchant's homily makes his "Blood run Chill." "I had something in me," he says, "by what secret Influence I knew not, kept me from . . . the general Wickedness of the rest of my Companions" (60). To have been identified with them nevertheless is an object lesson in the importance of clothing to selfhood.

The episode of the glass merchant in *Colonel Jacque* is part of a costume motif as elaborate as that in *Moll Flanders*. Not only must the hero be well turned out; so must his mistress, and even his money. As a child, Jack lacks pockets in which to keep his first loot, and has mortifying recourse to a "foul Clout" which he finds in the street (23). Later, while observing a potential victim, he fastidiously remarks the "Black Dirty Baggs" in which colliers put the rewards of their ungenteel calling (43). While still a ragged thief, he deposits his first substantial prize—a dishonestly claimed reward—at interest with a gentleman, and when he returns years later to make another deposit, he wears livery taken from his gang's wardrobe of disguises and claims to be in the service of a baronet. As a bond servant in Virginia, clad in "the ordinary Habit of a poor half naked Slave" (126), Jack is recognized as a man of quality by his master, a member of that mystic fraternity upon whom the fate of the Defoe hero always depends. But an overseer who is ordered to provide clothes for Jack adds the note of social realism when "he lets me into a little Room by it self; here *says he*, go in there a Slave, and come out a Gentleman" (127).

This is a scene of rebirth for Colonel Jack. From this point his fortunes undergo an unbroken rise. The further crises in his life are moral rather than material. Position and independence give free play to "that Original something . . . that used formerly to Check me in the first meannesses of my Youth" (155). He is able to think of his criminal life as a nightmare descent ("The thought of it was like Reflections upon Hell and the Damn'd Spirits"), of his period of bondage as a purifying ordeal ("I remember'd it as a state of Labour and Servitude, Hardship and Suffering"), and of his future as a reward for victory over his fate:

> how Happy I was, that I cou'd live by my own Endeavors, and was no more under the Necessity of being a Villain. . . .
>
> . . . tho' this was the Foundation of my new Life, yet this was not the Superstructure . . . I might still be born for greater things than these; . . . it was Honesty, and Virtue alone that made Men Rich and Great, and gave them a Fame, as well as a Figure in the World, and . . . therefore I was to lay my Foundation in these, and expect what might follow in time. (156–157)

But since the world is still addicted to false appearances, Jack continues to compensate by means of disguises. He will masquerade as a French officer and a Spanish Don before attaining his true estate, and will similarly compensate others who have been deprived of justice by the perversity of the world. As a plantation owner, Jack serves as a fairy godfather to a scholarly felon among his bond servants. In return, the servant gives Jack training in language and religion which brings him closer to his ideal of gentility. Having been deceived by the appearances of quality in two of his first three wives, the hero (now Colonel Jacque) marries a worthy country girl, but first corrects the disparity between her worth and her appearance by dressing her in the clothes of a former wife. When his first wife turns up as a bond servant on his Virginia plantation, he has yet another chance to perform for a fallen member of the genteel class the same service which his master had performed for him, and his first impulse is to "new Cloath her" (256). Having been purified, like the hero, by degradation and suffering, she now deserves to wear the clothing which had formerly been merely a part of her wordly imposture. His fourth wife having died, Jack is now free to complete the cycle by remarrying his first.

The role of the first wife at the conclusion of his adventures is similar that of the poor widow in *Captain Singleton*. He is her benefactor, she his protectress. Because of a misadventure in the Caribbean, Jack becomes separated from her for a long time after their marriage. Like Bob Singleton's Venetian period, it is a time of meditation and repentance in the company of a wise and benevolent patron. The patron, a Spanish Don, smuggles him to Europe in like disguise, and at length Jack is permanently reunited with his wife in London. In *Colonel Jacque*, as well as in *Captain Singleton*, it seems that the hero must at least temporarily change his identity in order to achieve the permanent relationship with a woman which is requisite to a "steady way of living." While the pattern is more prominent in the earlier novel, its meaning is clearer in the later one, where the role of women in the hero's effort to recover his birthright is given much more elaborate development.

In her office as protectress, Jack's wife, like Singleton's, makes it possible for the hero to return to England. When she learns that her husband had offered certain half-hearted assistance to the Jacobite rebellion of 1715, she uses her mysterious influence at court to get him a pardon. Although the Jacobite episode was by far the least of Jack's offenses against the Crown, he uses the pardon as a means of consolidating his moral debts. It represents atonement with his king and country, and it imposes an obligation defined in terms of a distinctly romantic or aristocratic code of honor:

> having now . . . receiv'd my Life at the Hands of King GEORGE, . . . I became sincerely given in to [his] Interest . . . and this from a Principle of Gratitude, and a Sense of my Obligation to his Majesty for my Life. . . . [To] those who graciously give us our Lives, when it is in their Power to take them away, those Lives are a Debt ever after, . . . and if my Prince has given me my Life, I can never pay the Debt fully. . . .
>
> . . . so I must lay it down as a Rule of Honour, that a Man having once forfeited his Life to the Justice of his Prince, and to the laws of his Country, and receiving it back as a Bounty from the Grace of his Soveraign; such a Man can never lift up his Hand again against that Prince, without a for-

feiture of his Vertue, and an irreparable Breach of his Honour and Duty, and deserves no Pardon after it, either from God or Man. (276–277)

For Defoe this declaration may have been chiefly a means of assurring his readers that he had not treated treason on a par with theft.[16] But the passage also justifies itself as an attempt by the hero to resolve his deepest emotional conflict. The theme of making one's life the property of the man who saved it is a familiar one in romance, and here it is invoked as a final assertion of that aristocratic nature which Jack has always claimed for himself. Earlier, in his struggle to realize his true nature, he had violated its first laws by disowning his country and taking up arms against his prince. Now, with the need for such disloyalty behind him, he seizes the chance to perfect his claim to gentility by living according to the rules.

The above manifesto makes obvious use of the traditional connection between king and father. From the king, Jack insists, he has "receiv'd [his] Life" and contracted a debt "that never ceases while the Benefit receiv'd remains." To raise one's hand against the king is to commit an unforgivable offense against God and man. To devote oneself to the service of the king is to obtain, in one's own degree, the princely virtues—grace, beneficence, and honor. Jack's offense against the king was overt and his atonement explicit, but neither receives any significant development in the narrative as a whole. They acquire their importance as a surrogate for a submerged and complex pattern of revolt and reconciliation with the Man of Quality who had literally "given [him his] Life," his unknown father.

Jack's offense against his father comes in the very act of trying to emulate him. Upon introducing himself as one whose "original may be as high as any Bodies," he was compelled to add wryly, "for my Mother kept very good company, but that part belongs to her Story, more than to mine" (3). Though this story is not told, it is epitomized in the history of Jack's successive wives. When he returns from France as Colonel Jacque, he is at the "height of [his] good Fortune" (185), and has genteel accomplishments enough to compete for the favors of a lady of fashion. He is soon attracted to one of the sort that keeps "very good company," and he protests in significant terms his own sexual innocence: "I was a meer Boy in the Affair of Love . . . as perfectly unacquainted with the Sex, and as unconcern'd about them, as when I was ten Year old, and lay in a Heap of Ashes at the *Glass-*

House" (186). When he goes on to describe with terror the very qualities in the woman which attract him, this innocence appears more like resistance to a tabooed relationship:

I know not by what Witch-Craft in the Conversation of this Woman, and her singling me out upon several Occasions, I began to be ensnared, I knew not how, or to what End; and was on a sudden so embarass'd in my Thoughts about her, that like a Charm she had me always in her Circle. . . .
She attack'd me without ceasing, with the fineness of her Conduct, and with Arts which were impossible to be ineffectual . . . and yet kept herself . . . on the Reserve . . . surrounded continually with Obstructions. (187)

After a clumsily elaborate battle of the sexes, he marries the Jezebel, who is promptly revealed as a compulsive gambler and adulteress. Later she will be the fallen woman whom Jack redeems and the solicitous wife who intercedes for him with the king. But the first marriage is a visitation on Jack for desiring gentility in an illicit form. It punishes both his pride and his fortune.

Jack never meets one of his first wife's lovers, unless Defoe intends the reader to suppose that a creditor of hers, a "Gentleman well Dress'd" who appears after the separation, is one of them. He plainly, in any case, becomes the object of all the rage and humiliation which Jack has accumulated during the marriage. The gentleman interprets Jack's refusal to pay his wife's bill as a slur on her honor, and he demands satisfaction on her behalf. Swordsmanship being one of the genteel skills which Jack has overlooked, he awkwardly demurs and is publicly humiliated: "they call him Colonel, *says he,* I suppose he might be born a Colonel, for I dare say, he was born a Coward . . . and a Coward is a Rascal; and with that he came to me, and strok'd his Finger down my Nose pretty hard, and laugh'd and mock'd most horridly" (202). The hero's response is one of those instances of emotional excess, here rendered as physical violence, which have been said to distinguish *Colonel Jacque* from Defoe's other narratives (What has not been observed is that all, except the sentimental instances noted by Professor Monk,[17] occur during Jack's marital career.): ". . . being in a Fury I threw my Head in his Face, and Closing with him, threw him fairly on his Back . . . and had not the Constable step'd in, and taken me off, I had certainly stamp'd him to Death, with my Feet, for my Blood was now all in a Flame" (202–203).

After this incident Jack has his nose slit and his ear severed by two rogues hired by the gentleman to avenge him. The hero has paid an inordinately high price for an experience ostensibly designed to show the evils of false gentility. What is more, he seems to have learned a different lesson from the one which the episode was contrived to teach. Instead of repudiating as archaic and brutal the attributes of his wife's "gentleman," he goes to war in order to make those attributes his own. "I was come to what I was Born to," he says after receiving his commission, "I had never till now liv'd the Life of a Gentleman" (207). He compares himself with the Count de Charolais, "who . . . had an utter Aversion to the War, and abhorr'd it, and every thing that belong'd to it, [but] was so chang'd by the Glory he obtain'd in . . . Action . . . that afterwards, the Army was his Mistress and the Fateigues of the War his chief Delight" (208).

Nor does the lesson of his first marriage cure him of his addiction to quality jades. Another overcomes his resistance, this time by means of wine, and he marries her, now at least confident that he can vanquish his rivals and overeager to do so. He establishes his second wife, an Italian bourgeoise with salon manners, in Paris where in his absence she begins to keep "some Company, that I had Reason to believe were not such as an honest Woman ought to have Convers'd with" (224). The "Company" is principally a marquis, older than Jack, "a very honest Gentleman, and a Man of Quality," whose apparently innocent visits make Jack extravagantly suspicious. Eavesdropping on their drawing room conversation, he interprets the gentleman's May and January story about a fashionable courtship as *prima facie* evidence of adultery. He bursts into the room ("*say you so*, Madam, said I, was he too old for her!" [226]) and provokes a duel in which his rival is gravely wounded. The marquis confesses his guilt and Jack returns home to abuse his wife triumphantly before fleeing the country.

Though Jack's suspicions have been confirmed, Defoe's emphasis is on their irrationality. The novelist in this way distinguishes between character and fate only to show how they conspire to turn the hero's marriages into love triangles. Even when he feels that he has broken the pattern by marrying a country girl, he learns after her death that she had once been seduced and deserted by a "Gentleman of great Estate." He had chosen a country girl for wife in reaction, it seems, to the disaster of his third marriage, a disaster in which the psychological pattern of Jack's marital career comes through with particular violence and clarity.

The third wife is the "exquisitely genteel" widow of a ship's captain.

Since Jack's figurative rebirth as a gentleman about half way through the novel, his adventures have amounted to an elaborate voyage homeward, corresponding to the perfunctory but significant windup given to Captain Singleton's affairs. In both novels, the attainment of a perfect mate is necessary for the completion of the hero's journey. Jack seems fated, after apparently finding such a wife, either to learn that another gentleman has already been there or to meet a rival who threatens to destroy the relationship.

In Jack's third marriage both events occur, the latter as sequel to the former. He is first attracted to the widow while she is still in a state of elegantly controlled grief over the death of her husband. In due time she agrees to make Jack "the most happy Creature in the World" (239–240). This felicity lasts for six years until, as a result of a difficult childbirth, his wife takes to drink. When she is thoroughly demoralized, another ship's captain comes into her life:

> a Villain, if it be proper to call a Man, that was really a Gentleman, by such a Name, who was an intimate Acquaintance coming to pretend a Visit to her, made her and her Maid so Drunk together, that he lay with them both; with the Mistress the Maid being in the Room, and with the Maid, the Mistress being in the Room; after which, he it seems took the like liberty with them both, as often as he thought fit. (241–242)

Despite his absurd scruple about vilifying a gentleman, Jack takes revenge on *this* gentleman, it seems, for all the humiliations he has ever received at the hands of the class. He rejects the idea of challenging him, for "after a Man had treated me as he had done, he deserv'd no fair Play for his Life." Murder in ambush would be a more appropriate method, but this shocks Jack's "Temper . . . as well as Principle," and he decides to accost his victim in the street. He first confronts him, as he might have confronted his own father, with "the Villainy he had been guilty of in my Family" (242). Then he forces the man to refuse a duel, recalling in detail his own humiliating encounter with his first wife's "gentleman":

> he could not believe [I told him], but that I must be a great Coward as well as a Cuckold, or that I would resent it, and that it was now a very proper Time to call him to an Account for it, and therefore [I] bad him, if he durst show his Face to what he had done, and defend the Name of a Captain of a Man of War, *as they said*, he had been, to draw.
>
> He seem'd surpriz'd at the Thing, and began to Parlee, and would lessen the Crime of it; but I told him it was not a time to talk that Way,

> since he could not deny the Fact; and to lessen the Crime, was to lay it the more upon the Woman. (243)

The subsequent chastisement of the gentleman recovers and transforms a still earlier scene from Jack's past, the scene in which he watched his scapegoat brother "roar out like a mad Boy" under a flogging administered as an example to young rogues like himself. In the present episode the street boy, now turned gentleman, reduces a rival gentleman to street boy:

> I took him fast by one Wrist, and can'd him as severely as I was able, and as long as I could hold it, for want of Breath, but forebore his Head, because I was resolv'd he should feel it; in this Condition at last he begg'd for Mercy, but I was Deaf to all Pitty a great while, till he roar'd out like a Boy soundly whipt; then I took his Sword from him, and broke it before his Face, and left him on the Ground, giving him two or three Kicks on the Back-side. (243)

It is clear that Jack in this scene has turned an individual into a symbol, that through this enemy he is getting at inaccessible ones. The rival has been made to represent social superiority deflated, paternal authority superseded, exploitative lust chastised. But such work of abstraction exacts its own emotional cost, which Defoe unexpectedly includes (though without emphasis or detail) in his account of Jack's experience: "I grew so disconsolate and discouraged, that I was next Door to being distempered, and sometimes indeed, I thought myself a little touch'd in my Head. But it proved nothing but Vapours, and the Vexation of this Affair, and in about a Years time, or there abouts, it wore off again" (244).

Aside from this instance, the only irrational trait that Jack is able to perceive in himself is a violent temper—evidence, it would seem, of his aristocratic nature. But in trying to explain his third wife's moral deterioration, he cites a fable whose Oedipal theme defines his own relationship with wives and rivals. The fable purports to illustrate how drink releases the demons of sexuality:

> That was a good Story, whether real or invented, of the Devil tempting a young Man to murder his Father. No, *he said,* that was un-natural. Why, then *says the Devil,* Go and lye with your Mother: No, *says he,* That is abominable. Well, Then, *says the Devil,* If you will do nothing else to oblige me, go and get Drunk; Ay, ay, *says the Fellow,* I'll do that, so he went and made himself Drunk as a Swine; and when he was Drunk, he murdered his Father, and lay with his Mother. (241)

By condescending to take a country girl for his next wife, Jack can assure himself of his social superiority in a completely new way, certain that he is not displacing some rival gentlemen in the affections of a promiscuous lady of fashion. (Yet Defoe, as we have noted, insists upon the triangularity of all Jack's sexual relationships by adding that even Moggy had been seduced by a gentleman before her marriage.) In remarrying his first wife, Jack finally reconciles his need for innocence with his need for perfect self-gratification. His wife is no longer the quality jilt she once was. Like Moggy, she is in a humble condition, and he can serve as her aristocratic deliverer without risking the humiliation, the jealous rage, the guilty anxiety, which have always resulted from his encounters with a rival. He is his own successor in his wife's affections; he is in the place of the father as well as that of the son. Although the reunion still involves him in a love triangle—a triangle which is in fact responsible for his decision to remarry—his role in it is both guiltless and wholly triumphant. While his former wife is still serving as his housekeeper, Jack learns that his tutor has fallen in love with her. The tutor, of course, is also a person of quality who has been brought low and then rescued by Jack. And he is the character in the novel who can best be described as a "good" father to the hero, for he has enabled Jack to satisfy his true father's ambitious demand that despite his abandonment he should be always "inspire[d] . . . with thoughts suitable to [his] Birth." When Jack tells the woman of his tutor's feelings toward her, he has the satisfaction of hearing her state her emphatic preference for himself: ". . . let me be your Slave rather than the best Man's Wife in the World. . . . I will never belong to any Man else . . . let me be as I am, or any thing else you please to make me, but not a Wife, to any Man alive but yourself" (261–262). This extraordinary act of submission releases Jack from the taboos which have destroyed his earlier attachments. His triumph over a paternal rival has been changed from an aggression against the man to an act of charity toward the woman. Jack's charity, indeed, has already turned both of these parental figures into his creatures, and they seem to exist in the last sixth of the novel only to gratify his unconscious will.

The theme of separation and reunion with the beloved derives, of course, from the Greek romances. Unity with the other is necessary for the unity of the self.[18] Jack must endure a second separation from his wife before their final reunion in England, and this Caribbean interlude is hard to justify in terms of either narrative or psychological interest; but when compared with the ending of *Captain Singleton* it reveals a remarkable consistency in Defoe's way of conceiving of the hero's return. Singleton returns to England with his patron, William Walters, to live under the protection of one of William's own relations. In order to marry this woman, who represents his own all-but-forgotten past, he must receive the blessing of his spiritual father and undergo a permanent change of identity. In *Colonel Jacque* the use of an aristocratic disguise reappears in a merely vestigial form. Jack cannot return to England without imitating the dress of the new patron whom he has acquired in the Caribbean. The disguise is not retained, but far more elaborate means have been used to remove the psychological and moral obstacles to Jack's recovery of his origins and his rectification of those wrongs which had left him an outcast in the streets of London with only a "strange original Notion" to give direction to his life.

IV

"Strange original notion" better describes Moll Flanders's self-image than Jack's, for there is nothing in her background to support her conviction that gentlewoman, not maidservant, is her appropriate station in life. Yet her father's anonymity and her gypsy guardians are appropriate credentials for a child-exile of romance. And against all the conventional signs of gentility, which she lacks, Moll is compelled from the beginning to assert her "nature." "I had no policy in all this," she says of her childish appeal for a reprieve from domestic service, "it was all nature."[19] From the standpoint of spiritual autobiography, which G. A. Starr has shown to have contributed heavily to the structure and theme of Defoe's fiction, "nature" means depravity. But such a conclusion would be misleading in the present context, where "nature" is evidently to be preferred to "policy." Moll's childish spontaneity is the innocent, policy the sophisticated, expression of natural depravity.

Starr follows Moll in identifying vanity as the dominant characteristic of her depraved nature. Commenting on her seduction by the Elder Brother, he observes that vanity "provides a radically simple basis for Moll's thoughts and actions at this point in the book."[20] It follows that the novel makes its initial appeal to the reader's concern over where Moll's vanity will lead her. To vice, says Starr, and a hardening of the heart followed by an imperfect, because excessively delayed, repentance. This development, taken from spiritual autobiography, gives *Moll Flanders* its "structural integrity," which is marred by the presence of materials and techniques not belonging to the religious genre.[21]

Starr's research draws attention to the unusually marked discrepancy between the apparent design of Defoe's narratives and their total effect. The modern criticism of *Moll Flanders,* preceding *Defoe and Spiritual Autobiography,* generally begins with a more inclusive definition of the novel's form and responds quite differently to the heroine's principal flaw. Her vanity can be consistently seen as inseparable from her distinctive and powerful appeal. For vanity is merely Moll (or Defoe) the moralist's word for self-love, a quality which Lionel Trilling has found to be "the basis of . . . energy and style and intelligence" in a heroine very differently situated, Emma Woodhouse:

> There is a great power of charm in self-love, although, to be sure, the charm is an ambiguous one. We resist it, yet we are drawn by it, if only it goes with a little grace or creative power. Nothing is easier to pardon than the mistakes and excesses of self-love: if we are quick to condemn them, we take pleasure in forgiving them. And with good reason, for they are the extravagance of the first of virtues, the most basic and biological of the virtues, that of self-preservation.[22]

Moll begins with the "extravagance" of that virtue, even though she has cause to settle for a simpler form of it. Although she defines her original idea of herself, with comic naïveté, in terms borrowed from the society in which she lives, her emphasis at this point is on the ineffability of the idea, which can be defined only negatively as a kind of independence, as an inability to endure having her identity depend on her relation to an employer. She knows no more about it than she knows about the identity of her father or the duration of her period with the gypsies; no more than Jack knew about being a gentleman or Crusoe about the impulse which drove him to reject the middle way of life. Moll's low circumstances and ignorance of the world lead her ominously to mistake a prostitute for the embodiment of her idea, and this antinomy is what first engages the reader's interest in her fate. He believes, as she does, in her obscure claim to an ideal station in life, and he is anxious that, Cinderella-like, she should take possession of it. But he is also aware that the most obvious social determinants as well as common prejudice dictate that she will end where she began, at Newgate. Defoe's art consists in developing both possibilities together in each phase of Moll's adventures, revealing them as indivisible aspects of the same character. It is Moll's dual identity which is the source of narrative interest and the principle of coherence in the novel, from her early romance of gentility to the reversal of her fortunes at Newgate to her ultimate regeneration in the New World.

While Moll is under the protection of her guardian, her strange original notion is allowed to grow in an atmosphere of maternal indulgence. Then it is actively cultivated by her first genteel benefactor, the Mayoress: "Nay, she may come to be a gentlewoman, says she . . . ; she has a lady's hand" (14). Later, during her first visit to America, Moll will remark the same trait in her mother, whom she still supposes to be her mother-in-law. The whiteness of hand in that scene will be a confirmation of what the older woman is saying—that the inhabitants of Virginia have been liberated from their Old World identity—and the full pertinence to Moll of this fact will not be revealed until the end of the story. At present the "lady's hand" is rewarded by a shilling, fostering Moll's tendency to associate personal with negotiable "value." By ten she is "grave," "mannerly," and "proud," qualities which are translated by virtue of monetary gifts into "head-dresses, linen, and gloves" (15). The method is established by which Moll will try to advance her romantic cause in the world.

We are not allowed to suppose that she has merely added the vice of greed to that of vanity. Her response to "genteel living" is an aesthetic one, and her claim to it seems so natural or "original" that after being a guest in the house of a lady she is permanently alienated from her real home: "I was not so easy in my old quarters as I us'd to be, and I thought it was fine to be a gentlewoman indeed, for I had quite other notions of a gentlewoman now than I had before; . . . I lov'd to be among gentlewomen, and therefore I long'd to be there again" (16). Like Pip, who after a day at Satis House dreams of what he "used to do" there, Moll has acquired an instant nostalgia for the higher condition. Her liberal accomplishments too, picked up while she was in the hated position of servant, demonstrate "gifts of nature"; they are treated as secular signs of grace:

the lady had masters home to teach her daughters to dance, and to speak French, and to write, and others to teach them musick; and as I was always with them, I learn'd as fast as they; and tho' the masters were not appointed to teach me, yet I learn'd by imitation and enquiry all that they learn'd by instruction and direction. . . .

By this means I had . . . all the advantages of education that I could have had if I had been as much a gentlewoman as they were with whom I liv'd; and in some things I had the advantage of my ladies, tho' they were my superiors, *viz.* that mine were all the gifts of nature, and which all their fortunes could not furnish. (18)

This assurance enables Moll to believe herself "loved" by the Elder Brother, an excellent portrait of the merchant's son playing aristocratic rake. The attraction, of course, is a form of self-love: the gentleman's attentions seem to Moll another instance of her special qualities being recognized by the great. But this vanity continues to be her most natural and engaging quality, especially by contrast with her equivocal moralism in reviewing the episode: "if I had known . . . how hard he supposed I would be to be gain'd, I might have made my own terms, and if I had not capitulated for an immediate marriage, I might for a maintainance till marriage, and might have had what I would" (24–25). This calculation is called "act[ing] . . . as virtue and honour re-quir'd," and her joyous spontaneity at the time is called "vanity and pride": [I] was taken up only with the pride of my beauty, and of being belov'd by such a gentleman" (25).

As a result of the brother's manipulation of her feelings, this pride in being loved is linked with an identical passion for gold: "I spent whole hours in looking upon it; I told the guineas over a thousand times a day." The gentleman, as Robert R. Columbus demonstrates,[23] has contrived to make Moll respond to money as an index of his "value" for her, and therefore of her objective value. The following passage illustrates his technique:

he thought he had heard some body come up stairs, so he got off from the bed, lifted me up, professing a great deal of love for me, but told me it was all an honest affection, and that he meant no ill to me, and with that put five guineas into my hand, and went down stairs.

I was more confounded with the money than I was before with the love; and began to be so elevated, that I scarce knew the ground I stood on. (23)

Throughout this affair the reader's censure is reserved for the mean calculations of the Elder Brother. Moll's exuberance continues to be a redeeming trait, even of her avarice, so that even after she has pursued her criminal career beyond material necessity, her attraction to "fine" cloth and "very good" plate cannot be regarded as a mere hard acquisitiveness. Linen, lace, and silver have become magical objects by virtue of the attributes with which Moll has invested them. Their fineness and goodness are qualities which she demands for herself. She is not a materialist but an economic idealist.

After learning the world from the Elder Brother, Moll can continue to romanticize wealth, but not her method of acquiring it. The death of her first husband, the mawkishly democratic Robin, leaves her comfortable and disgusted, and she expresses the attitude of her widowhood with uncharacteristic cynicism: "I had been trick'd once by that cheat call'd love, but the game was over, I was resolv'd now to be married or nothing, and to be well married or not at all" (53). The attitude is revealed more accurately in her choice of a second husband, the shopkeeper with aristocratic tastes who insists on separating his means of making a living from the figure he cuts in the world. This "gentleman-tradesman" seems admirably suited to the dualism in Moll's own situation; but the tradesman, instead of supporting the gentleman, is destroyed by him. As Moll will discover again in Jemy, her "highwayman husband," the aristocratic qualities which attract her are not only otiose, but self-destructive: "He said some very handsome things to me indeed at parting; for I told you he was a gentleman, and that was all the benefit I had of his being so" (56).

Moll's true feelings about her bourgeois gentleman are belied by the prim remark, "Vanity is the perfection of a fop" (55). They come through clearly in the only two episodes concerning him. First, the extravagant trip to Oxford, Moll's first masquerade:

> we had a rich coach, very good horses, a coachman, postillion, and two footmen in very good liveries; a gentleman on horseback, and a page with a feather in his hat upon another horse; the servants all call'd him my lord, and I was her honour, the countess, . . . and a pleasant journey we had; for, give him his due, not a beggar alive knew better how to be a lord than my husband. (55)

The second is his flamboyant escape from the sponging house:

> . . . letting himself down from almost the top of the house to the top of another building, and leaping from thence, which was almost two stories,

and which was enough indeed to have broken his neck, he came home and got away his goods before the creditors could come to seize. (56)

This character's charming bravado, his generous pride in Moll, his destruction and flight, illustrate a Marxian dictum cited by Ian Watt, that "enjoyment is subordinated to capital, and the individual who enjoys to the individual who capitalises."[24] Moll's future course will be to continue the masquerade, to impersonate her ideal self even as she works at a sordid profession. But she does not squander her capital. The costume of gentility itself becomes her means of prospering as fortune hunter, thief, and prostitute.

In Moll's next marital enterprise, her own imposture is doubled by her half-brother's. The incest motif, that vestige of romance so familiar in the early novel, becomes in this episode a way to explore the ultimate implications of the heroine's narcissism. The courtship of sister and brother is a study in symmetry. They are brought together by greed, but discover a strong mutual sympathy. They play the coy game of trying to learn each other's motive and fortune, each unaware that their motives and fortunes are identical. The game is played on a windowpane, where the gentleman inscribes a line of verse and Moll completes the couplet. By marrying her brother, Moll figuratively steps through the looking glass into the New World, where her selfhood and her destiny will receive their final definition. The figure behind the mirror, though Moll does not yet know it, is her mother, whose new status in America vindicates Moll's origin and prefigures the end of her adventure:

with a great deal of good humour'd confidence she told me she was one of the second sort of inhabitants . . . a criminal. And here's the mark of it, child, says she, and shewed me a very fine white arm and hand, but branded. . . .

This story was very moving to me, but my mother (smiling) said, You need not think such a thing strange, daughter, for some of the best men in the country are burnt in the hand, and they are not asham'd to own it. (76)

The melodramatic crisis following Moll's discovery of the truth has the primarily structural function of forestalling that atonement with her beginnings which is the goal of all romantic heroes, and all of Defoe's. The pattern of separation and reunion, which generally dominates the love relationships in romance, is followed also in Moll's relationships with two of her husbands, but both are rendered anticlimactic—the first by the half-brother's decline into imbecility, the second by the aristocratic highwayman's uselessness on the plantation. The important occurrence of the pattern concerns Moll's need for union with a thoroughly regenerated parent in a new Eden.

By fleeing back to London, however, Moll charts an antithetical course for herself—one that will lead her to the Sign of the Cradle, emblem of a distinctly unregenerate "mother" who leads her back to the dread place of her birth. From Bath to Newgate, Moll undergoes a steady metamorphosis in her pursuit of quality. At first she is as successful as Colonel Jack in making disguise serve her own version of the truth. With the help of her genial panderess of a landlady (another ambiguous maternal figure), she passes at Bath for a gentlewoman of declining circumstances and wins the affections of a "compleat gentleman." Her duplicity in this affair, like that of a successful *picara,* exposes deeper and less engaging duplicity in a respectable character. Moll's disguise is a metaphor for the disparity she perceives between her nature and her fortune. The gentleman's is a means of deceiving himself and distorting sexual feelings. His desire for Moll appears first in the guise of paternal benevolence:

> He ask'd me to come into his chamber; he was in bed when I came in, and he made me come and sit down on his bed side. . . . .
>
> . . . taking me by the hand, [he] made me put it [into a drawer full of gold], and take a whole handful; I was backward at that, but he held my hand hard in his hand, and put it into the drawer, and made me take out as many guineas almost as I could well take up at one. (97–98)

Then it appears in the guise of fanatical purity:

> And now he made me deep protestations of a sincere inviolable affection for me, but with the utmost reserve for my virtue, and his own. I told him I was fully satisfy'd of it; he carried it that length that he protested to me, that if he was naked in bed with me he would as sacredly preserve my virtue as he would defend it if I was assaulted by a ravisher. I believ'd him, and told him I did so; but this did not satisfy him; he would . . . give me an undoubted testimony of it. (100)

Moll is deceived by the "noble principle" ("I was much wickeder than he" [101]), but firmly aware of how the failure of this purity test has changed her identity: "I exchang'd the place of friend for that unmusical harsh sounding title of whore" (102). With this new status, Moll has yet something to learn from her lover about gentility. The gentleman repents, and "whenever sincere repentance succeeds such a crime as this, there never fails to attend a hatred of the object" (107). Moll acts promptly on the observation that one requires "leisure for repentance," an observation which throughout Defoe's fiction defines the place of religion in the life of the aspiring hero. Moll writes the gentleman a note declaring that she "desir'd to repent as sincerely as he had done, but intreated him to put me in some condition that I might not be expos'd to temptations from the frightful prospect of poverty and distress" (109). Repentance, of course, is what at last certifies Moll's hard-won respectability.

The spurious attractions of the Bath gentleman, like those of the Elder Brother and Jemy, are used by Defoe to correct the aristocratic bias in Moll's romanticism. The only leisure or status acquired in the Bath affair comes during her lying-in, when she replaces the "harsh sounding title of whore" with the pseudonym "Lady Cleave." By contrast, her happy marriage to a bank clerk is a period of genuine "leisure for repentance." The clerk personifies Crusoe's middle station in the same way that Jemy embodies her original dream of gentility. The former is a "quiet, sensible sober man, virtuous, modest, sincere, and in his business diligent and just" (164). The latter is "tall, well-shap'd and had an extraordinary address; talk'd as naturally of his park, and his stables, or his horses, his game-keepers, his woods, his tenants, and his servants, as if he had been in a mansion house, and I had seen them all about me" (124). Her "ordinary" way of life with the bank clerk seems to Moll a "safe harbour, after the stormy voyage of [the] past": "I began to be thankful for my deliverance. I sat many an hour by myself, and wept over the remembrance of past follies, and the dreadful extravagances of a wicked life, and sometimes I flatter'd myself that I had sincerely repented" (163). That final note of instability foretells the bank clerk's ruin and Moll's return to sin. The "safe harbour" could never have held her as long as the "infinite variety" of life with the highwayman. The intensity of Moll's love for Jemy is dramatized in an episode which recalls at once the separation-and-reunion motif of classical romance and the evangelical spiritualism with which Defoe's readers were familiar. From twelve miles off, the departing husband hears Moll's passionate appeal: "O Jemy! . . . come back, come back, I'll give you all I have; I'll beg, I'll starve with you" (133).

Moll's weakness for the aristocracy is not cured until she and her demoralized adventurer settle in the colonies. At first, still under his spell, she takes his funk as evidence that "the greatest spirits . . . are subject to the greatest dejections" (274). At last she learns that in America the style of the landed gentry is at odds with the substance. When luck, endurance, and resourcefulness bring her "a maid-servant and a Negro boy to wait on me, and provisions ready dressed for my supper," she recognizes that she is in a "new world," and begins "almost to wish that I had not brought Lancashire husband from England at all" (291).

The period between Moll's first and final reunion with Jemy is like a parody of that ordeal of separation in early romance where the heroine meets and withstands a series of threats to her constancy. Moll meets and succumbs to them all. Whereas marriage to the bank clerk had been a safe harbor after a stormy voyage, marriage to the gentleman brings her into the establishment of a midwife for prostitutes: ". . . whether I was a whore or a wife, I was to pass for a whore here" (141). At this point her progress toward Newgate is accelerated under the tutelage of "Mother Midnight."

This "necessary woman" is a powerful source of ambivalence. She is created to appeal to the dualism in the heroine's nature. Her gratuitous generosity toward Moll has a status similar to, say, Bob Fagin's in the life of the young Dickens. It makes her an embodiment of the city's seductions. By occupation and temperament she is in the tradition of the Fagin of *Oliver Twist* and of Richardson's Mrs. Sinclair, who try to "mother" their victims into moral ruin. She lives by the vices of the city. At the Sign of the Cradle, illegitimate children are aborted or sold, stolen goods bought, thieves trained. Like Fagin or Mrs. Jewkes of *Pamela,* the governess enjoys physical intimacy with her charges, and seems to know their secrets:

> Are you sure you was nurs'd up by your own mother? and yet you look fat and fair, child, says the old beldam; and with that she stroak'd me over the face. . . .
> . . . Sure, said I to my self, this creature cannot be a witch, or have any conversation with a spirit that can inform her what I was before I was able to know it my self? (151–152)

What this new "mother" seems to know—the dark potential implied in Moll's origin—she exploits, using "necessity," that ambiguous force throughout Defoe's fiction, to add a skillful thief to her stable of doomed felons. "Give me not poverty lest I steal," is Moll's way of simplifying the complex motives behind her thefts. But most of her crimes reveal, apart from material necessity, a compulsion to secure for herself the appearance of social dignity or to discredit such appearances in others. "Necessity" takes on the connotation of "fate" as well as "need," when Moll defines the motive behind her first thefts as a diabolic compulsion prompted by Satan; she begins her criminal career with the theft from a careless maidservant of a bundle whose contents she admiringly catalogues, notwithstanding her horror at the deed: "a suit of child-bed linnen . . . very good and almost new, the lace very fine . . . a silver porringer . . . a small silver mug and six spoons . . . a good smock, and three silk handkerchiefs" (167). The next crime is more clearly an assault against a genteel mother committed under the auspices of a villainous one. It is the theft of a string of beads, "worth about twelve or fourteen pounds," from an overdressed child: "I suppose it might have been formerly the mother's, for it was too big for the child's wear, but that, perhaps, the vanity of the mother to have her child look fine at the dancing school had made her let the child wear it" (169).

Moll's genteel dress at this time is, unfortunately, not vanity but policy. Yet it is important to her ideal of respectability, for it is her only link with the respectable world. When she alters her thief's strategy by dressing as a beggar woman, the change seems ominous and unnatural to her. The mask of gentility on the other hand, enables her, in the midst of picking a pocket, to revert quickly and naturally to her "decent" self while her wretched alter ego is "deliver'd up to the rage of the street." It enables her to divert such rage from herself to a merchant who has accused her of theft. And it gives her a chance to act out, for profit, an old dream of familiarity with the gentry as she deceives another privileged child.

The fragmentation of Moll's identity during her criminal life, a process symbolized by her multiple costumes and pretenses, lends subtle reinforcement to G. A. Starr's emphasis on the progressive hardening of her heart. While we get almost no useful account of Moll's motives at this point, we can infer from the effects of what she does a new element of vindictiveness in her personality. An effect of her old "vanity," or her firm possession of an ideal self, was that it enhanced in her view the quality of others, like her guardian, the Mayoress, and the Elder Brother. The disintegration of that selfhood into a set of utilitarian disguises and ploys has the effect of degrading others, like the mother of her first child victim, the London gentleman, and the tradesman who mistakenly accuses her.

The seduction and robbery of the London gentleman, and the subsequent reunion with him, is the coldest of Moll's sexual adventures. An earlier episode, mock-romantic in effect, has prepared us to recognize the androgyny of Moll the thief (as opposed to the femininity of Moll the servant). She has assumed a male disguise which conceals her sex even from the robber with whom she works and sleeps; when her partner is caught she reverts to female, apprehensive that she will be informed upon, and awaits the "joyful news that he was hang'd" (191). In the heavily moralized affair of the London gentleman, she assumes an archetypally destructive role—that of the urban harlot, too old and experienced to have desires yet bent on exploiting the desires of others. The whole episode is a fable of the dualism of city life and how it is created and sustained by the dualism in man. Sir ——— is a "civil . . . gentleman . . . there is not a finer man, nor a soberer, modester person in the whole city" (200). So much the better for Moll, who makes her appeal to the side of his nature that corresponds to the underground life of London, the life she has come to represent. Alternately sinning and repenting with the gentleman (the governess serving as go-between) becomes Moll's way of vindicating her "character" at the expense of his.

In the incident of the mercer, Moll is ironically mistaken for a thief identically dressed in widow's weeds, who has just fled from a shop. The mistake is corrected when Moll's double is captured and made the object of a mob's self-righteous frenzy:

> [Two journeymen] and a great rabble with them [brought] along with them the true widow that I was pretended to be; and they came sweating and blowing into the shop, and with a great deal of triumph dragging the poor creature in the most butcherly manner up towards their master. (212)

Like the boy in the street, this captured felon serves as scapegoat for Moll's crimes, securing for her the role of heroine in the popular melodrama that follows:

> we all went very quietly before the justice, with a mob of about 500 people at our heels; and all the way we went I could hear the people ask, what was the matter? and others reply and say, a mercer had stop'd a gentlewoman instead of a thief, and had afterwards taken the thief, and now the gentlewoman had taken the mercer, and was carrying him before the

justice. This pleas'd the people strangely, and made the crowd encrease, and they cry'd out as they went, Which is the rogue? which is the mercer? and especially the women. Then when they saw him they cry'd out, *That's he, that's he*! and every now and then came a good dab of dirt at him. (214–215)

I had the satisfaction of seeing the mob wait upon [the mercer and his journeyman], as they came out, holooing, and throwing stones and dirt at the coaches they rode in, and so I came home. (216)

It is a leveling kind of satisfaction, a falling off from that absolute belief in her own distinction which earlier (and later) uses of the crowd have tended to confirm. The Defoe hero does evil things, but not, characteristically, for evil reasons. The crowd, respectable or other, shows the dark side of this optimism, manifesting at all times a gratuitous hostility toward the ideals and interests of the individual. That Defoe should be able to sustain such a subjective ordering of experience is not just the result of "point of view," his conception of which is loose enough to accommodate his journalistic and evangelical purposes. It is equally the result of those details of plot and metaphor which define for Moll a special place in relation to her surroundings, that of child exile and finally of romantic quester. She is most tarnished by the world when she can join the crowd and watch someone else in the role of scapegoat. But she is quick to resume that role. Paradoxically she recovers the prestige which Defoe has reserved for her when she is caught stealing.

Objectively, thieves are in the wrong, their captors in the right. In Defoe's account, Moll enters a darkened house in quest of a treasure guarded by two dragons, "two wenches that came open-mouth'd at me just as I was going out at the door . . . two fiery dragons cou'd not have been more furious, they tore my cloaths, bully'd and roar'd, as if they would have murther'd me" (237). The way past these dragons carries Moll into the pit.

When the romantic motif in *Moll Flanders* reaches a crescendo, so does its significance as a novel. The book has been a most convenient early example of the literary genre which is committed to giving an authentic account of the relations between the individual and society, for in *Moll* the relations are of the most rudimentary order: from the first the people and institutions are seen exclusively as allies or obstacles to Moll's self-realization. It is a higher achievement, formal and thematic, when a novel can depict society as a mirror of the individual. For a moment, in the Newgate episode, *Moll Flanders* reaches that level,

> that horrid place! . . . the place where my mother suffered so deeply, where I was brought into the world, and from whence I expected no redemption but by an infamous death. To conclude, the place that had so long expected me, and which with so much art and success I had so long avoided.
>
> . . . the hellish noise, the roaring, swearing, and clamour, the stench and nastiness, and all the dreadful afflicting things that I saw there, joyn'd to make the place seem an emblem of hell itself, and a kind of entrance into it. (238–239)

But it is one thing to recoil in horror from one's fellow prisoners and another to become one with them. A descent into hell brings the hero into contact with aspects of his character or fate which he cannot acknowledge in the rational, daylight world, and Moll's descent is not complete until she sees herself in "Poor Jenny," the grotesquely complacent felon:

> how hell should become by degrees so natural, and not only tollerable, but even agreeable, is a thing unintelligible but by those who have experienc'd it as I have. (240–241)

> I degenerated into stone, I turn'd first stupid and senseless, and then brutish and thoughtless, and at last raving mad as any of them were; in short, I became as naturally pleas'd and easy with the place as if indeed I had been born there. (242)

She was, of course, born there, and her spurious conception of gentility dies there. It is survived by the more rugged virtues—ingenuity, vigor, and perseverance—which have always been at the basis of her character and which now, at the nadir of her career, bring about the reversal of her fortunes. The old ideal survives in the person of Jemy. He steadily loses his identity in America while Moll establishes a new one for herself, based on her adoration for those household gods who will enable her to return to England as the sturdy representative of a new order of gentility.

V

Charlot, heroine of a *récit* in Mary Manley's *New Atalantis* (1709), is an orphan of quality adopted by a great duke and trained in the love of virtue. In time the duke becomes infatuated with her, reverses the tendency of her education, and seduces her in his villa. Charlot's mentor, a widowed countess, has advised her to follow the example of Mlle de Scudéry's Roxelana, "who by her wise Address brought an imperious *Sultan*, contrary to the established rules of the *Seraglio*, to divide with her the Royal Throne."[25] But through Charlot's disinterestedness and her lover's prudence, the affair comes to be carried on away from court and villa in the anonymity of a rural hideaway. The worldly countess, finding that Charlot "possessed all she could desire in the Duke's company," pronounces her a "*pauvre Fille trompez* [*sic*]," and decides to act on her own advice.[26] The duke consequently discards Charlot and marries her mentor.

The cynicism of the countess is expressed most precisely by her use of the Roxelana story. She reads it with solipsistic assurance as an exemplum on the need for policy to govern inclination. Scudéry's Roxelana is, in fact, an archetypal vixen whose relation to sexuality and power is the antithesis of all virtue illustrated in the romance. The daughter of an exiled nobleman and a slave, she is at first the instrument of her father's ambition to reestablish himself at court, but after the death of her father she continues to pursue and use power with diabolic animus.

In drawing lessons from Charlot's history, Mrs. Manley shows little more sensitivity than the countess to its romantic antecedent. The story, we are told, "warn[s] all believing Virgins from Shipwracking their Honour upon . . . the Vows and pretended Passion of Mankind." The other lesson, still more mundane, is "That no Woman ought to introduce another to the Man by whom she is beloved."[27] This is closer to Defoe than to Mlle de Scudéry, and together with the analogies among the stories of Roxelana, Charlot, and the Fortunate Mistress, it suggests how the work of such writers as Mrs. Manley, Mrs. Heywood, and Aphra Behn constitutes a bridge between Defoe and romance. The connection is most evident, of course, in his attempts to treat high life.

Roxana is the daughter of an exile, a Huguenot "of better Fashion, than ordinarily the People call'd REFUGEES at that time were,"[28] who retains enough wealth after emigrating to England to marry his daughter, with an ample dowry, to an "Eminent Brewer in the City." This is "the Foundation of [her] Ruin" (7), for the brewer's offense against Defoe's credo—financial incompetence—is compounded by his offense against Roxana's—commonness. Her French heritage consists of gifts of art and nature which qualify her as a budding *précieuse* but serve her ill as the wife of a blundering English tradesman:

> I was . . . tall, and very well made; sharp as a Hawk in Matters of common Knowledge; quick and smart in Discourse; apt to be Satyrical; full of Repartee, and a little too forward in Conversation; . . . tho' perfectly Modest in my Behaviour. Being *French* Born, I danc'd, *as some say*, naturally, lov'd it extremely, and sung well also. (6)

When her husband squanders both of their fortunes and absconds, she must turn these liberal qualities into capital.

The decline into poverty is Roxana's fall from grace. Her first deliverer discovers her plight in the ruined condition of her garden, which he promises to restore. The price of restoration is the heroine's virtue, and the need to pay it is urged against Roxana's demure protestations by her maid Amy, the personification of her fallen nature. The same is true, with modifications, of all of Defoe's "helper" characters: whether casuistically shrewd like William Walters or corruptly generous like Moll Flanders' "governess," they all enable the initiate to meet, on its own terms, the fallen world; and the reader himself, anxious for the hero to prevail in that world, is consequently of their party. Roxana's maid provides the most lurid instance.

Serving without pay after the heroine's fall, Amy offers to prostitute herself for her mistress, spies and panders for her, and finally disposes of the daughter who threatens her long-sought security. This last is a self-immolating act, for while Roxana cannot afford her daughter's existence, neither can she countenance her murder. Amy's crime is merely the climax of a career of amorally selfless devotion to her mistress, and it reminds us that her function all along has been to act out the basest impulses belonging to Roxana's situation, to absorb just enough of the guilt attendant upon social rise so that the heroine (and the reader) is free to enjoy some of the exaltation of the romance. Like Mary Manley's countess, Amy is the heroine's worldly advisor in matters of love, but she is also her servant, and never acts in her own behalf. This gives her the status of a "shadow" character. Mistress and maid embody two sides of a single personality. Taken together they correspond to the wicked-queen archetype represented in Scudéry's *Ibrahim,* the one inheriting Roxelana's beauty and address, the other her ruthlessness.

The dual nature of Scudéry's heroine is symbolized by her parentage, which can be said to have provided her with both the energy and means for self-aggrandizement. Only with a slave can the sultan fornicate without sin, but he can marry only a free woman. When slavery, therefore, has served Roxelana's purpose, her nobility asserts itself and enables her at last to achieve total dominion. In *Roxana*, the functions of slave and gentlewoman are divided between the two major characters, but the symbolic identity between these characters is carefully established. When Amy begins urging the liaison between Roxana and her gentleman, she becomes, like that inner compulsion which leads Moll Flanders to crime, a type of Satan, or "one of his Privy-Counsellors" (37). ". . . had I consulted Conscience and Virtue," says Roxana, "I shou'd have repell'd this *Amy*, however faithful and honest to me in other things, as a Viper, and Engine of the Devil" (38). The strange partnership is carried further when Amy, fearing that Roxana's sexual scruples will prevail, offers herself as a surrogate, citing the slave who bore Rachel's children. The mistress rejects the offer, but makes a more subtle use of her double. In a darkly playful mood after yielding to the gentleman, she assumes the role of maid and puts Amy to bed with her master. The servant proves after all more particular about her own innocence than about Roxana's. She is overcome with remorse which her mistress cannot feel, having been hardened by the recent barter of her virtue. When Roxana tries to console the girl with the Rachel story, the reversal of roles is complete, and Roxana understands why she needed it:

> Had I look'd upon myself as a Wife, you cannot suppose I would have been willing to have let my Husband lye with my maid, much less, before my Face, for I stood-by all the while; but as I thought myself a Whore, I cannot say but that it was something design'd in my Thoughts, that my Maid should be a Whore too, and should not reproach me with it. (47)

The character who instigated her corruption must now experience her loss of innocence.

Roxana's first lover becomes her means of returning to France—not merely to recover but to surpass the genteel prospects with which she was born. When her pretended husband, a jeweler, is murdered while carrying samples to a foreign prince at Versailles, Roxana is left with his estate, much of the supposedly stolen jewelry, and an introduction to the prince, who falls in love with her. She easily sheds her English identity, pretending to be a French Catholic from the province in which she was in fact born. (Amy, of course, cannot pass for French and remains the heroine's necessary link with a squalid past.) Roxana's beauty and provincial origin make her the fair unknown at the French court, the "*Belle veuve de Poictu*":

> the Prince profess'd, I was the most beautiful Creature on Earth; *and where have I liv'd?* says he; *and how ill have I been serv'd, that I should never, till now, be shew'd the finest* Woman *in* France? (61–62)

A look in the mirror shows the superficial completeness of her transformation from abandoned *bourgeoise* to *belle inconnue*: "Look there, Madam, *said he*; Is it fit that Face, pointing to my Figure in the Glass, should go back to *Poictou*?" (60) She enjoys a Roxelana-like rise among the prince's mistresses, and he urges that they enjoy together the "Freedom of Equals" ("your Beauty exalts you to more than an Equality" [62–63]).

But Roxana's aim is not power. At the height of her affair with the prince her affinities are with the victimized Charlot, who "possessed all she could desire" in the company of her lover, rather than with the ambitious slave of *Ibrahim.* The conquest of the prince is a private one, achieved at the cost of her public identity. When the affair is over, she recognizes it as a self-indulgent fantasy comparable to madness. As she trifles with a rich and devoted merchant, the prince, she tells us, "*or the Spirit of him,* had . . . Possession of me" (234):

> I think verily, this rude Treatment of [the merchant], was for some time, the Effect of a violent Fermentation in my Blood; for the very Motion which the steddy Contemplation of my fancy'd Greatness had put my Spirits into, had thrown me into a kind of Fever, and I scarce knew what I did.
>
> I have wonder'd since, that it did not make me Mad; nor do I now think it strange, to hear of those, who had been quite *Lunatick* with their Pride; that fancy'd themselves Queens, and Empresses, and have made their Attendants serve them upon the Knee; given Visitors their Hand to kiss, *and the like;* for certainly, if Pride will not turn the Brain, nothing can. (235)

The prince makes his profit of this delusion. "Now you shall be a Princess" (64), he tells her, but only as a prologue to sexual relations. Her only domain will be that erotic "no place" which Steven Marcus has called "pornotopia."[29] The prince's need for secrecy requires that Roxana be confined to her house (which he enters through a back alley), that the number of her servants be limited, that she discontinue the use of her equipage. When he offers her the greater mobility of a country house, she responds with the faceless subservience of a pornographic female: "[I] told his *Highness,* no Place could be a Confinement where I had such a Visiter" (67):

> Never Woman, in such a Station, liv'd a Fortnight in so compleat a fullness of Humane Delight; for to have the entire Possession of one of the most accomplish'd Princes in the World, and of the politest, best bred Man; to converse with him all Day, and, *as he profess'd,* charm him all Night; What could be more inexpressibly pleasing, and especially, to a Woman of a vast deal of Pride, as I was? (68)

"Pride," paradoxically, is the trait which defines Roxana's role in an episode that reads like a male fantasy of female compliance. This typifies Defoe's method of sustaining at once a romantic (Roxana the heroine's) and an antiromantic (Roxana the narrator's) perspective on the affairs of the principal character. The love between prince and "princess" is a kind of mutual idolatry (which in Defoe's fiction commonly means narcissism): "the Prince was the only Deity I worshipp'd, so I was really his Idol" (70). While the young heroine sees her destiny taking an appropriately romantic shape, the hardened narrator repeatedly intrudes with moral ridicule: "I think I may say now, that I liv'd indeed like a Queen; or if you will have me confess, that my Condition had still the Reproach of *a Whore*, I may say, I was sure, the Queen of Whores" (82). A parody of the high and low love relationships of romance occurs when Amy takes up with the prince's valet: ". . . as they had many leisure Hours together below . . . when his Lord and I were together above; . . . they could hardly avoid the usual Question to one another, namely, Why might not they do the same thing below, that we did above?" (83). Along with the metaphor of altitude, the romantic distinction between styles of love collapses here under the pressure of Defoe's literalism. Amy's function is to reveal the identity between high and low, the essential depravity concealed by the accident of style. To the narrator, the whole affair "amounted to no more than this . . . *like* Mistress, *like* Maid" (83).

This persistent deflation of the romantic possibilities in Roxana's early experience tends to give events themselves the character of illusions and to reserve for moral reflection alone the character of reality. Roxana occasionally doubts her ability to convey plausibly the facts of her life: "It wou'd look a little too much like a Romance here, to repeat all the kind things he said to me, on that Occasion" (72). Since facts must be disarmed of their romantic potential in the interest of moral truth, Roxana ironically refers to her wholly mercenary love parlays as "Platonicks" (232) and to the attentions of her Dutch merchant as "Knight Errantry" (218, 226).

The deceitfulness of actuality gets more objective treatment in the scenes of Roxana's greatest social triumph—the masked balls at which she receives the members of the court of Charles II. Roxana has passed at court for "the Widow of a Person of Quality in France," and is harassed by other impostors, "*Fortune-Hunters* and Bites . . . , *Beaus,* and *Fops* of Quality" (171). But, she declares, "nothing less than the KING himself was in my Eye" (172). Her eye, of course, fails her at the ball. A hint that the King is present among the masks (even the reader is not yet disabused), causes Roxana to feel a real and strong emotion over an illusory object: "I colour'd, as red as Blood itself cou'd make a Face look . . . ; however there was no going back" (173). She chooses instead to enter this world of illusion more fully, to dominate it:

> A-while after, the Masks came in, and began with a Dance *a la Comique,* performing wonderfully indeed; while they were dancing, I withdrew . . . ; in less than Half an Hour I return'd, dress'd in the Habit of a *Turkish Princess.* (173)

> my Lord ——— , who happen'd to be in the Room, slipp'd out at another Door, and brought back with him one of the Masks, a tall well-shap'd Person, but who had no Name, *being all Mask'd,* nor would it have been allow'd to ask any Person's Name on such an Occasion; the Person spoke in *French* . . . and ask'd me, if he should have the Honour to dance with me? (174)[30]

Their dance is followed by the solo which earns her the name Roxana. Later the name, the dance, and the costume will be facts of her past which she must suppress. At present, in the atmosphere of exoticism and imposture which she calls her "Element," they belong to the order of fantasy: "I hardly knew where I was; but especially, that Notion of the KING being the Person that danc'd with me, puff'd me up to that Degree that I not only did not know any-body else, but indeed, was very far from knowing myself" (177).

Such reflections as this remind us of the narrator's function in *Roxana*: to discover the moral truth behind the mere phenomena of the heroine's experience. This responsibility is happily diminished in the masked ball episodes, where the theme of illusion is dramatized. Another objective means of undermining the romance is to put the heroine in constant—and not always rational—fear of exposure, to make her sensitive to the deep-hidden facts of her past and her motives which always threaten to emerge and shatter the glittering surface of her life. These intimations of disaster are presented with the egocentric vividness of the early rather than the moralistic wryness of the late Roxana.

One form which Nemesis might take is the reappearance of her husband: "this *Nothing-doing Wretch* . . . , the only thing that was capable of doing me Hurt in the World, I was to shun . . . , as we wou'd shun a Spectre, or even the Devil" (95). Another is the Jew to whom she tries to sell her late benefactor's treasures:

> As soon as the *Jew* saw the Jewels, I saw my Folly; and it was ten Thousand to one but I had been ruin'd, and perhaps, put to Death in as cruel a Manner as possible. . . .
>
> . . . [He] held up his Hands, look'd at me with some Horrour, then talk'd *Dutch* again, and put himself into a thousand Shapes, twisting his Body, and wringing up his Face . . . as if he was not in a Rage only, but in a meer Fury; then he wou'd turn, and give a look at me, like the Devil; I thought I never saw any thing so frightful in my Life. (112–113)

The Jew's power over Roxana is the result not only of knowledge but of his immunity to those charms which have made the world support her egoism. He fits a Jewish stereotype from Shylock to Fagin: antic, sinister, obsessed, knowing, asexual, and consequently free of those susceptibilities which make the Dutch merchant, at this point, sacrifice in order to protect the heroine and make Amy abase herself throughout in order to serve her. The penalty for such freedom is mutilation:

> the Prince's Gentleman . . . Can'd him very severely . . . ; and that not . . . curing his Insolence, he was met one Night late, upon the *Pont Neuf* in *Paris,* by two Men, who muffling him up in a great Cloak, carried him to a more private Place, and cut off both his Ears, telling him, It was for talking impudently of his Superiours; adding that he should take Care to govern his Tongue better, and behave with more Manners, or the next time they would cut his Tongue out of his Head. (133–134)

Roxana has rational cause to fear the Jew, but not so the series of "hags" who serve as companions of her social rise. Like Colonel Jack's marital suspicions, Roxana's dread of these female attendants illustrates Defoe's instinct for separating recurrent feelings from their rational causes in order to demonstrate their independent character. While Jack's emotional excesses are an index to his unconscious motives, Roxana's serve as a providential warning or a guilty intimation of approaching Nemesis. When the prince sends the heroine into rural seclusion for her lying-in, he provides her with the first of these "Witches," and she perceives for the first time the sordid and dangerous aspect of her liaison with royalty: "I did not like this Old Woman at all; she look'd so like a Spy upon me, or, (as sometimes I was frighted to imagine) like one set privately to dispatch me out of the World" (77). By appealing to that fear of exposure which has determined the prince's whole conduct of the affair, Roxana persuades him to replace the stranger with Amy.

But this does not free her from the rule of anonymity or the company of old women. On an incognito journey to the Mediterranean, the prince assigns to Roxana an "old Witch" who instructs her in the secrets of Italian society, and who had in Naples "liv'd but a loose Life, as indeed, the Women of *Naples* generally do; and . . . I found she was fully acquainted with all the intrieguing Arts of that Part of the World" (102). Since Italy is getting familiar treatment here as the seat of those amoral energies which underlie civilized life, it follows that the "strange old Creature" should go on to acquaint Roxana with "that Part" of the prince's life and with the heroine's own place in it: "[She] told me a Thousand Stories of his Gallantry, as she call'd it, and how, as he had no less than three Mistresses at one time, and, as I found, all of her procuring, he had of a sudden, dropt them all, and that he was entirely lost to both her and them" (107). This is intended as a tribute to Roxana's power over the prince, but it merely shows her the spuriousness of that royal status which he has proffered so cheaply, and it makes her think, by contrast, of the true princess, "the most valuable of her Sex; of Birth equal to him, if not superiour, and of Fortune proportionable; but in Beauty, Wit, and a thousand good Qualities superiour not to most . . . but even to all her Sex; and . . . her Virtue . . . was that of, not only the best of Princesses, but even the best of Women" (107).

The two crones who attend her and the Jew informer who threatens to destroy her are all intruders into Roxana's fantasy. They represent, in her "dream world of romance," as Northrop Frye has said in a different connection, "the shrunken and wizened shape of practical waking reality."[31] They embody those ineluctable facts of life, physical decay and corruptive experience, which have not figured in Roxana's romantic calculus. They have forced her to recognize the disparity between her true nature and the one which she has imagined for herself. Roxana in Italy, like Moll at Bath, becomes the victim of her lover's repentance but achieves a somewhat firmer grasp of her real designs on the world. She has been initiated into the sisterhood to which she properly belongs, and in compensation for her lack of a regal character, she has obtained the princess-costume in which she will achieve counterfeit distinction at the English court.

Roxana's introduction to "Persons of very great Figure" in the court is accomplished with the help of "an old Lady or two," "Female hangers-on," who "play'd high, . . . stay'd late, [and] only ask'd leave to make an Appointment for the next Night" (172). She is disturbed by the assistance of these old women, because she sees in their grotesque vivacity not only the wages of social ambition but the impulses, epicene and aggressive, behind such ambition. Roxana's royal costume merely keeps these impulses before us in their enhanced form. Suggestively alien, heavily armored with gems, the disguise liberates within the heroine an overt and powerful eroticism which expresses the animus as well as the brilliance of her personality. In terms of that romantic paradigm which governs her illusions, Roxana inescapably combines the qualities of ruthless queen and *belle inconnue.*

At the climax of the novel the sensibility and the ruthlessness of her own early career will confront her in the menacing shape of her daughter. By this time, that symbol of her past will be the only threat to the rational order of Roxana's life, for she will have managed in a way characteristic of Defoe's heroes to resolve the conflict between dream and morality. Even before her performance at court, this reconciliation is prefigured in a conversation with her financial advisor, Sir Robert Clayton, in which she is able to acknowledge her epicene traits as the result of the social disabilities of women instead of concealing them from herself as dark and personal compulsions. She explains the "Amazonian" language of her "Platonick" repartee as follows: "[Though] it was my Misfortune to be a Woman, . . . I was resolv'd it should not be made worse by [men]; and seeing Liberty seem'd to be the Men's Property, I wou'd be a *Man-Woman*" (171).

Clayton, who combines in his own person aristocratic elegance and practical wisdom, is the spokesman for Defoe in these scenes. His speeches condition the reader to accept marriage with a merchant as a satisfactory denouement to Roxana's story:

> Sir *Robert* said . . . that a true-bred Merchant is the best Gentleman in the Nation; that in Knowledge, in Manners, in Judgment of things, the Merchant out-did many of the Nobility. . . .
>
> That an Estate is a Pond; but that a Trade was a Spring; . . . and upon this, he nam'd me Merchants who liv'd in more real Splendor, and spent more Money than most of the Noblemen in *England* cou'd singly expend, and that they still grew immensely rich. (170)

The baronet's tribute to the sagacity of merchants is later balanced by the merchant's comment on the moral efficacy of titles:

> He told me, that Money purchas'd Titles of Honour in almost all Parts of the World; tho' Money cou'd not give Principles of Honour, they must come by Birth and Blood; that however, Titles sometimes assist to elevate the Soul, and to infuse generous Principles into the Mind. (240)

Marriage to the merchant (who obtains two titles for her) becomes Roxana's means of placing social prudence at the service of her quixotism, of realizing her romantic dream in a manner subject to the limits of "practical waking reality." Her conversion to reality, like Bob Singleton's, is effected by a Quaker, who at this point conspicuously supersedes Amy as the heroine's confidante. Like William Walters, Roxana's Quakeress illustrates the efficacy of an austere life style, arranges an advantageous match for the heroine, enables her to make—at small sacrifice—retributive use of her ill-gotten wealth, and relieves her, through a rare blend of innocence and casuistry, of much of the self-disgust which accompanies repentance. It would seem that Roxana is symbolically freed from her past when, perceiving the nobility of her friend's bearing ("sufficient to her, if she had been a Dutchess" [211]), she resolves to assume a Quaker disguise, the moral antithesis of the Turkish costume and the denial of her old identity.

Such is the predictable resolution of one of Defoe's paradoxical bourgeois romances: the hero, through a series of impersonations, comes to realize the truth of his ideal nature; having discovered the illusoriness of his former goals, he takes possession of them. But Defoe was plainly unwilling to settle for so facile a conclusion to his most scandalous narrative. He destroyed the unity of his bourgeois romance by adding at the end a sternly moralized intrigue.

The concluding fable of retribution is notoriously unfinished and yet regarded as potentially Defoe's greatest achievement in plotting. Its fusion of suspense and didacticism anticipates *Caleb Williams*. But it ends with an abrupt assertion of poetic justice:

after some few Years of flourishing, and outwardly happy Circumstances, I fell into a dreadful Course of Calamities, and *Amy* also; the very Reverse of our former good Days; the Blast of Heaven seem'd to follow the Injury done the poor Girl, by us both; and I was brought so low again, that my Repentance seem'd to be only the Consequence of my Misery, as my Misery was of my Crime. (329–330)

However attenuated, the moral thriller can be seen as Defoe's most painstaking effort to counteract the amoral yearnings implicit in the romantic design of his fictions—the yearning for sexual freedom, for the ego's dominion over life. And its failure cannot be attributed to a lack of preparation. It begins early enough to be considered part of Defoe's scheme for the last third of the novel. During this concluding third, therefore, romance and fable dramatize (without reconciling) alternative fates for the heroine. In both, a "helper" character is used as *ficelle*: the Quakeress reunites the lovers and secures Roxana's future; Amy reunites child and parent and confirms her subjection to the past.

The daughter is introduced, after Roxana has achieved independence, as an object of her reparative charity. She offers no explicit threat at first, but Defoe's method of defining her character and circumstances establishes her at once as the most formidable challenger to the heroine's position in the novel. The daughter has been visited, in effect, by a fairy godmother, and has adjusted quickly to the drastic change in her fortunes. She is in more than one way a creature made in Roxana's image. Amy directs her

to put herself into a good Garb, take Lodgings, and entertain a Maid to wait upon her, and to give herself some Breeding, that is to say, to learn to Dance, and fit herself to appear as a Gentlewoman; being made to hope, that she shou'd, sometime or other, find that she shou'd be put into a Condition to support her Character, and to make herself amends for all her former Troubles. . . .

The Girl was too sensible of her Circumstances, not to give all possible Satisfaction of that Kind, and indeed, she was Mistress of too much Understanding, not to see how much she shou'd be oblig'd to that Part, for her own Interest. (204–205)

She has not only the same given name as her mother, but the same practical intelligence and passionate egoism. It therefore seems natural at this point that she should not risk her present bounty by pressing for more knowledge and inevitable that later she should demand to know who she is and attempt to control her own destiny.

Each scene in which she lays ardent, tearful, cunning siege to her mother's feelings reveals desperate ambition supported by filial sentiment and by a desire for the truth. This richness of dramatized motive enables us to see the daughter at once as a monster of Roxana's creation and as the heroine of her own romance.

Because the daughter is characterized externally, it is left to the reader to infer the nature of her egoism from his knowledge of Roxana's. With the latter he has been sympathetic, for to be a protagonist, as W. J. Harvey has said, is to "incarnate the moral vision of the world inherent in the total novel."[32] It can be said that the protagonist is in a large measure the creator of the fictional world which he inhabits, since order and value in that world are defined in relation to his history and motives. The world which Roxana has created, out of highly refractory materials, is a romantic one subject to certain middle-class modifications. Her romance ends with marriage to a merchant and the acquisition of titles. At this point, the reader's sympathy with the character forces him to recoil from her "vision" as it is now taken up by her antagonist. All that is squalid, ruthless, and primitive about this egocentric view of life can be forcefully dramatized when it is presented, from without, as a threat to the heroine's security. Such egoism as Roxana's, projected upon an antagonistic "flat" character, turns the romance into a melodrama, a tale of flight and pursuit which has its place in the novel as the culmination of the antiromantic theme which the narrator has been obtruding all along.

The "moral" of this antiromantic fable concerns the ultimate self-destructiveness of selfish pursuits. Its dramatization requires tight control of the symbolic identification among characters. Our horror at the murder of Roxana's daughter depends in part on our sympathy with Roxana's own youthful, lonely aspirations. The fable's attack is against such aspirations, but Roxana's is against a person who has them—figuratively against her own early self. The crime, of course, is committed on her behalf by the character who has consistently been the agent of her own lawless propensities. The banishment of Amy indicates a denial by the heroine of complicity in her daughter's death. The hasty final paragraph corrects this failure of conscience by showing mistress and maid reunited and suffering together. There is no mention of the lover who represents the happy ending of Roxana's romance of gentility.

The faulty ending of *Roxana* can be taken as Defoe's most strenous effort to deal as artist with the conflicting demands of his imagination. Both demands are for a kind of freedom: the kind which enables the love of one's ideal self to triumph over practical circumstance and the kind which makes moral judgment possible and vindicates common morality. What helps to make Defoe so important in the history of the English novel is that this conflict subsequently proves to be intrinsic to the genre. Formal analysis of Defoe's novels persistently confronts us with specific moral concerns and techniques for dealing with them which are only refined and amplified, not added, by the later novel. Romance, as appropriated to the novelist's use, is always tacitly redefined as that myth of personal preeminence which the ego projects upon the outside world. As such, romance becomes the novel's principal "criticism of life" and principal source of moral conflict.

The present analysis has concluded with an episode whose form and meaning anticipate, however embryonically, the most illuminating kind of moral encounter in modern fiction. It is elementary to the novel that a protagonist should exist on a different level of reality from the other characters in his world, that he should "create" that world, making everything else exist in relation to him. The novel, says Harvey, "exists to reveal" him.[33] But in order to do justice to the intricacy of moral relations, the context that reveals the protagonist must be able to accommodate another kind of "hero," a character with independent claims to preeminence which seem to issue from a differently imagined world. It is as if he were the hero of a different novel, come to reveal the limitations of the context which defines, say, Emma Woodhouse or Gwendolen Harleth, Isabel Archer or Stephen Dedalus. The history of Jane Fairfax suggests social frustration, of Daniel Deronda spiritual commitment, of Madame Merle tragic passion, of Leopold Bloom mundane affection, which are just outside the protagonist's imaginative range. They challenge the hero's conception of himself, or the novel's conception of the hero. There is no need to dramatize extensively the inner life of such a character. This approach, indeed, might endanger the novel's coherence. The paradigms for such self-consciousness as theirs all exist in the higher mimetic forms—in romance, epic, and myth—and the novelist's instinct for formal economy will lead him to identify that character's line of descent from the ideal order of fictions and, in the interest of realism, to "*dream the myth onwards* and give it a modern dress."[34]

JOYCE'S WASTE LAND
AND ELIOT'S UNKNOWN GOD

Robert Adams Day

When T. S. Eliot, in his celebrated appreciation of Joyce's *Ulysses,* wrote the rather startling words, "I hold this book to be the most important expression which the present age has found . . . a book to which we are all indebted, and from which none of us can escape," he may have felt that he was indulging in a hyperbole justified by genuine enthusiasm and by a desire to do everything possible to further the book's fortunes; or he may have been thinking only of *Ulysses'* impact on the history of poetic expression, its use of the "mythical method," which he felt had "the importance of a scientific discovery." On the other hand he may have been expressing, in the faintly paranoid tones of the phrase "from which none of us can escape," some of the feelings he had revealed in a letter to Joyce two years before, just prior to the composition of *The Waste Land* and just after reading the manuscript of the Circe episode: "I have nothing but admiration, in fact, I wish for my own sake that I had not read it." Are "indebted" and "escape" to be taken seriously in Eliot's case? It is hard not to see in these statements an element of irritation and dismay, of being overwhelmed and perhaps forestalled by the triumphant virtuosity of a work which was accomplishing precisely what Eliot himself was trying to formulate at the time—an appalling vision of the spiritual desolation of the modern world, presented with techniques drawn from associative psychology and literary allusion, firmly grounded on a foundation of mythological correspondences, showing forth simultaneously "the boredom, the horror, and the glory" of life in the twentieth-century metropolis.

To the best of our present knowledge, Eliot never stated that *The Waste Land* was indebted to *Ulysses*. Yet critics have persisted in suggesting, if not indebtedness, at the very least a remarkable affinity between the two works. As early as 1935, F. O. Matthiessen remarked in *The Achievement of T. S. Eliot*: "If the natural demands of their mediums took Joyce and Eliot to the opposite poles of expansion and compression, the qualities of experience they were endeavouring to present were enough alike to lead to marked parallels in certain of their qualities of expression." And he immediately and suggestively followed this cautious observation with a quotation from an unpublished lecture by Eliot on the method of *Ulysses*: "In some minds certain memories, both from reading and life, become charged with emotional significance. All these are used, so that intensity is gained at the expense of clarity."[1]

Many others have remarked upon the more obvious similarities of *Ulysses* and *The Waste Land* in structure and themes, as panoramas of modern life; some have pointed out in passing scattered verbal echoes, but most have avoided the question of indebtedness. The most recent of the very few detailed explorations of this matter, however, reaches the following conclusion:

> . . . the parallels between the two works are too extensive to be explained as purely independent developments. Although it appears that *Ulysses* did not explicitly or consciously enter into the composition of *The Waste Land,* it seems probable that Joyce's great work exercised a powerful influence on the unconscious level. Eliot's mind was singularly retentive, and much of his reading gestated below the conscious level, later to appear in his writings assimilated and transformed to Eliot's own purposes. . . . Very likely unbeknownst to Eliot, *Ulysses* seems to have helped to crystallize his thinking and to provide him with the framework, motifs, events, and symbols which emerged in *The Waste Land.* . . . The creative mind is a great mystery, and absolute certainty in these matters is impossible . . . . Nevertheless, the existence of significant parallels on so many levels indicates that the influence of *Ulysses* was very great, and it seems reasonable to call *Ulysses* the most powerful contemporary influence on *The Waste Land.*[2]

This conclusion, though provocative, is too hypothetical and hesitant to be very satisfying, and its author is commendably cautious. He comments that "in no case can the critic point to a specific passage in *Ulysses,* as he can in Marvell's "To His Coy Mistress" . . . and say that Eliot has lifted that passage and incorporated it into his work," and he regrets that evidence is lacking to demonstrate Eliot's knowledge before writing *The Waste Land* of "Circe" and "Oxen of the Sun," which he believes to contain the most striking extended parallels. Moreover, there is little consistency in the kinds of parallels he adduces, or closeness in their content: that Sweeney and Mrs. Porter and her daughter resemble Boylan, Molly, and Milly, or that Eliot's Thames and Joyce's Royal Canal contain garbage, for example, proves little.[3]

Are we then to conclude that there is no demonstrable indebtedness of *The Waste Land* to *Ulysses*, and that similarities between them are too vague to be significant or, if true verbal parallels, are merely the result of coincidence? It would be futile and foolish to contend that Eliot borrowed his "mythical method" from Joyce's book, or that he consciously lifted phrases and images from it for his poem as he did with Marvell. Both methods had been masterfully developed in his earlier poetry and needed no reinforcement. Yet a close study of the evidence for Eliot's transactions with *Ulysses* and with its author before he wrote *The Waste Land*, of Eliot's own discussions of the poetic process in operation, and of the two twentieth-century epics themselves leads to the conclusion that the matter of *Ulysses* did indeed penetrate *The Waste Land*, but in a much more complicated and significant manner than can be explained by such concepts as the borrowing of framework or the lifting of passages. The key to reconstructing this process is to be found in Eliot's "intensity . . . gained at the expense of clarity" and Matthiessen's "opposite poles of expansion and compression."

It will appear that an intense and enthusiastic reading of *Ulysses* bred at some level in Eliot's mind the perception of a particular "figure in the carpet," concealed in the maze, but of crucial importance to the total structure. The elements of this pattern provided him, in his own words, "a set of objects, a situation, a chain of events which [would] be the formula of [a] particular emotion" which he was struggling to give form in the embryonic poem. He dwelt with special intensity on certain brilliant nodes of this pattern that blended with or echoed images on which he himself had brooded almost obsessively. Some of these he dramatized into "scenes" of *The Waste Land* which parallel scenes in Joyce's novel; some he used repetitively, as Joyce had, for the musical structure of his work; some he powerfully condensed by combining their essentials into new, ambiguous figures with multiple significations. What Eliot took from *Ulysses* was not taken at random; paradoxically, it might have been so had he consciously "borrowed." No one should maintain that *The Waste Land* might not have come into being without the influence of *Ulysses*, but without *Ulysses* it could not have been what it was. But to demonstrate this requires a lengthy discussion, and (to paraphrase again from Eliot's essay on *Hamlet*) "we shall have to understand things which Eliot did not understand himself."

I

On the broadest level of technical and artistic similarity, it is clear that Eliot and Joyce solved in like manner, by literary or historical allusion and the manipulation of styles, the problem of creating an all-inclusive epos in a little space; both were preoccupied with the problem of transcending time in art. At the other extreme, "microscopically" examined, the two works show an abundance of readily discernible similarities in word, phrase, and motif. But general resemblances and verbal echoes do not carry us very far; both may be adventitious, and neither separately nor together do they prove a connection or establish its significance. What we need is an approach midway between these two extremes—one which could show connections important to the formulation of particulars in Eliot's ideas and technique, which could demonstrate that Eliot must have found in *Ulysses* materials that enriched his accumulating store of images—an approach mediating importantly between *The Waste Land* as it may have been first projected, or as it existed in early fragments,[4] and the poem as accomplished fact.

If *Ulysses* and *The Waste Land* are related significantly, each should illuminate the other. Not a mere resemblance, but a resemblance conveying *claritas* or *quidditas, integritas,* and *consonantia* should be demonstrable, so that a repeated phrase or figure of Joyce can be clarified in meaning by seeing it through *The Waste Land,* and so that the figure thus understood can be shown reducible to a concentrated form in Eliot's poem, while retaining its full implications to enlarge the significance of Eliot's allusive poetic distillation. Thus Prufrock's "I am not Prince Hamlet" can immediately be seen as a witty but perhaps rather flat allusion, while a back-and-forth examination of the dissimilarities between the two characters, exploring the whole conduct of Shakespeare's protagonist and drama, with excursions into the history of *Hamlet* criticism, will involve implications of great richness; yet at the end J. Alfred Prufrock has not ceased to be totally relevant in his inapplicability. If this method is valid, we can guess at what

Eliot meant in some of the more puzzling passages of *The Waste Land* by exposing him to Joyce; we may add dimensions to Joyce's meaning by reading him through the eyes of Eliot.

Eliot, like Joyce, was composing an epic in terms fit for his time, paradigmatic of man's situation in the modern world as he saw it. Both utilized such devices as musical-thematic rather than linear structure, a seeming hodgepodge of confused, disjunctive scenes and impressions, mythological framework, multiplex literary allusions, jarring alternations of the sublime and the ridiculous. But if we hope to demonstrate convincingly any complex and important connections between the minds and works of the two writers, it is best to begin with an intensive examination of more limited and manageable areas of their work. Such an area—basic to both yet remarkably similar—is comprised in the pattern of a quest and in a method of irony. The quest, structurally important enough in each case to amount to the "plot" of the work, is essentially religious, since its goal is redemption, life, and something to live by; yet both Eliot and Joyce were far too serious as artists to suppose that the answer could be readily and irrevocably found, or presented in simple and unambiguous terms. Hence Hieronimo's mad "play" in divers tongues and the open-ended *Ulysses*—both characterized in the 1920s as the work of madmen. Paradoxically, too, the seriousness of both men led them perpetually to present the most profound matters concealed in the most frivolous terms. For example, both use the calling of "Time" as a pub closes (at the end of "Oxen of the Sun" and of "A Game of Chess") in two senses: as the end of a scene of vulgar pleasure on the literal level, but in context and as a *poetic* statement to indicate, if the reader wishes, the calling of sinners to repentance. Continually, in both *Ulysses* and *The Waste Land*, the highest things may be found in the lowest.[5] But this philosophical or religious paradox leads to an interesting consequence in the world which each work creates—the characters or speakers perpetually take these things literally and hence go astray (perhaps the best-known example is the false card-reading of Madame Sosostris), leaving the reader the option of constructing the higher meaning from the author's imagery, context, and allusions.

It is within this ironic quest for redemption that *The Waste Land's* indebtedness to *Ulysses* can be chiefly and most clearly traced. The quest was central in what Eliot had been reading and in what he would write, but the essence of what is sought is atomized or dissipated in the fabric of *Ulysses* as it cannot be in *The Waste Land. Ulysses* is enormous in every sense; but Eliot, doing what he did in the final compass of 433 lines, worked by concentration and selection. If we examine all the parallels of *The Waste Land* with *Ulysses* which can reasonably be seen in motifs, situations, figures, and images, we shall discover that they are concentrated in a few parts of the poem; that they occur many times in *Ulysses,* but most notably in certain episodes which Eliot can be shown to have read with particular concentration; and that they are chiefly ironic reductions of traditional religious figures. It appears that Eliot's borrowings from *Ulysses* may have been unconscious but were not haphazard—that they were largely governed by his seizing upon certain disparate, repetitive images surrounding two of Joyce's figures and crystallizing them around two similar figures in his poem. These figures of Joyce are the dog, as he is manifested throughout the novel, and the mysterious man in the macintosh; in Eliot they become the puzzling "Dog . . . that's friend to men" and the never-identified person "Gliding wrapt in a brown mantle, hooded" of "What the Thunder Said." These dogs and unknown men may seem to have but the most superficial resemblances to one another; Eliot indicated sources for both figures in his notes, yet did not mention *Ulysses*; and the meaning of the dog and man to Joyce both in life and in his book have long engaged biographers and critics, who have evolved a variety of theories. Yet the evidence, as we shall see, points to the conclusion that Eliot perceived the existence in *Ulysses* of a chain or cluster of miscellaneous imagery which Joyce associated with rebirth or redemption, which constantly recurs, and which invariably marks the appearance of either or both of these figures—both made, by a typically outrageous and typically Joycean extended paronomasia, into manifestations of God, as the imagery comments upon them.

II

If we follow Macintosh and the dog through Joyce's poetic labyrinth, carefully noting the image clusters that surround them and the shapes they take in the minds of Stephen and Bloom (through whose eyes they are nearly always seen), we discover that they seem to be fibers of the same strand, complementary parts of a huge submerged metaphor. This trope, perhaps better characterized by Frank O'Connor's term "dissociated metaphor," since its basis—the statement of which it is an extension—is "never apparent and sometimes carefully disguised,"[6] hovers around the conception of death and rebirth as expressed by many religions in symbol, but most importantly in Christian terms centering about the death and resurrection of Christ. Many of its elements, moreover, singly or combined, are not found in *Ulysses* alone; their fundamental importance in Joyce's repertoire of poetic statement is attested by the fact that they occur in *A Portrait of the Artist as a Young Man* and are metamorphosed in *Finnegans Wake*. Further, if we examine the parts of this complex metaphor, overt and hidden, we discover that they constantly impinge upon the stated and implied metaphors of Eliot's *Waste Land*. It becomes difficult or impossible not to conclude that Joyce's matter of death and rebirth impressed itself on Eliot's gathering store of images—more significantly, that Eliot perceived it according to the mode of random accumulation and final fusion of images which he himself so often emphasized, and that he concentrated the most striking members of this vast submerged structure into his own enigmatic dog and hooded figure.

Ulysses, says a recent critic,

> Besides being an ingenious, intricate pattern . . . is a cataclysmic plunge into the black pit of the self, into the darkness of the inarticulate. Joyce . . . practiced assiduously . . . the pursuit of maddeningly subtle and elaborate association patterns. . . . He allowed the book to grow, in large part, by a process of accretion and cross-patching, which involved a huge ragbag of miscellaneous words and phrases. Some of these elements coagulated more or less spontaneously. . . . He thought of his book as a growth, a meadow of blooms, not a formal demonstration . . . what kind of plunge would it be which produced only a tidy package of allegorical messages? . . .[7]

This seemingly contradictory, though just, summation is a useful introduction to the dissociated metaphor which surrounds dog and Macintosh. Ragbag and intricate pattern are both evident in it; though if it were not tied together after the fashion of music by juxtaposition, repetition, and variation on themes, there would be little justification for seeing the pattern. The note sheets for *Ulysses,* however, which have been shown to be similar to the elaborate and seemingly miscellaneous strings of images which Joyce set down for *Exiles* in 1913, show that the ragbag-and-pattern method was an essential feature of Joyce's art from the crucial revision of *Portrait* onward.[8] Furthermore, there is evidence that at some points in *Ulysses* elements of this particular metaphor were added at late stages of composition, evidently to preserve the desired tonality of poetic statement enveloping these two enigmatic figures. We can, in short, deduce the existence of a pattern deliberately made from the recurrence of its elements in relevant situations. At the same time, we must avoid rushing to the conclusion that this metaphor is a key to the ultimate meaning of *Ulysses,* or that Joyce was working out a "tidy package of allegorical messages" with the precision (or the faith) of a Dante. The critic quoted above remarks, concerning the play on the words "God" and "dog" in particular:

> In this whole matter of dogs and their function in the novel, it seems best to assume that Joyce started with certain "given" properties of his story and actors, and worked them into the fiction wherever they seemed to fit on one level or another. He did not start with a categorical Dog-God relation or equation and deliberately exploit it by working gods and dogs into all the significant juxtapositions he could discover.[9]

This may be true; but if Joyce did not work dogs and gods into *all* significant juxtapositions, he worked them into a great many, enough to be strikingly noticeable on close reading; and in *Finnegans Wake* (188)* Shem is asked, "Do you hold yourself then for some god in the manger, Shehohem, that you will neither serve nor let serve, pray nor let pray?" echoing the repeated *non serviam* of Stephen Dedalus, the artist-Lucifer. Metaphorical statement is permitted to be somewhat shapeless, and to go underground for long periods.

The concrete terms—the string of images—in which Joyce's dissociated metaphor is expressed, and which are either presented directly or alluded to by figurative language, may seem at first to be completely heterogeneous; but they can be sorted into several categories, though most belong in more than one:

1. Biblical references, particularly to Moses in the bulrushes and to the burial and resurrection of Christ.
2. References to the reenactment of the Passion in the Mass, and to the Crucifixion with its implements—the nails.

* Page references to the texts of Joyce's novels, and page and volume references to his correspondence, will be given in parentheses in the text and will refer to the following editions: *A Portrait of the Artist as a Young Man,* ed. Chester G. Anderson and Richard Ellmann (New York: Compass Books, 1964); *Ulysses,* corrected Modern Library ed. (New York, 1961); *Finnegans Wake* (New York: Viking, 1947); *The Letters of James Joyce,* ed. Stuart Gilbert and Richard Ellmann, 3 vols. (New York, 1966).

3. Literary references, particularly to *Hamlet, The Tempest,* and *Lycidas.*

4. Animal figures (many of them digging in the earth)—cock, rat, ass, vulture, dog, fox, wolf, pard, pig (these usually associated with religious or rebirth imagery), worm, maggot, cockle or scallop, phoenix, barnacle goose (a sort of aquatic phoenix, according to legend).

5. Allusions to burial or drowning and to arising from the earth or the waters, centering around a dead-alive body ("changed" if drowned, a living corpse if buried).

6. Lastly, three images which seem to have been partly idiosyncratic with Joyce, but which pervaded his entire work from *A Portrait* to *Finnegans Wake,* and each of which he associated with the death-rebirth idea: the Viconian thunder as the voice of God heralding a new order, the number eleven, and a brown garment, which may be either a shroud or a religious habit, and which is often ragged.

We shall see these, few or many, continually recurring in connection with the dog figure and the man in the macintosh, and associated in every conceivable combination, either by juxtaposition or suggestive imagery; always or nearly always they are perceived and elaborated by Stephen or Bloom rather than being presented by the authorial voice.

As an example of how elaborately and pervasively Joyce wove the materials of his image cluster into the fabric of *Ulysses,* we may take a rather ordinary passage from the first pages of the Calypso episode, as Bloom on his first errand of the day eyes the maidservant in Dlugacz's butchershop (59). His fancy lights upon two details: her hands ("Chapped: washing soda") and her hips ("The way her crooked skirt swings at each whack"). Hands and skirt fuse with the image of a heifer, and as the girl leaves the shop Bloom thinks, "Sodachapped hands. Crusted toenails too. Brown scapulars in tatters, defending her both ways." He is evidently thinking that she might scratch an assailant with both hands and feet; but "brown," "scapulars," and "tatters" are new elements, "scapulars" introducing religious connotations. The brown fingernails and toenails might suggest by their shape, color, and size the kind of "scapular" worn by Catholics as an amulet and therefore a defense against evil, a small holy picture sewn to an oblong of cloth; Bloom thinks of a sailor in "Nausicaa," "Off he sails with a scapular or a medal on him for luck" (378). But a scapular is also a part of the *habit* of certain religious orders, a brown or black garment with front and back panels but no sides, defending its wearer "both ways" as the girl's swinging skirt does. Her skirt is no doubt tattered, and perhaps her fingernails are shredded. But this image also reaches forward to the dog on the beach in "Proteus," the burial of Paddy Dignam, Macintosh, Stephen's riddle of the fox burying his grandmother, and the Crucifixion. Paddy Dignam's shroud is a "brown habit" (98), and when he is metamorphosed into a dog in "Circe" he wears a "brown mortuary habit" (472). The man in the macintosh has a brown garment (254ff.), the dog on the beach is called "Tatters" (46), the man in the macintosh is "tattered and torn" (427), both fox and dog dig with their nails, and Bloom will emphasize the "nails" in his own crucifixion and Christ's in the next two episodes (81, 92). It is worth noting that "brown," "scapulars," and "tatters" are introduced together, that all constitute a "poetic" comment by Bloom's free association on what he actually sees, that "habit" is not mentioned, but merely suggested by "scapular," occurring only in later appearances of the cluster of images, and that "nails" are underplayed. All these facts suggest that Joyce is deliberately adding symbolic flavoring, even to a tiny scene of the utmost triviality, as a thematic anticipation of what will recur again and again.

The brown scapulars have relatively few links with other members of Joyce's strings of images, but such members as have both literary and religious associations are made to ramify much more widely, however trivial they may be in themselves. To give a single example—the cockle, or scallop,* is first encountered by Stephen in Mr. Deasy's study. It is juxtaposed (29) with "leopard shells"—a forecast both of the dog and of Bloom, who repeatedly become leopards—and with a shell "whorled like an emir's turban," which may prefigure Bloom as Haroun al-Raschid in Stephen's prophetic dream (47); it is "the scallop of Saint James"—the badge worn by pilgrims to the shrine of Santiago de Compostela, hence an emblem of Christian pilgrimage. Joyce has Stephen relate cockles to *Hamlet* by way of Ophelia's song about her true love's cockle hat and staff, and thereby also to the play's many references to death by water and to burial; later cockles are connected with Macintosh, with the number eleven, with the Crucifixion, with Moses in the bulrushes, and by Bloom with *Hamlet* and burial. With

* The word is cognate with the French *coquille,* which also means "scallop."

the aid of literary and standard religious references which the astute reader is likely to grasp at once and elaborate upon, Joyce is enabled to perform a second and more complicated kind of linkage within his metaphor. The symbol relates to a literary work or a body of tradition; this in turn is likely to contain or to be associated with yet another symbol in the cluster; this may relate to another part of the tradition, and so on—one is tempted to say ad infinitum.

Before tracing this huge submerged metaphor through the fabric of *Ulysses,* we need to discuss a third kind of linkage which Joyce used —the working out in concrete terms of "quotations" which are not quoted. This method appears in Joyce's use of *Hamlet,* a play whose relation to *Ulysses* is immensely complicated. A thorough investigation of the relationships, direct and by association or metaphor, between the two works would furnish subject matter for a book; but in connection with the cluster of images which we shall explore, a passage from Stephen's exposition of *Hamlet* and three passages from the play itself are crucial.[10]

Throughout *Ulysses* it appears that Stephen is doing more with *Hamlet* than we might at first suppose—it is obvious that he constantly seeks flattering parallels between the prince's plight and his own, but on a deeper level he conducts a continual meditation, both logical and alogical, on the text of the play in his efforts to work out a solution to the problems of life and art which face him. If the artist is like the God of Creation, as Stephen has indicated in *A Portrait,* may it not be that God after all will turn out to be like the artist?[11] Some such equation, at least, is suggested in Stephen's oracular utterances on Shakespeare and *Hamlet* in the library scene. Much of his discourse is fragmentary and broken by interjections from others, much of it is superior fooling; but just before Mulligan's entrance Stephen discourses at some length and with apparent seriousness (196–97). The passage plays ambiguously throughout upon a confusion between life and art, and upon the term "creator"—with God as Creator of the world, and Shakespeare as creator of a world of art. But it also makes use of important figures from the image cluster with which we are concerned. Stephen says:

> The soul has been before stricken mortally. . . . But those who are done to death in sleep cannot know the manner of their quell unless their Creator endow their souls with that knowledge in the life to come. The poisoning and the beast with two backs that urged it king Hamlet's ghost could not know of were he not endowed with knowledge by his creator.

> That is why the *speech* (his lean unlovely English) *is always turned elsewhere, backward.* . . . He goes back, weary of the creation he has piled up *to hide him from himself, an old dog licking* an old sore. But because loss is his gain, he passes on towards eternity in undiminished personality, untaught by the wisdom he has written or by the laws he has revealed. . . . He is a ghost . . . a voice heard only in the heart of him who is the substance of his shadow, *the son consubstantial with the father.* (Italics mine)

Mulligan enters, saying "Amen," and Stephen's thought greets him with "O mine enemy." (He has already thought of the dog on the beach [45] as "Dog of my enemy.") We may be in doubt as to whether Stephen's speech was about God, or Shakespeare, or both,[12] but Mulligan is not: "You were speaking of the gaseous vertebrate, if I mistake not?" Nor is Stephen, for his unspoken thoughts turn to pseudohistorical mockers of God, a burlesque Creed (which should not be dismissed as mere burlesque),[13] and a Gloria, with medieval musical notation.

The question of all the possible implications of this passage, its potentialities as a key to the whole of *Ulysses,* and what Stephen and Joyce truly mean cannot occupy us here; but as purely poetic statement it is of great importance. We find God, Shakespeare, the creator, the father consubstantial with the son (both in the human and divine senses), and the ghost of Hamlet's father metaphorically equated. We find a triple statement: divine or ontological (God), natural or human (Shakespeare), and literary or artistic (the character of the Ghost in the play) equated by means of ambiguous nouns ("creator"), pronouns ("he"), and figurative statements. All three speak in language that is "backward," each is "a dog," and for each the creation has been piled up to hide the creator from himself. The images of a dog (God, backwards), ghosts of the dead, especially of Hamlet's father, and a farrago of traditional Christian epithets or characteristics for the divine, usually parodied or distorted but attached to dog and *Hamlet* in every possible way, will occur throughout *Ulysses.* They will also surround Macintosh, a sort of ghost.[14]

Besides this set of images put into the mouth of Stephen, Joyce seems to have incorporated into his extended metaphorical equation three specific motifs or quotations from *Hamlet.* These are Ophelia's words "his cockle hat and staff" (IV.v.25), Hamlet's "If the sun breed maggots in a dead dog, being a god kissing carrion" (II.ii.181–182), and his meditation on how "a king may go a progress through the guts of a beggar" (IV.iii.33). Though only one is quoted directly, each pervades the fabric of the novel, constantly in association with dog and Macintosh, and each is linked to the idea of metamorphosis, rebirth, resurrection.

Ophelia's "cockle hat and staff" are assimilated by Stephen to himself at the end of "Proteus": "*Lucifer, dico, qui nescit occasum.* No. My cockle hat and staff and his my sandal shoon. Where? To evening lands" (50). Stephen negates his comparison of himself to rebellious Lucifer, and recreates himself as a Christian pilgrim with cockle hat, staff, and sandals. His pilgrimage, he correctly prophesies (pilgrimages are to seek God) will be to "evening lands," where he will find God and his true father. The "shoon," however, are annoyingly Mulligan's, and the hat and staff—the hat is "my Hamlet hat" (47) later to become "diaconal" (698)—are Stephen's identifying symbols, "familiars," throughout. But the line from *Hamlet* has in its context implications which Joyce will exploit further. Ophelia will die by water, but Laertes says that she will be a ministering angel, thus resurrected; later on in the song she will assert that her lover (in the song's words) or her father, is "dead and gone" and in the grave, words which Joyce will apply to dead Paddy Dignam (474), who speaks them from underground, like the Ghost. The cockles, taken from the water, and as Christian symbols, will frequently reappear.

The concept of metamorphosis is also provided by Hamlet when he says to the king regarding the worms that are eating the corpse of Polonius: "Your worm is your only emperor for diet. We fat all creatures else to fat us, and we fat ourselves for maggots. . . . A man may fish with the worm that hath eat of a king, and eat of the fish that hath fed of that worm . . . to show you how a king may go a progress through the guts of a beggar" (IV.iii.21–33), and when he says to Horatio: "Why may not imagination trace the noble dust of Alexander, till he find it stopping a bunghole?" (V.i.205–206). It may be that "'Twere to consider too curiously, to consider so," as Horatio observes, but Joyce makes Stephen echo these passages in "God becomes man becomes fish becomes barnacle goose becomes featherbed mountain. Dead breaths I living breathe, tread dead dust" (50).[15] The barnacle goose, which was believed to hatch from the shell of the wormlike barnacle, a phoenix of the sea, serves to blend the ideas that death by land and by water results in resurrection, that all things are in all things ("Dead breaths I living breathe"), and that the highest may be found in the lowest.

Lastly, the same idea is provided by Shakespeare, together with God and dog, in a speech of Hamlet's which, while it is not quoted, is exemplified with variations both in Stephen's fox riddle and his contemplation of the dead dog being "nosed over" by a live dog on the beach: "For if the sun breed maggots in a dead dog, being a god kissing carrion . . . haply your daughter may conceive."[16] It is worth noting that Bloom, at the same moment, is "considering so" on the other side of Dublin, and is making use of the same string of images; both implicitly and explicitly his thoughts are hovering about *Hamlet* and resurrection: "It's the blood sinking in the earth *gives new life*. . . . bones, flesh, *nails*. . . . But they must *breed* a devil of a lot of *maggots*. Wonder how [the caretaker] looks at life. Cracking his jokes too; warms the *cockles* of his heart. . . . Gravediggers in *Hamlet*" (109; italics mine). And on the same page we find "going to heaven," a joke about "eleven," and the first appearance of Macintosh.

Having enumerated the ingredients of Joyce's vast dissociated metaphor of death, resurrection, and redemption, and examined some of the ways in which he introduces and interweaves its parts, we are ready to trace its presence in *Ulysses*. But a cautionary point needs to be made before we do so: while it is a remarkably prominent metaphor, unparalleled in its richness of figurative statement and containing an abundance of traditional religious symbolism, it doubtless does not lead to a clear solution of Joyce's or Stephen's questionings concerning life and art; doubtless Joyce did not intend it to. Our concern is rather with the reiterated words and images of *Ulysses* as nurturing agents for the words and images of another modern epic whose "message," for that matter, has remained equally ambiguous. *Ulysses* has led one diligent reader to observe, for example: "Stephen Dedalus entertains a sacramental conception of the universe throughout the novel. He is on the point of stating and accepting his version of it, but does not quite recognize it, or is not quite ready to make the reorganization of his attitudes that it will require."[17] Another reader maintains on the other hand that

> Stephen is post-Christian, in that he finds new secular meanings to fill the husks of religious words he regards as dead. . . . In the Proteus episode Stephen argues in great and complex detail the relation of Christ to his mother's husband and to his true father, God. There is no reason to suppose that he believes in either manifestation of the godhead, but the imagery helps him to phrase his alienation from his own father, who is a mere Joseph, and his longing for kinship with some greater self.[18]

But in the same essay he remarks that the similarity of technique between *Ulysses* and *The Waste Land* "has made it difficult to read Joyce without reading into his books something of Eliot's scorn of the modern world and of the world in general. . . . The essence of Eliot's charge against the modern world is that it has no real faith, but to Joyce it has, if anything, too much."[19] What this particular image cluster ultimately means to Bloom and Stephen, or ultimately meant to Joyce, is difficult to say; its importance to our investigation is that it is *there,* and was there for Eliot to read.

III

We shall need to trace the quests of Stephen and Bloom at length and rather digressively before returning to Eliot, since Joyce enmeshes his two characters in a web of complicated symbols which fan out to some distance, like Stephen's equation in the *Portrait,* before coming together again and exhibiting their underlying relationships. As *Ulysses* progresses, Stephen is at first principally associated with the dog figure, Bloom with the man in the macintosh. When the climactic Circe episode approaches, all four draw together and meet. Symbols, images, and themes associated with Christ, God, burial, and resurrection sometimes run parallel to the two figures, sometimes blend, sometimes cross as if to indicate an interrelationship. For the purposes of clarity, however, let us first follow Bloom, then Stephen, in connection with the two figures and the usually conventional, though sometimes distorted or parodied, Christian symbols that surround them.

As Bloom pursues his roundabout course from his home by way of the bath to the funeral of Paddy Dignam, he encounters whispers of immortality, mocking reminders of the Passion. He wanders into Mass at All Hallows. "Crown of thorns and cross," he thinks. "*Corpus*. Body. Corpse. Good idea the Latin. Stupefies them first. . . . Rum idea: eating bits of a corpse" (80). The faithful, for Bloom, are partaking merely of something dead; the resurrection that gives meaning to the Host is absent from his thoughts, the communicants too are dead. He ignorantly wonders if the IHS (Jesus) on the priest's chasuble may be INRI, and concludes that the two monograms mean "I have sinned" or "I have suffered" and "Iron nails ran in" (81). The prayers in English after low mass he ironically characterizes as "Throw them the bone" (82). Bloom stands "unseeing" while two worshipers "dipped furtive hands in the low tide of holy water" (83); "This is my body," he says as he visualizes himself in the bath (86). Here for the first time (though far from the last) dog, corpse, nails, the Passion, the Eucharist, are confusingly combined and parodied in the mind of a secular "unseeing" man, with suggestions of religion in hiding ("furtive") and dearth of (holy) water, as in *The Waste Land.* Some elements of this combination are repeated in the carriage on the way to Glasnevin as Bloom, like Eliot's fisher by the dull canal, reflects on his father's death and as rain impends (89–90). The sight of dogs copulating may have resulted in Rudy's conception. Bloom thinks; by the waters (the Grand Canal) raindrops fall as he remembers his father's death (God's or Christ's, by Joycean consubstantiality and metempsychosis): "Dogs' home over there. . . . Be good to Athos [the elder Bloom's dog]. . . . Thy will be done." When Boylan passes, causing Bloom a spasm of pain, he thinks "The nails, yes. . . . My nails" (92) as his own "crucifixion" is heralded; here Boylan has been epiphanized to "the white disc" of a straw hat, suggesting the Host. At the Royal Canal (once more by the waters) nails in a coffin and a bleeding corpse, cast out of it, are again evoked, together with passage over water and "carrion dogs" (98–99). Here Bloom's thought transforms the corpse to Dignam's, clad in "a brown habit too large for him," our first full glimpse of the *brown* garment which will be the emblem of the man in the macintosh and of Eliot's hooded figure. On arrival at the cemetery "simnel" or Easter "Cakes for the dead" are "dogbiscuits," anticipating the later associations of dog and biscuits in the Cyclops and Circe episodes with the Host and the burial of Dignam (300–305; 473), but Bloom does not know who ate them.

As he did with the Mass, and as Eliot's speaker will do in the "Dog" passage, Bloom scoffs ignorantly at the Burial of the Dead. His strictly nonsacramental thought, however, is filled with secular love and sympathy. And as he turns to leave the cemetery, the thoughts that flit through his mind link him by way of images with Stephen's thoughts at the same moment on Sandymount strand (and with Eliot's Phlebas) —death by water, the fox or dog scraping up the earth, and the resurrection: "Pick the bones clean. . . . Or bury at sea. . . . Drowning they say is the pleasantest. . . . But being brought back to life no. . . . Poor Papa too. . . . And even scraping up the earth at night. . . . I will appear to you after death. . . . I do not like that other world. . . . Let them sleep in their maggoty beds" (114–115). Here Bloom perfectly sums up the attitudes of Eliot's Wastelanders on the painful subjects of raising the dead and of religion.[20]

These last reflections of Bloom may be influenced by the fact that the mysterious man in the macintosh has just made his first appearance and disappearance. This enigmatic figure appears twelve times, all told, in the pages of *Ulysses*. He is chiefly beheld, however, rather than merely mentioned or thought of, at Dignam's funeral and in Bella Cohen's brothel (there through the medium of hallucination), and he figures chiefly in conjunction with Bloom, not with Stephen. Many attempts have been made to identify him and to solve the persistent question, which continually plagues Bloom, of who he is. Three investigators have independently concluded that he is Mr. Duffy of the *Dubliners* story "A Painful Case,"[21] but even if we accept this identification on the literal level we may still ask whether the allegorical or anagogical levels are not also to be considered, why Joyce has set up such an elaborate puzzle, and why he harps until the end of "Ithaca" (the last section to be finished) on this "selfinvolved enigma" (729). It is worth mentioning also that for several years Joyce used to delight in teasing some American friends by asking them to guess the answer to this riddle; apparently they never solved it.[22] We must either dismiss Macintosh as another of Joyce's elaborate jokes on the reader or conclude that the answer to a puzzle on which he lavished so much ingenuity can be found and is worth finding. Since "mac" means "son (of)" in Gaelic, Macintosh may be in some sense a son. If we consider all the information that Joyce gives us about him, we may see him not only as *connected* with Christ, as has already been surmised,[23] but Christ himself, son of God, living proof of the possibility of raising the dead, who appeared and disappeared mysteriously after the resurrection but was usually not recognized on first encounter, and whose identity or very existence was questioned by those of little faith.[24]

Returning to Bloom meditating in Glasnevin Cemetery between eleven and noon, we see him glance up from the graveside. Macintosh first appears as from nowhere at Dignam's burial, precisely at the moment when the body is being lowered into the earth (109), and significantly on the *third* day after Dignam's death: "Monday he died. . . . Three days" (111). His entrance is not described; he is simply there. Three times, as in a ritual, Bloom demands to know who he is and says, ironically for us, that he would give *a trifle* to know (109) and that "Always someone turns up you never dreamt of." Macintosh is a "lankylooking galoot"—odd language for Bloom, but a perfect description of an emaciated Christ in the language of the American evangelist J. Alexander Dowie, a precursor who in "Oxen of the Sun" will apply similar epithets to his Saviour (427). The apparition turns Bloom's thoughts to loneliness, burial, and to Robinson Crusoe, a man alone—but as with Christ (Bloom distorts Defoe), "Friday buried him." Bloom then considers (110) that Macintosh is "thirteen. Death's number," but it is also the number of Christ and the twelve apostles; Bloom cannot tell, however, "where the deuce [devil, appropriate to the Harrowing of Hell] did he pop out of?" "Pop out of" gives the reader, on the other hand, more to work on. It clearly suggests a rising motion, sudden and violent, from an enclosed space, as Bloom later realizes in "Circe" when he sees Macintosh in hallucination (485) springing up through a trapdoor, suggesting in theatrical terms the nether regions. "He wasn't in the chapel"—the resurrected Christ appeared in a garden, on the shore, in private houses, and walking on the roads,[25] but nowhere else, certainly not in the Church in Ireland (for Joyce) nor in the "empty chapel" (for Eliot). Rain again impends, Bloom thinks, on hearing the braying of an ass—perhaps Balaam's, wiser than its master in the matter of detecting heavenly presences, for Bloom says, "No such ass."[26] (Joyce no less than Eliot seems to associate the coming of rain with both material and spiritual fertilization, a widespread tradition as old as the Eleusinian mysteries, in which the cry "Let there be rain, conceive!" signified the union of Heaven and Earth.[27]) Appropriately Bloom, like Stetson's interlocutor, is led to speculate on the possibility of life within the grave, but with the same result: "No, no; he is dead, of course. Of course he is dead. . . . Just as well to get shut of them as soon as you are sure there's no" (111). When Hynes the reporter approaches Bloom to ask who the mysterious man may be and to make the error of writing his name as M'Intosh, Bloom does not know who or where he is, but observes oddly that he has "become invisible," and punningly says, "Good Lord, what became of him?" (112). God works in mysterious ways, however; when Bloom asks himself at this point "Has anybody here seen?" he is referring to the popular Irish song "Has Anybody Here Seen Kelly?" but when he completes the fragment with "Kay ee double ell" he has unknowingly thrust a key into a complex of interlocked symbols which surround Macintosh and help to identify him.[28]

"Kay ee double ell" is clearly a reference to the Book of Kells, in which Joyce apparently saw an emblem of *Ulysses'* ornate intricacy, and thus seems to hint that something of central importance is concealed here. It is also a reference to Kino's eleven-shilling trousers, which will presently attract Bloom's attention on the Liffey bridge (153), and later play a decisive, if symbolic, role in the action of "Circe" (523ff.); most importantly it is a triple reference to the mysterious number eleven and to the name of God. So Bloom thinks, at least; "El" in Hebrew is God as the Lord, a circumlocution for the Ineffable Name, and Bloom has already associated "El" with God, the funeral, and the eleventh hour. "He crossed Townsend street, passed the frowning face of Bethel [an evangelical chapel]. El, yes: house of: Aleph, Beth. And past Nichols the undertaker's. At eleven it is" (71).

The meaning of the number eleven for Joyce in *Ulysses* is highly significant for our discussion—particularly because of its continual presence before Bloom and Stephen as they encounter the dog and the man in the macintosh—but somewhat hard to determine. According to Hanley's word list, the number occurs no less than fifty-eight times; more if we allow for the various ways in which it can be written or suggested. Eleven is the hour of Dignam's funeral and Stephen's meditation on the beach, as well as the hour when Macintosh, heralded by proclamations of the Second Coming and the Last Judgment in the language of the evangelist Dowie, appears to the drunken revelers staggering from Burke's pub as it closes (427). Little Rudy died at eleven days and would be eleven if he were alive; the cockle-picking midwives, or "maries" of the Crucifixion, carry in a midwife's bag eleven of these mollusks, surely a very light repast, and surely therefore symbolically intended (254); and eleven occurs in other important contexts. It is probable that Joyce intended the number to have a single, constant significance in *Ulysses*, but what was it? The answer would seem to lie in Joyce's extensive knowledge of Christian tradition and of occult lore.

The "eleventh hour" is a commonplace in Western thought for the penultimate moment when repentance or right action will avail; we lay paradoxical stress on the idea that God will attach no blame to us for delaying so long. The locus classicus for this tradition is Christ's parable of the laborers in the vineyard, in which "the last shall be first, and the first last; for many be called, but few chosen."[29] Here the eleventh hour is a time of repentance and spiritual rebirth, if we will but accept the grace offered. Both Joyce and Eliot take advantage of the fact that eleven is also the closing time of Irish and English pubs; a turning away from worldly pleasure is demanded ("HURRY UP PLEASE ITS TIME") by an unidentified voice in both "Oxen of the Sun" (427) and "A Game of Chess," but in each scene no response from the blind, or blind-drunk, worldlings is heard; the message is in vain, for it is perceived only on its literal level, even though Joyce reinforces it, as we shall see, with explicit references to its religious significance.

Two books of arcane lore, one of which Joyce owned, the other probably known to him since it was much in vogue in Dublin theosophical circles,[30] give eleven as a number associated with rebirth and arising from death or from the waters.[31] But it was the teachings of Madame Blavatsky that were most pervasive and powerfully influential among the Hermetists of the time. These in essence, apart from their Vedantic sources, were basically a variant and reworking of what is to be found in the Kabbalah;[32] and it is in the doctrines of the Kabbalah that the number is associated both with rebirth and with the letter K. One system by which the Kabbalah helps to interpret the Scriptures is to arrange the twenty-two letters of the Hebrew alphabet in two horizontal rows, with assigned numerical values. Since K (kaph) is the eleventh Hebrew letter, as it is in the Roman alphabet, it is on the left of the first row and thus has the value eleven. Anyone accustomed to reading from left to right and coming upon the rows, which frequently appear in works of Kabbalistic lore, is immediately confronted with "K 11," and perhaps nothing more esoteric than this accidental conjunction originally imprinted the combination in Joyce's mind.

Doctrines originating in the Kabbalah, however, as developed in the modern pseudoscience of numerology, interpret eleven as being the number of revelation and of martyrdom. Numerologists see it as representing God (one) added to the ten which represents the material world; thus it signifies revelation, the beginning of the spiritual knowledge of God, and martyrdom, entry into the higher life of heaven. Those whose "number" is eleven are prophets and teachers, bearing a supernatural message to the world.[33]

Whatever the source, the connection of eleven with rebirth and revelation is not idiosyncratic with *Ulysses*. In *Finnegans Wake* Joyce has fully developed and rearranged Kabbalistic doctrine for his own purposes. Here Ainsoph, represented by 1 (*En Soph*, God, also the male principle) unites with 0 (the female, "that noughty zeroine") and the resulting 10 produces eleven, or the new generation (261–262). Hence eleven represents renewal, revival, and thus rebirth or resurrection.[34] But the number had already acquired its symbolic significance for Joyce by the time he finished *A Portrait of the Artist as a Young Man*. In Chapter V, after his emblematic death and his rebirth as artist, Stephen, significantly crossing one of the bridges of the novel, has an encounter which Joyce makes curiously portentous:

the consumptive man with the doll's face and the brimless hat . . . tightly buttoned into his chocolate overcoat [an anticipation of the *brown* macintosh], and holding his furled umbrella a span or two before him like a diviningrod. It must be eleven, he [Stephen] thought. . . . The clock in the dairy told him that it was five minutes to five, but, as he turned away, he heard a clock somewhere near him, but unseen, beating eleven strokes in swift precision. . . . Eleven! . . . What day of the week was it? . . . Thursday. (177)[35]

(We may observe that *Ulysses* also takes place on Thursday, and that Stephen had an English class at ten, French at eleven; reborn, he will leave English-speaking Ireland for France.) If we consider that Joyce places Dignam's funeral and Macintosh's "popping out," plus a dead-yet-alive dog on the beach, at the eleventh hour, and that other symbolic manifestations, such as the appearance of the three-masted *Rosevean*[36] and the apotheosis of Little Rudy, are linked with it, we may justly conclude that eleven, with K or without it, signifies resurrection for Joyce; Bloom's "Kay ee double ell" is a "key of knowledge" that unwinds an important thematic arabesque in his verbal Book of Kells.[37]

This phrase is not the first appearance of the number in Ulysses. Besides Bloom's funeral–Beth El association already indicated, it has been connected by Stephen with burial and "going to heaven" in his riddle at Mr. Deasy's school (26); and Bloom's "joke for the dead" thematically heralds Macintosh's first appearance (109) with the same images that will announce him outside the pub twelve hours later: "Spurgeon went to heaven 4 A.M. this morning. 11 P.M. (closing time). Not arrived yet. Peter."

After his enigmatic first manifestation at Glasnevin, Macintosh next pops up in "The Wandering Rocks," a chapter of cross-purposes and ships that pass in the day: "a pedestrian in a brown macintosh, eating dry bread, passed swiftly and unscathed across the viceroy's path" (254), while a few lines later two women, the "two maries" of Stephen at Sandymount (45) appear, bearing symbols of Christian pilgrimage, birth, and water—"a [midwife's] bag in which eleven cockles rolled." (The women have appeared earlier in the chapter, placed next to Stephen and his set of rebirth symbols.) The risen Christ, on foot and alone, like Macintosh, no longer had anything to fear from the "viceroy," Pilate the procurator of Judea; and according to the accounts in two of the Gospels he ate bread among the humble people to whom he appeared.[38] "*Dry* bread" is also the Host; Macintosh is walking through the desert of sterile Dublin, and here only one of the two necessary elements of a complete priestly Eucharist is present.

Somewhat later, in "The Sirens," Macintosh is conjured up in Bloom's mind as the latter walks by his own "tumid river," along Ormond Quay (289–290). The idea that drumheads are made of asses' skins, and a glimpse of a passing whore, trigger fragments in his reverie that combine the cemetery scene, dead Rudy, a muffled brown male figure, and femininity: "Asses' skins. Welt them through life, then wallop after death. . . . Haw. . . . Waken the dead. . . . Dignam. Poor little *nominedomine*. . . . Muffled up. Wonder who was that chap at the grave in the brown mackin. . . . Heehaw. . . . What is she? . . . Stout lady does be with you in the brown costume." Given a change of poetic tone, from Bloom's voice to Tiresias', it is not frivolous to consider this passage with *The Waste Land*'s

> Gliding wrapt in a brown mantle, hooded
> I do not know whether a man or a woman
> — But who is that on the other side of you?
> (v, 363–365)*

Next, in one of the Rabelaisian catalogues of "Cyclops" we are told that "The man in the brown macintosh loves a lady who is dead" (333). Christ loves the Church, for she is his bride; but the Church, as we have already seen, is "dead" for Bloom and for Stephen and Joyce, though in different senses. In "Nausicaa" Macintosh appears in Bloom's mind on Sandymount strand as he meditates by the waters after Gerty MacDowell's departure (376). "Ask yourself who is he now. *The Mystery Man on the Beach*. . . . And that fellow today at the graveside in the brown macintosh. . . . Whistle brings rain they say. . . . Signs of rain it is. . . . And distant hills seem coming nigh." It was

* The text of *The Waste Land* used here is that found in T. S. Eliot, *Collected Poems: 1909–1935* (New York, 1936).

triply a "mystery man" who appeared on the beach in the Gospel of John, for at first "the disciples knew not that it was Jesus," the resurrection had occurred, and the miraculous draught of fishes signalized the stranger's identity.[39] We have already seen Macintosh associated with the coming of rain, but here the new image of distant hills combined with rain suggests the imagery of Eliot's lines which occur before and after the "hooded figure" passage (V, 330–49, 385–400).

The last manifestation of the mysterious figure before all the thematic threads are brought together in the "Circe" episode comes at the end of "Oxen of the Sun" through the voice of the 1904 John the Baptist, J. Alexander Dowie, proclaiming resurrection amid a chaos of slang, mostly American; the quest for Macintosh's identity is still on. This drunken medley has been compared to the confusion of tongues in *The Waste Land* (the builders of Babel were punished for presumption against God).[40] Yet here as in his previous appearances Macintosh is surrounded with distorted symbols and epithets appropriate to Christ's victory and triumph. The time is almost eleven: "Closingtime, gents" (427), as in *The Waste Land*'s second section and Bloom's joke for the dead (109); Macintosh is seen passing Burke's pub by the drunken revelers as they stagger out.[41] His apparition is preceded by a voice crying out in the confusion a perverse parody of the vernacular prayers after Low Mass prescribed by Leo XIII in 1884, earlier characterized by Bloom as "throw them the bone" (82). These are mingled here with sexual puns, and since it is the priest who recites these prayers, we may assume that the voice which speaks the fragments is that of Stephen, a spoiled priest. An extremely "low," or black mass, has been celebrated: "*Nos omnes biberimus viridum toxicum* [absinthe, drunk by all but Bloom, who drinks "Rome boose"] *diabolus capiat posteriora nostra*" (427). The "congregation" prepares to leave. "Gospeltrue. . . . O, lust, our refuge and our strength. . . . Through yerd [yard-rod-penis] our lord, Amen. . . . And snares of the poxfiend. . . . Kind Kristyann will yu help, yung man hoose frend tuk bungalo kee to find plais whear to lay crown off his hed 2 night. . . . Cot's plood. . . . Thrust syphilis down to hell and with him those other licensed spirits. Time. Who wander through the world. Health all." Here we have a suggestion that "the Son of Man hath no place to lay his head" (especially since the same passage in the Gospel tells us that even "foxes have holes," a conjunction that would have pleased Joyce),[42] for a kind Christian is appealed to and the head wears a "crown"; the Dutch or Scandinavian pronunciation of "God's blood" is a reminder both of Mass and Crucifixion. "Gospel-true" hints at the last Gospel, or termination of the Mass. The prayer itself is the source of Eliot's line "And after this our exile" in *Ash-Wednesday*; it is in part a supplication to the Virgin and to the archangel Michael.

> O God, our refuge and our strength, look down in mercy on Thy people who cry to thee . . . through the same Christ our Lord. Amen. Holy Michael, archangel, defend us in the day of battle; be our safeguard against the wickedness and snares of the devil. May God rebuke him, we humbly pray, and do thou, prince of the heavenly host, by the power of God thrust down to hell Satan and all wicked spirits, who wander through the world for the ruin of souls. Amen.[43]

Satan having been properly invoked, and aid besought against the dangers of liquor and sex, the congregation is dismissed, and Macintosh ironically comes into view. "Golly, whatten tunket's yon guy in the mackintosh?" ("Tunket" is in origin a nineteenth-century American euphemism for hell.) "Dusty Rhodes." (The comic turn-of-the-century hobo figure may also suggest the wanderer on the road to Emmaus.) "Peep at his wearables. By [God Al]mighty! What's he got? Jubilee mutton." (The Paschal Lamb.) "Bartle the Bread we calls him." (The Host, the "dry bread" of "The Wandering Rocks.") "Man all tattered and torn [the Crucifixion] that married a maiden all forlorn." (The Church, the "lady who is dead.") "Walking Macintosh of lonely canyon. . . . See him today at a runefal [funeral]? Time all. There's eleven of them." (Eleven strokes of the clock, but also eleven disciples.) It is indeed "time"—the eleventh hour—and Christ has come like a thief in the night as the bells of earth strike eleven. The passage rises to a crescendo of drunken confusion as the voices mingle, but among the broken phrases some are significant in our context: "even now that day is at hand when he shall come to judge the world by fire. . . . *Ut implerentur scripturae*. . . . Washed in the Blood of the Lamb. . . . You'll need to rise precious early, you sinner there, if you want to diddle the Almighty God" (428). Here Stephen and Bloom together are witnesses of the passing of the risen Christ, who has harrowed Hell, and hear voices proclaiming that he has come in judgment; but neither, though for different reasons, is in a condition to attend.

This passage contains an epithet for Macintosh which requires further discussion, since it shows so many complex relationships with the chain of images we have been pursuing and throws light on its origins in Joyce's structural elaboration of *Ulysses*. The "man all tattered and torn" of course comes from the familiar Mother Goose rhyme "The House That Jack Built," but this rhyme seems to have exercised a peculiar fascination for Joyce. Frank Budgen in 1918–19 saw Joyce collecting, among other things, "a parody on the House that Jack Built,"[44] and the rhyme in one version or another ramifies widely into the novel's thematic structure. It connects Christian and Jew, Stephen and Bloom, for its origin has been traced to a medieval Hebrew chant, first printed in a *haggadah* of 1590. This chant, now known as "A Kid, A Kid," is a similar accumulative rhyme, organized around kid, cat, dog, staff, fire, water, ox, butcher, Angel of Death, and is a traditional feature of the Passover Seder, familiar to all Jewish children. Bloom mentions it with his usual vagueness and distortions as being in "poor Papa's haggadah book" (122); the book itself appears in "Ithaca" (723). "The House That Jack Built" has been especially attractive to scholarly cranks; at least two books were written before Joyce's time on its Hebrew origins and possible esoteric meanings. It has been more often parodied than any other Mother Goose rhyme, and at least two versions provide a strange compendium of the figures associated with Joyce's dog and man: "This is the farmer sowing his corn" (Stephen's "my father gave me seeds to sow" in his fox riddle), or, "This is Sir John Barley-corn / That treated the Boy that every morn / Swept the stable snug and warm / That was made for the Horse of a beautiful form / That carried Jack with his Hound and Horn / That caught the Fox that lived under the thorn / That stole the cock that crowed in the morn / That waked the priest all shaven and shorn / That married the man all tattered and torn / That kissed the maiden all forlorn / That milked the cow with the crumpled horn / That tossed the dog / That worried the cat / That killed the rat / That ate the malt / That lay in the house that Jack built."[45] Here we have Irish alcoholism, the dog, the chase after the fox in "Circe" with "Hornblower of Trinity" (586), the thorn (close to a hollybush, associated with the Crucifixion, and found in the original version of Stephen's fox riddle),[46] the cock, the tattered man and maiden, the "obese gray rat" of the cemetery, and for that matter, Bloom's cat. We can hardly avoid concluding that Joyce used the elements of the nursery rhyme to give structural stiffening to the image cluster adhering to the dog and Macintosh, and to prescribe the poetic directions which it would take.

IV

After their riotous departure from Burke's pub, Stephen, Bloom, and the man in the macintosh travel together, so to speak, until Stephen's exit in "Ithaca." Stephen, however, has been already introduced to the crucified, dead, and resurrected Christ in another manifestation; and Stephen's confrontations with him, though we cannot be dogmatic about Joyce's conscious intentions, are particularly ironic if seen in the light of Christian symbolism. It is appropriate that Stephen, further from grace than Bloom by his own will and constantly seeing himself as the fallen Lucifer, should encounter the Son of God not as man but as beast, and concealed under the inverse language of the damned (what the Devil says can always be read backwards) not as God, but as dog. The figure of the dog is continually caught up by Joyce in the complex of images that we have already noted, centering about death and rebirth; but with Stephen and the dog the burial is by water, not in the earth. While Bloom is kind to all animals and loves water (671), Stephen hates and fears dogs and is a "hydrophobe" (673), a term which we may take as a punning nudge toward the idea of dogs. Stephen, unlike Bloom, is quick to perceive religious symbols and give them their Christian names, but he identifies them coldly and mechanically, unable or unwilling to see that they may have a special significance for him. Like Bloom, he has unconsciously received and given hints of what is in store.

Long before the action (and the writing) of *Ulysses,* Joyce has seen to it that imagery of dog and death by water should impinge on a kind of rebirth in Stephen. We have seen how the figures of "eleven" and the brown garment appeared at a crucial moment for him in *A Portrait of the Artist as a Young Man;* somewhat before this, just after his rejection of the Jesuit principal's temptation, as he is going forth to dedicate himself to art and to be vouchsafed the vision of the wading girl, he feels that "His soul had arisen from the grave of boyhood, spurning her graveclothes." The faintly blasphemous image is appropriate enough to the lush, romantic egotism of adolescent Stephen, but the ironic commentary on his rapture furnished by the shouts of his swimming classmates is prophetic of *Ulysses:* "Bous Stephanoumenos! Bous Stephaneforos! Duck him! Guzzle him now, Towser! . . . Oh, Cripes, I'm drownded!" (167–170) The "bullockbefriending bard," the pervasive idea of drowning, and the devouring Christ-dog of *Ulysses* in such intimate combination can hardly be accidental.

They are to reappear in "Nestor." A few pages before Stephen first applies the epithet "bullockbefriending" to himself (36), after receiving Mr. Deasy's letter on foot-and-mouth disease, he stumbles through his pedagogical duties and prophesies to his students with the riddle of the fox (related to dog and wolf) burying (rather than digging up) his grandmother (rather than mother). Yet Stephen prefaces his remade folk rhyme with a Christian gloss: "a riddling sentence to be woven on the church's looms" (26), and the rhyming line that he aptly inserts into the traditional version, "My father gave me seeds to sow," can be applied to the parable of the sower and to Christ's mission on earth. The riddle is made of Christian symbols. The cock crowing suggests Peter, who in "Hades" sends a telegram from heaven at eleven; but the cock, as Joyce doubtless knew (and likewise Eliot, with his cock on the rooftree that crows amid lightning to bring rain), is also a type of Christ dispelling the darkness—a famous early Christian hymn makes it explicit that the cock's crowing is *figura iudicis nostri.*[47] The blue sky and the bells striking eleven suggest the Virgin and resurrection. Later, on the strand at eleven, Stephen will say, "Signatures of all things I am here to read" (37), giving the title of a mystical work of Jakob Boehme that Joyce owned,[48] but Stephen in his pride cannot read any signatures correctly. In the schoolroom he encodes the message of the riddle, as it were, for instead of Christ-God digging up Father Adam, we have dog-fox *burying* his grand*mother* under a hollybush (not a thornbush; Christmas, not Easter). Stephen is equally blind to prophecies of Christian resurrection after baptism, or death and rebirth by water. When a student recites, as a priest might, "gabbled verses" (25)

> *For Lycidas, your sorrow, is not dead,*
> *Sunk though he be beneath the watery floor . . .*
> *Through the dear might of Him that walked the waves. . . .*

Stephen says, "I don't see anything" (26) in anticipation of closing his eyes on the beach: "shut your eyes and see" (37). But his mind immediately goes on to produce his riddle. Nor does he see anything when these hints are symbolically repeated in "Proteus" on Sandymount strand; he is unable to do more than merely register the Christian symbols which sweep through his mind and before his eyes. Perhaps this is the result of his hatred of "partial contact by immersion or total by submersion in cold water," and of the fact that he lacks one month of having completed a symbolic gestation period without a bath (673); in any case, like Eliot's Wastelanders, he is in perpetual *fear* of death by water. He wonders (37) "Am I walking into eternity along Sandymount strand?" The answer is clearly no.

Whatever may be lacking in Stephen's conscious cerebration about symbols, his associative processes in fantasy are wiser than he. He sees on the beach the carcass of a dead dog; almost at once a live dog, as though by metamorphosis, "grew into sight," and he cries out, invoking dog-reversed, "Lord, is he going to attack me?" (44–45), then immediately recalls his Luciferian *non serviam,* "you will not be master of others nor their slave." The two cockle-picking women he has noticed immediately become "The two maries" who stood at the foot of the cross and who found the empty tomb, but they are also Pharaoh's daughter and her handmaid ("Egyptians"), who took Moses (a type of Christ) from his "death" in the water, or the mother and sister of Moses, who put him there: "They have tucked it safe among the bulrushes. . . . No, the dog."[49] Thus Christ (by way of his prefiguration), the crucifixion and resurrection, and death and rebirth through water are brought together in Stephen's mind by the cockles and the dead-live dog.

Now the dog, to Stephen-Satan, becomes "Dog of my enemy," and sends Stephen into a complicated meditation on his own cowardice and Mulligan's bravery.

> He saved men from drowning and you shake at a cur's yelping. . . . Would you do what he did? A boat would be near, a lifebuoy. *Natürlich,* put there for you. Would you or would you not? The man that was drowned nine days ago off Maiden's rock. . . . The truth, spit it out. I would want to. I would try. I am not a strong swimmer. . . . His human eyes scream to me. . . . With him together down. . . . Waters: bitter death: lost. (45–46)

While these thoughts are perfectly explicable on the literal level, the allegorical level refers them to the imitation of Christ. Stephen distrusts his own courage and capacity to abandon himself, in the care of a higher power, for the sake of another who is "drowning." These reflections parallel Eliot's lines on the same critical moment of decision, "The awful daring of a moment's surrender," in which a boat would also be provided for the man who has learned the lesson of faith and self-abnegation (ll. 400–423). But like a timid Wastelander, Stephen fears death by water and denies the possibility of resurrection through the dear might of him that walked the waves.

The dog next undergoes a series of significant metamorphoses in Stephen's mind. "Looking for something lost in a past life" (46) and thus clearly reborn, he goes into the water and returns transformed, "a rag of wolf's tongue redpanting from his jaws." From wolf, foe to man, he quickly reverts to doggishness as he sniffs the carcass of his dead "brother." "Dogskull, dogsniff, eyes on the ground, moves to one great goal. Ah, poor dogsbody. Here lies poor dogsbody's body." As was the case with Bloom's doggy thoughts on the Mass, it is not God's body that lives for Stephen in Christ's person, but dogsbody, as he himself has been called by Mulligan (6) that "lies." Again, however, Stephen's aimless associations tell him more truly of the dog's identity than his conscious thought, for the words "moves to one great goal" are an echo of Mr. Deasy's easy Victorian teleology in "Nestor," which Stephen politely rejected: "All history moves towards one great goal, the manifestation of God" (34). Stephen, who is convinced that God is a shout in the street (though what he means by this will take the rest of the novel to unfold) thinks history, as it is in *The Waste Land* and *Gerontion,* merely a nightmare from which he is trying to awake.[50] The dog, which is a "mongrel" like the Garryowen of "Cyclops" and the multiple dog of "Circe," is named "Tatters," and thus he is Christ and the man in the macintosh as well, "tattered and torn that married a maiden all forlorn" (427). He refuses to leave the vicinity of the carcass, and "dabbled and delved. Something he buried there, his grandmother. He rooted [suggesting a pig and the later comparisons in "Circe" of dog and pig] in the sand . . . a pard, a panther, got in spousebreach, vulturing the dead" (46–47).[51] Here the dog has become the fox of Stephen's riddling vision, and in his eyes it is nothing more than the grave robber of Bloom's thoughts at Glasnevin or the Dog of *The Waste Land.* This particular dog, however, is a panther, got in spousebreach, and thus has become Christ. The panther, *pantheros,* is "all beasts," like the Protean dog (Joyce intended this punning allusion), while the identification of the panther with Christ was a commonplace in the medieval bestiary.[52] Got in spousebreach, however, it is doubly Christ for Stephen and Joyce, since a legendary

Roman centurion, Panthera,[53] was said to have been the father of Jesus (cf. 521); alternatively, a supernatural form of spousebreach occurred: "My mother's a jew, my father's a bird" (19) and *"C'est le pigeon, Joseph"* (41, 521). Stephen's roving fancy has murmured to him that Christ has risen both on earth and from the waters, but he drives out such implications: *"Omnis caro ad te veniet* . . . Oomb, all-wombing tomb" (48), as the "Egyptians" (gypsies, Pharaoh's daughter and her maid, or Maries) carry what they have taken from the sea away with them. Yet once more the idea of gypsies causes Stephen's fancy to explode into imagery, this time forming a link between Bloom's thoughts and his own: "Loose sand and shellgrit crusted her bare feet ("Crusted toenails"). . . . calling under her brown shawl from an archway where dogs have mired" ("brown scapular in tatters") (47; cf. 57).

Following this symbolic encounter, Stephen slowly leaves the beach. His mind is still idly running over what he has seen, amalgamating both secular and Christian references to rebirth from the sea, the Crucifixion, himself as Satan rejecting all this, and contrariwise as a faithful pilgrim accepting it ("cockle hat"). He anticipates, in a similar context, *The Waste Land*'s references to *Hamlet* and *The Tempest:*

> Full fathom five thy father lies. . . . Sunk though he be beneath the watery floor. . . . God becomes man becomes fish [ICHTHUS, the early Christian symbol of Christ, Son of God, Saviour]. . . . A seachange this. . . . I thirst. Clouding over. Thunderstorm. Allbright he falls, proud lightning of the intellect, *Lucifer, dico, qui nescit occasum.* No. My cockle hat and staff and his my sandal shoon. Behind. Perhaps there is someone . . . high spars of a threemaster, her sails brailed up on the crosstrees. . . . (50–51)

This is not the end of these associated figures, for with their framework of imagery evoking rebirth they pursue him through the "Wandering Rocks" chapter; the sight of a jeweler with a "Moses' beard" calls forth the thought "you who wrest old images from the burial earth" and the name of Antisthenes, later called "a *dog* [or Cynic] sage" (523), while at the same moment "Two old women fresh from their whiff of the briny trudged . . . one with a midwife's bag in which eleven cockles rolled" (242). The jeweler scene provides us with further indications that Stephen's fantasy is performing prodigies of recapitulation and prophecy as it spawns images associated with figures of dog-fox, resurrection, fatherhood, and Bloom. "Old Russell" recalls "Daun Russell, the fox" of the medieval beast fable, notably

Chaucer's "Nun's Priest's Tale"; his "vulture nails" suggest the Protean dog "vulturing the dead" (47), Stephen's own "vulture talons" in "Circe" and Rudolph Bloom's "feeble vulture talons" (572, 437); Old Russell is a "Grandfather ape" like Virag as baboon and vulture-Thoth (521, 511); and the rubies, from the "dark wormy earth" like the "maggoty beds" of the dead in Bloom's thoughts at the cemetery (115), have come from where "fallen archangels flung the stars of their brows" suggesting Stephen as Lucifer (50). In Stephen's imaginings the rubies have been oddly mined: "Muddy swinesnouts, hands, root and root, gripe and wrest them," suggesting the union of God, dog, and pig in "Circe" (520) and Virag's "truffles of Perigord, tubers [like Eliot's "dried tubers"] dislodged through mister omnivorous porker" (516). The ruby, moreover, traditionally symbolizes both Eden and the risen Christ.[54] The idea of something precious or holy lost in the earth through the agency of a fallen archangel and ironically brought to light through the muddy means of a pig, dog, fox, or vulture, odious animals all, is clearly basic to Joyce's (and Eliot's) structure of imagery.[55]

The thunder and rain associated with Stephen's Luciferian unbelief in "Proteus" recur in "Oxen of the Sun," immediately preceded by references to "Hamlet his father," Moses ("saved from water of old Nile, among bulrushes"), and "The House That Jack Built" (394). We are told in plain language (Elizabethan country dialect and Bunyanesque prose) that Stephen regarded the thunder as the voice of an angry God,[56] and that he had been turned from the true faith (394–396). The thunder here is beginning to assume its role as the Viconian thunderclap which awakens man to the demands of the supernatural and ushers in a new fourfold cycle, and Joyce anticipates its function in *The Waste Land*; it is significant in connection with Eliot's themes that in the same passage the death of Dignam and drought through the land are linked (in the language of Pepys) with sexual sterility.[57]

It is difficult to say whether Garryowen, the Citizen's companion in "Cyclops," is a true continuation of Joyce's dog imagery as it has been established around the thematic dog of "Proteus," but if we allow for ironic distortion on Joyce's part and the ignorance of unbelievers in Barney Kiernan's pub, Garryowen, though not a friend to all men, is presented in terms that continually give him a parody-religious dimension. The narrator of the episode tells us that it would be "a corporal work of mercy if someone would take the life of that bloody dog" (295), an appropriate sentiment for a Wastelander and an upside-down description of the Eucharist; and Garryowen has a growl "that'd put the fear of God in you" (299). The resurrection theme immediately appears, for while Dignam's death is not an improper topic at this point, there is considerable doubt as to whether he has not just appeared in the flesh to Alf Bergan, and maudlin Bob Doran mutters that Christ is not "good," but "a bloody ruffian, I say, to take away poor little Willy Dignam" (300–302). Garryowen is very much interested in the timorous Bloom, since "Jewies have a queer odour for dogs" (304), as they well may, in their character as a peculiar people, for an inverse God. Since "cakes for the dead" are "dogbiscuits" (100) Garryowen, in this land of the spiritually dead, becomes a cannibalistic communicant; he is given "a few bits of old biscuit" (305) out of a "Jacob's tin" (or ciborium), which he eagerly devours. Joyce had previously made this significant association; in *A Portrait of the Artist as a Young Man,* while Stephen is evoking "the radiant image of the Eucharist" (220–221) he is also thinking of a girl from "Jacob's biscuit factory." The narrator continually expresses hostility to Garryowen, a dry dog, "his eye all bloodshot from the drouth in it and the hydrophobia dropping out of his jaws" (311). Nevertheless this dog is also a wolf and much like a man, or a friend to man, since in the succeeding burlesque description we have a "marvellous exhibition of cynanthropy given by the famous old Irish red wolfdog setter." He is given water to quench his thirst (312).

In this chapter Bloom, who has hitherto been visited by the disguised Christ figure in the person of the man in the macintosh, meets him in the form of a dog, perhaps in preparation for the final crossing of all four thematic threads in the "Circe" episode—Bloom, Stephen, man, dog. At the end of "Cyclops," Bloom becomes Christ: "Christ was a jew like me" (342); a parody of religious services has been enacted —Communion (305), the Creed (329), the Last Gospel (343). The Citizen intends to "crucify" Bloom with the biscuit box or ciborium (342–343) and Garryowen, now perhaps a mere dog again, pursues the fleeing Bloom. Symbols crowd thick and fast—the burlesque description includes an earthquake as at the Crucifixion, but with *eleven* shocks (344); Bloom ascends as Elijah, with God, Jesus, and Moses as witnesses.[58]

V

The Circe episode is a chapter of dream, hallucination, and metamorphosis. In it all the related figures and images which we have examined occur at least once, and usually in illuminating conjunction or amalgamation. The chapter is of course a thematic summary of *Ulysses,* but because the narrative technique is that of dream, the figures more often than not *become* one another. Joyce, using the method of Freudian *Traumdeutung,* translates causal relationship, wish, dread, or simile into metaphor, and dream-equations repeat and explain relationships that have previously been merely suggested and concealed. For example, the dog figure first appears as a "spaniel" (432) while Stephen by symbolic or magical gestures produces the "light of the world" (Christ) and illustrates the Eucharist; it then appears eight times to Bloom on the streets of Nighttown (432–468) as a spaniel, a retriever, a terrier, a wolf, a wolfdog, a mastiff, a bulldog, a boarhound, and a greyhound. We are not told that various dogs appear, or that a single dog changes from one breed to another; the metamorphosis which Stephen imagined in "Proteus" is dramatized without explanation, shown in action. The dog is Pantheros.

Bloom connects him with the overfriendly Garryowen (453), feeds him, and tells the watchmen that (like Eliot's Dog) he is "The friend of man." It is true, as Helen Gardner has remarked of Eliot's line, that this is a copybook phrase,[59] but Bloom utters it in self-defense, for he has been accused of committing a nuisance and has replied rather oddly, unless we see a religious implication in the words, "I am doing good to others." Bloom himself becomes a dog as the Honourable Mrs. Mervyn Talboys prepares to chastise him: he has a "hangdog mein," is a "mongrel" and a "Pig dog and always was since he was pupped" (468–69). At this point the man in the macintosh or someone with his characteristics enters and becomes a dog, for Bloom's jury consists of eleven named persons, six from Dignam's funeral, and a "Nameless One," the only juror who speaks solo (469–470), and who "snarls" doggishly.

Now Bloom's dreamwork fuses a set of significant images into one. Triggered by the words "I was at a funeral" (472) his fantasy converts the risen corpse of Paddy Dignam into both a dog and Macintosh: "The beagle lifts his snout, showing the grey scorbutic face of Paddy

Dignam. He has gnawed all. He exhales a putrid carcasefed breath [reminiscent of the dog on the beach at Sandymount]. . . . His dachshund coat becomes a brown mortuary habit." Dignam-dog-Macintosh "bays lugubriously," says, "List, list, O list!" like the ghost of Hamlet's father, and seeks to "satisfy an animal need" against a lamppost (473); he has appeared by "metempsychosis." Now the Victor Talking Machine dog, he pricks up his ears, then listens with an ear to the ground: "My master's voice!" (474). He disappears, "his brown habit trailing its tether," suggesting the "obese grey rat" of Bloom's and Stephen's visions at eleven (44, 114). Just as Bloom had been sure at the funeral that Dignam's resurrection was impossible, Dignam's voice underground "bays" (combining dog and the Ghost in *Hamlet*) "Dignam's dead and gone below." He is buried in the "House of Keys" (the Church), and the parody-Eucharist of "Cyclops" is also evoked, together with "cakes for the dead": "Namine. Jacobs Vobiscuits. Amen," says Father Coffey from Glasnevin (473). Thus is it made clear that the dog and the man in brown, hitherto manifested separately and with their connection only obscurely hinted at, are one, and that Joyce wanted them to be connected by imagery with the resurrection of the dead and with the Eucharist, though masked from Bloom's conscious thought or understanding.

His fantasy, however, like Stephen's, is more penetrating. During Bloom's apotheosis as Lord Mayor of Dublin we have a clarified repetition of the thematic material, this time with Macintosh alone, in which Bloom denies the risen Saviour and sets himself up as a false Messiah, Antichrist, and Pope. Bloom has become Caesar, for a group of sightseers cry "*Morituri te salutant*" and die (485). Their death, like Dignam's, instantly produces resurrection: "A man in a brown macintosh springs up through a trapdoor" and accuses Bloom of lying and imposture: "Leopold M'Intosh [a nonexistent name, Hynes's mistake in the *Telegraph*], the notorious fire-raiser. His real name is Higgins [Bloom's mother's maiden name]." Bloom, master of the world and Antichrist, deals with the situation promptly. Taking over the anti-canine words of Stephen-Antichrist from "Proteus,"—"Hired dog! Shoot him to bloody bits with a bang shotgun" (42)—he cries, "Shoot him! Dog of a christian! So much for M'Intosh!" and a cannon shot makes Macintosh "disappear." Bloom's bodyguards at once take care of asserting his status as Antichrist and Pope, for among the fantastic catalogue of their donatives to the crowd are "Maundy money," "loaves and fishes," and "40 days' indulgences."

Macintosh is still to be heard from. In the genealogy of Bloom (496) he appears as the "Dusty Rhodes" of the Dowie prophecies in "Oxen of the Sun," and we are told that he begat "Benamor" (son of love). Now detached from Macintosh, the dog and his rebirth symbols are nearby, for on the next page dogs defile Bloom and the tailor's bill of Mesias (Messiah) is *eleven* shillings. To complete the inverted identification of Christ, "Reuben J. Dodd, blackbearded Iscariot, bad shepherd, bearing on his shoulders the drowned corpse of his son" appears. A death-by-water figure (Dodd's son had been *rescued* from an attempted suicide by drowning) has now become the lamb of the travestied Good Shepherd of iconography.*

As Bloom finally enters the brothel he is brought together with Stephen, and appropriately from this point on the symbols of Stephen, Bloom, dog, and Macintosh are elaborately interwoven. On the hall table Bloom notices the first of Stephen's rebirth figures, "the spaniel eyes of a running fox" (502; cf. 432, 572, 586); dog and fox are amalgamated. Stephen's definition of God from "Nestor" (34) reappears with "that fellow's noise in the street," and the theme of Antichrist is reiterated, both in the words of the whore Florry and in the recurring figure of Dodd with his drowned son over his shoulders (505–506). Elijah proclaims the Last Judgment in the idiom of J. Alexander Dowie and the three whores, like Eliot's three Thames-daughters though in more broadly comic terms, tell in turn the story of their first undoing (508–509).

It may be hard to tell which of Joyce's apparitions it is that comes in response to Dowie-Elijah to judge the quick and the dead, but Bloom's grandfather Leopold Virag is an interesting candidate. He is a dog, for he "chases his tail" and "worries his butt," has "forepaws" and "yelps" (520); he wears a brown macintosh (511). He is also costumed as Osiris, the resurrected god and judge of the dead, who is depicted with "an Egyptian pshent," the double crown of the two kingdoms, in Egyptian pictures of the judgment; he is vulture-headed

* The associations of Mesias and Dodd with Christ are affirmed by a note sheet for "Circe," which contains the phrases "Messiah the tailor" and "LB [Bloom, already a Christ-figure] carries sheep on back."—Reproduced by Robert M. Adams in *Surface and Symbol* (New York, 1962), p. 259.

Thoth ("he holds a roll of parchment. . . . Two quills project over his ears"), the god of scribes and Stephen's patron, the just judge and weigher of souls as well, who is sometimes pictured as a dog-headed ape.[60] In Virag the motifs of grandfather, god, resurrection, dog, macintosh, judge, scribe, are united, but Virag also parallels Bloom and Stephen as Antichrists by denying the true Messiah, adopting classical calumnies: "Verfluchte goim! He had a father, forty fathers. He never existed. Pig God! [Bloom was characterized a few pages earlier as "pig dog"] . . . He was Judas Iacchias . . . the pope's bastard. . . . Panther, the Roman centurion, polluted her [Mary] with his genitories" (520–521). Meanwhile Stephen, as Philip Drunk and Philip Sober, repeats his joke about Christ's parentage: *"C'était le sacré pigeon, Philippe."* The Last Judgement modulates to a close with a reiteration of "K 11" and Stephen's themes—Antisthenes the Cynic (Anglicized to "dog sage") and the end of Arius the heresiarch, "The agony in the closet" (523).

Stephen is vaguely aware, as he was at the end of "Proteus" (51) that some unknown but important personage is present. For the first time he makes the transition to Macintosh, Christ, and love: "Who was it told me his name. . . . Aha, yes. *Zoe mou sas agapo* [My life, I love thee]. . . . Mac somebody. Unmack I have it" (518–519). His gropings for the mysterious person come to naught because "Spirit is willing but the flesh is weak," though Zoe immediately suspects that he must be a seminarian—"Are you out of Maynooth?"—for *agape* is not the appropriate kind of love for this Zoe.

Bloom's metamorphosis into a woman (523–556) is suitably almost free of the associated images we have been tracing, but as soon as Bloom has recovered his talismanic potato from Zoe and begun the ascent from the depths to his role of father, these images reappear as Bloom commences his protective efforts to look after Stephen's money. The phrase "it's long after eleven" as the whores and Bloom squabble over payment immediately evokes Stephen's fox riddle, this time with the last lines significantly altered: it is now time for "her [his mother's] poor soul / To *get out* of heaven" (558, italics mine) so that she may appear to haunt him for the last time and provoke him into the symbolic, Wagnerian-Blakean shattering of the lamp chimney with his augur's rod, the climactic assertion of his freedom and the establishment of his true rebirth as artist. "Eleven," repeated by Bloom, elicits from Stephen a laughing acceptance of his guilt and responsibility:

"Why striking eleven? . . . Proparoxyton. Moment before the next . . . Thirsty fox. (*He laughs loudly.*) Burying his grandmother. Probably he killed her" (559).* The prophetic phrase "moves to one great goal" of the "Proteus" chapter (46) is now spoken again and made clear (563), for Stephen, who is "twentytwo too" (twice eleven), identifies himself mathematically with Bloom.[61] "Sixteen years ago I twentytwo tumbled, twentytwo years ago he sixteen fell off his hobbyhorse."† The "great goal" is not the spiritual goal of the manifestation of God in Mr. Deasy's sense, but the saving secular goal, for Stephen, of identification with Bloom's humanity. "*Pater*! Free!" (572).

At this point the dog figure ceases to have Christlike attributes and becomes pure dog, in pursuit of Stephen, now "Christfox," eluding his followers. Stephen's fleshly father (572) gives tongue like a beagle as the Stephen-fox, now "*stout . . . having buried his grandmother*" or his guilt, seeks cover ahead of a pack of hounds. It is perhaps with reference to Stephen's new state that a "noise in the street" (574), which is God for Stephen, is now, as the dog had been, "our friend." No longer a figure of menace, God has been assimilated into Stephen's secular vision. Now his mother's appearance, though it can terrify him (582) cannot make him submit, and the forces and persons that oppose him have become dogs which he no longer fears: "Break my spirit if you can! I'll bring you all to heel!" After smashing the lamp chimney with his ashplant Stephen flees, and the fantastic fox hunt which had followed his first proclamation of freedom (572–573) is repeated in grossly augmented form (586). Bloom too is a fox and a "pard" that scatters false scents ("aniseed") for the drag hunt. The "bloodhounds" which pursue include the retriever of earlier pages, the mystery man on the beach, Garryowen, the Nameless One, Alexander Keyes, and "Hornblower of Trinity." This last figure, whose name suggests the angel Gabriel proclaiming the end of the world, brandishes a dogwhip and wears "an old pair of grey trousers," the hand-me-downs of Buck Mulligan which Stephen could not wear (6). "Biscuitboxes" are among

* *Proparoxytonos* is defined by Liddell and Scott as "[a word] with the acute accent on the antepenultimate." "Eleven" is not quite such a word; but Stephen's (or Joyce's) unconscious or deliberate wrenching of the definition to permit the transformation of "syllable before the last" to "*moment* before the *next* [stage? era?]" suggests that Joyce wants him to be well aware of the implications of "the eleventh hour" and of eleven as a number of rebirth and revelation.

† Unless the word "hobbyhorse" is completely gratuitous, it must serve to bring in the theme of *Hamlet*, and hence of atonement with the father: "For O, for O, the hobbyhorse is forgot" (III.ii.145).

the miscellaneous objects hurled after the fleeing pair. Thus it appears that Stephen and Bloom were intended by Joyce to have broken free—at least on the symbolic level—from both men and things of their past, though hotly pursued and pelted with rubbish of every category, sacred and profane.

In the witches' sabbath and black mass which occur during Stephen's encounter with the soldiers, Joyce, as though to make his dog-God palindrome unmistakably clear, has Adonai himself proclaim that God to the blessed and dog to the damned are one and the same, for the damned, we discover, think and speak in reverse, as they do in *The Waste Land*—"Htengier Tnetopinmo Dog Drol eht rof, Aiulella!" (599), while Adonai is "Dooooooooooog" to them and "Goooooooooood" to the blessed, with eleven o's in each instance (600). And it is clear from the recurring figures and actions which Joyce gives us that this mass is to be associated with the true Masses and parody masses of earlier chapters. The retriever appears sporadically, barking, in the decrescendo of the final pages of "Circe," but imagery associates him with Christ, the Eucharist, and Stephen, for in Private Compton's words he is "the bleeding tyke," and Cissy Caffrey, mistakenly thinking that Stephen is meant, cries expectantly, "Is he bleeding?" (602). Finally, the apotheosis of Rudy is marked by a faint echo of the dog imagery as "A dog barks in the distance" (609).[62]

The dog has vanished, his mission done, but Macintosh makes two more significant appearances in the *Nostos* of *Ulysses*. Hallucination has given way to the exhausted idiom of "Eumaeus" and we return to the purely literal plane of expression. Bloom reads the account of Dignam's funeral in the *Telegraph* (647–648), and while he is "Nettled not a little by *L. Boom*," he is "tickled to death" (his conscious thought about Macintosh can never get beyond death) by the mention of persons who were "conspicuous, needless to say, by their total absence (to say nothing of M'Intosh)."[63] He shows the article to Stephen, whose response is puzzling. "—Is that first epistle to the Hebrews, he asked, as soon as his bottom jaw would let him, in? Text: open thy mouth and put thy foot in it." A possible solution to the puzzle may be found, as well as a clue to Macintosh's identity, if we remember that the Epistle to the Hebrews is an affirmation of the universal significance of the resurrected Christ: "we have a great high priest, that is passed into the heavens"—and that among other admonitions it contains one on skepticism and shortness of sight: "Be not forgetful to entertain strangers: for thereby some have entertained angels unawares." (*Finnegans Wake* is a "farced epistol to the hibruws.")[64] Bloom, however, though he is to some extent versed in the Kabbalah and is told something of the Book of Kells (688), remains oblivious to this roundabout revelation of the Messiah. We know that he has performed numerous rites and ceremonies of the Old Dispensation (728–729), but they have not prepared him to apprehend the New. He does not finally comprehend the highly significant because "self-involved" enigma, "Who was M'Intosh?" His ignorance is easy enough to understand if one chooses to read from the Christian point of view, however, since he suddenly does comprehend another enigma, "Where was Moses when the candle went out?" The answer, to be supplied by the reader, is, alas, "In the dark." To the end of *Ulysses*, Bloom and Stephen remain, if one pays attention only to a literal or to a Christian interpretation of their enlightenment, blind guides, Wastelanders.

It can of course be said that a merely literal or a merely Christian reading of this particular strand in *Ulysses*' web denies the richness of the novel's total meaning and falsifies Joyce's intentions by narrowing their presumed scope. But the supreme importance of this dissociated metaphor is demonstrated by its prominence in the novel's figurative, symbolic structure, its ubiquitousness in the episodes, and its testimony of coherence and of deliberate planning on the part of Joyce. Indeed, it has already been elaborately and persuasively argued, on the basis of Joyce's Shakespearean material alone (especially *Hamlet*) that this matter bears the burden of a redemption motif, pervasive yet entirely in symbolic terms; and also that Joyce, in his manipulation only of material connected with Shakespeare and with the sea, has indicated a means of redemption or salvation and metamorphosis for Stephen in the realm of his future behavior as man and artist.[65] Whichever view we take, the imagery is undeniably present; to deny its significance is to say that Joyce was wasting his time. Further, it is not necessary or even pertinent to maintain that Joyce, because he employed Christian symbolism to suggest rebirth and redemption, was or had again become in any real sense a Christian when he was writing *Ulysses*. Much of the traditional Christian imagery of rebirth or redemption is archetypal, common to many religions; and Joyce, in view of his own Irish Catholic culture and the English-speaking audience which he was ultimately addressing, could hardly be expected to select imagery from any source other than Christian if he expected his meaning to be effectively conveyed. The result, as a significant vision of the modern world or a paradigm of modern man's predicament, may be satisfying or poignant to Christian, atheist, or seeker alike. Douglas Knight, in one of the most influential treatments of *Ulysses* in its totality, is led to sum up Joyce's ultimate vision of the state of Bloom, Stephen, and the Dublin-microcosm they inhabit, as follows:

> With a relative mastery of formal religion and metaphysical concepts, Stephen cannot see their relevance to experience. Bloom on the other hand sees the place of love and charity in the active world but can bring to their support only a materialist humanism . . . there exists most pervasively . . . a symbolic narrative of suffering without redemption, but in the presence of the possibility of redemption. . . . [Bloom and Stephen] are simultaneously [the inferno's] victims and its unconscious potential saviors.[66]

Just such a paralyzed world, whose inhabitants perpetually miss the clues to their salvation, has been seen by many readers in *The Waste Land*. The following comments by C. M. Bowra, for example, can be tellingly applied to Bloom at the end of *Ulysses*, and to Bloom's and Stephen's puzzled contemplation of Macintosh:

> Nothing has happened to him, and he is incapable of any decisive action. He is the passive consciousness which combines a wide understanding and knowledge with a singular ineffectiveness in doing anything that matters. His crisis is the crisis of the modern soul as [the author] diagnoses it. His life, which is also the life of his people, is terribly impoverished and weakened, and he needs some tremendous act to restore him and them.
>
> The figure seen by the disciples becomes an illusion of exhausted men and the sense of Christ's presence a mockery. . . . His presence in a way haunts them, without seeming real or truly important. In the collapse of their confidence . . . this presence becomes more insistent but has no more meaning . . . the figure of Christ is no more than a haunting phantom.[67]

Yet the first is Bowra's description of the Fisher King at the end of *The Waste Land*, the second is his interpretation of Eliot's "hooded figure." The same bleak vision can be seen in *Ulysses* and *The Waste Land*; but, more significantly, it can be shown that external circumstances forced its principal ingredients—figures and images—upon Eliot's attention just at the period when *The Waste Land* was growing in his mind.

VI

A profitable enquiry into the effect of *Ulysses* on Eliot's thought and writing must be based upon as precise a knowledge as possible of what Eliot knew of Joyce before he wrote *The Waste Land,* and what opinions he had formed of Joyce's work by that time. It has been suggested that Eliot's close connections with Ezra Pound, with the *Little Review* as contributor (it published approximately the first half of *Ulysses* in instalments, March 1918–December 1920) and with the *Egoist* as assistant editor from July 1917, had familiarized him with the first half of the book, and perhaps with some of the later episodes in manuscript.[68] But the recent full edition of Joyce's letters completed by Richard Ellmann, together with those of Pound to Joyce in Forrest Read's *Pound / Joyce* and those of Eliot to John Quinn in B. L. Reid's *The Man from New York,* make it possible to reconstruct a much more detailed picture of the relationship between Joyce and Eliot.[69] From early 1917 onward, Eliot was as ardent and well informed a Joyce partisan as Pound or Harriet Weaver; and he as well as Pound was seeing the episodes of *Ulysses* as soon as Joyce sent them to London.

When Joyce and Eliot first knew of one another has not been precisely established; but as early as October 23, 1915, Pound mentions Eliot to Joyce in a postscript with an offhandedness which argues considerable familiarity; and on November 27 he promises to send Joyce a copy of his *Catholic Anthology* "for the sake of a couple of poems by Eliot."[70] On March 13, 1917, only a few weeks after the publication of *A Portrait of the Artist as a Young Man,* Pound writes Joyce that Eliot "approves" of it and is trying to secure a commission to review it, and on the seventeenth that he hopes to send Joyce a copy of Eliot's *Prufrock* volume.[71] Joyce acknowledged the book later in the year (III, 510). In his letter of September 10, 1917 (to Mrs. Joyce, her husband being convalescent from an eye operation), Pound announces a payment of ten pounds from the *Egoist,* and says that both it and the *Little Review* will serialize *Ulysses,* beginning, he hopes, with the March issues.[72] And on December 19 he writes Joyce that the first seventeen pages of *Ulysses,* in duplicate, have been received in London.[73] (The first chapters of the novel arrived in December, and it appears that if all had gone well the manuscript would have been processed throughout in this way: one copy through Pound to the *Little Review,* one through Eliot to the *Egoist.*) Unfortunately,

English publication plans ran into trouble; on March 29, 1918, Pound wrote Joyce that "the Egoist printers wont set up the stuff at all."[74] Although the printing of episodes for the *Egoist* could not be arranged until 1919, Leonard Woolf mentions that at the end of 1917 or the beginning of 1918 Eliot was trying to secure the publication of *Ulysses* by the Woolfs' Hogarth Press, describing it as a "remarkable work" which no printer would touch; and this was considerably before Harriet Weaver's arrival at the Woolfs' with the first four episodes in April 1918.[75] Evidently by late 1917 she and Eliot were determined (or had promised Joyce) to do everything that could be done for the still-incomplete *Ulysses*; and in 1918–19 Eliot must have continued to receive duplicate manuscripts of the episodes from Pound as Joyce sent them—"Proteus" in June 1918, "Sirens" in June 1919, "Cyclops" in October.[76]

But Eliot's efforts on behalf of Joyce and the forthcoming *Ulysses* were not confined to negotiations with possible printers. He was the author of the *Egoist's* unsigned review of the second edition of *Chamber Music* in 1918.[77] In the summer of 1919 he was prepared to print in the *Egoist* John Quinn's brief in defense of *Ulysses* in its troubles with the U.S. Post Office Department, which Pound had sent him, but Quinn refused to allow this.[78] (Eliot was also in regular correspondence with Quinn regarding the publication of his own poems at this time; and in November 1919 he first referred to the future *Waste Land* as "a poem that I have in mind."[79]) A few months before this, on July 9, 1919, he had written to Quinn regarding "Scylla and Charybdis," which despite deletions had been stopped by the Post Office and occasioned Quinn's brief: "I have lived on it ever since I read it." He went on to say that the *Egoist* had been unable to get *Ulysses* printed, detailed his difficulties in trying to "impose" Joyce on London opinion-makers, and described himself and his wife as "carried away" by Joyce.[80]

Aside from whatever Eliot may have been accomplishing in literary conversations, his contributions to periodicals in 1918–1919 contained extremely flattering references to Joyce:

> Mr. Joyce ought to disturb this view of prose [as a "humbler vehicle" than verse]. . . . Mr. Joyce can wait his turn [for justification] until *Ulysses* (immeasurably an advance on the *Portrait*) appears as a book. . . . *Ulysses* is volatile and heady . . . terrifying.[81]

> [Yeats's] crudity and egotism are present in other writers who are Irish; justified by exploitation to the point of greatness, in the later work of Mr.

James Joyce. Mr. Joyce's mind is subtle, erudite, even massive; but it is not like Stendhal's, an instrument continually tempering and purifying emotion; it operates within the medium, the superb current, of his feeling.[82]

These comments of Eliot's on the qualities of Joyce's prose did not have to rely on reading *Ulysses* instalments in the *Little Review,* as we have seen; but four of the early episodes had to receive a particularly intense scrutiny, for professional reasons if for no others. The *Egoist* printed "Nestor" in its number for January–February 1919, "Proteus" in March–April, "Hades" in July and September, and the first half of "The Wandering Rocks" in December. Harriet Weaver, who served as "business manager" of the *Egoist,* leaving the editorial side to Eliot (Miss Dora Marsden, who wrote the "leaders," had little to do with its actual production), recalled that chapters of *Ulysses* used to arrive at the *Egoist* office in typescript, sometimes directly from Joyce, sometimes from Pound.[83] Eliot had to read and reread these with the concentration demanded of a proofreader; and it is worth noting that the dog in "Proteus" would have been forcibly called to his attention. The episode as it appears in the *Egoist* is less full in its description of the dog on the beach than the final text, and it is clear that the printer required deletions (no doubt because of the offensive word "pissed"; he also objected to "snot").[84] These would have demanded Eliot's painstaking editorial attentions.

Pound attempted to have Eliot join him and Joyce at Sirmione in June 1920,[85] but Eliot proved unable to make the trip, which would presumably have led to a discussion of *Ulysses* among other matters, since Joyce in a letter to Pound on June 5 hoped that Pound had received "Oxen of the Sun" and sent it to London and New York (II, 469); in any case, Eliot must have seen that episode in its early version, as well as the preceding ones.

Although the first meeting between the two did not occur until August 15, 1920,[86] it is easy to understand the note of respectful urgency in Eliot's letter of August 11 requesting it (III, 14) and the wistful tone of his "I should very much like to meet you, at last." Several further meetings must have followed quickly, for on the twenty-ninth Joyce wrote to his brother Stanislaus that "Eliot, Wyndham Lewis, Rodker and their wives keep moving between London, Paris, and the country. Dinners and lunches are the order of the day" (III, 17). Joyce apparently insisted on paying for meals, transportation, and tips at this time. His motives may have been vanity, esteem, gratitude, insurance for the future, or any combination of these; but whatever they were, we may be sure that he encouraged detailed discussions of *Ulysses* at these social gatherings.

If Eliot had known *Ulysses* at the end of 1921 only from what had appeared in print up to the time when the *Little Review* was forced to discontinue its serial publication, he would have been ignorant of three-quarters of "Oxen of the Sun" and of the remaining episodes, and he would have known those in the first half of the book only from the unrevised and therefore relatively thin versions in which they had then appeared. But the evidence of the newly printed letters makes it probable that before the late fall of 1921, when *The Waste Land* was composed at Margate and Lausanne and *Ulysses* had received its final revisions, Eliot had seen all of the book, that he was reading it with the eye of a poet, a future reviewer, and a literary adviser, with great care and concentration on its exact wording, that his famous *Dial* article, "*Ulysses,* Order, and Myth,"[87] may have been composed or meditated at about the same time as *The Waste Land,* and that Joyce was making an effort to insure that he saw *Ulysses* in final form.

On February 4, 1921, Joyce wrote to Harriet Weaver that "Circe" was being typed and that "Eumaeus" would be finished in a week or two. He continued:

> Mr. Eliot, who was here lately, told me of Mr. Aldington's article to which, it seems, he (Mr. Eliot) is replying by arrangement with Mr. Aldington. The latter's standpoint, so far as I could gather from Mr. Eliot, seems to me legitimate criticism but I expect that his article will go beyond those limits. . . . ["Circe"] offers a good front for attack (I, 157).

On April 23 he told Miss Weaver:

> I do not think it is necessary to say anything about Mr. Aldington's article. . . . While I consider his article quite fair (though somewhat irrelevant to my mind) perhaps it would be well to pass on to Mr. Eliot when you have read them the two episodes Mr. Pound sent [evidently "Circe" and "Eumaeus," as is indicated earlier] and also the typescript of *Oxen of the Sun* which I could send if you approve. I mention this because he told me it was arranged that Mr. Aldington was to write an article and he to reply to it. In that case he ought to see the book in its present (penultimate) stage (III, 41).

Richard Aldington's article had appeared in the April issue of the *English Review,*[88] but it is clear from what Joyce says that Eliot's reply, considering the conditions of magazine publication, will not appear for some months at least. Joyce's letter of May 2 to Miss Weaver remarks, "I would have sent on the typescript of *Oxen of the Sun* with this for Mr. Eliot but that this . . . was lent to Mrs. Harrison. . ." (I, 164). Meanwhile, however, Mrs. Harrison's husband had puritanically burned part of the "Circe" manuscript, and on April 19 Joyce agitatedly wrote to John Quinn, to whom he had sent "Circe" and "Eumaeus," that he needed several pages of the former returned so that he could repair the damage (III, 40–41). Quinn obliged with photographs of the missing pages, and Joyce thereupon wrote to Claud Sykes, his Zurich actor friend, ". . . Quinn has had the pages photographed . . . so that I shall not need to trouble you. . . . You can return the typescript here registered if sending by return. . . . I am glad you liked *Circe* and *Eumeus*. . ." (I, 164). But a postcard to Sykes on June 6 said, "Did you return the typescript. A copy arrived about a week ago but my family opened the wrapper so I don't know if it is yours or Eliot's" (III, 44).

It is evident, then, that in May 1921 Eliot had manuscripts of *Ulysses* episodes which were identical with those Sykes had at the same time, and these included "Circe" and "Eumaeus." But the following letter from Eliot to Joyce, dated May 21, 1921, indicates a good deal more:

My dear Joyce,

I am returning your three mss by registered post as you require and am exceedingly obliged for a taste of them. I think they are superb—especially the Descent into Hell, which is stupendous. Only, in detail, I object to one or two phrases of Elijah: "ring up" is English, "call up" American; "trunk line," if applied to the telephone service, is English, the American is, if I remember, "long distance." I don't quite like the wording of the coon transformation of Elijah, either, but I cannot suggest any detailed alteration. But otherwise, I have nothing but admiration, in fact, I wish, for my own sake, that I had not read it.[89]

The passage to which Eliot refers in this letter occurs about halfway through the "Circe" episode (507–508); Elijah is proclaiming the Last Judgment in the manner of an American revival spellbinder of 1904, and presumably Joyce had asked Eliot, as an American, to include in his comments detailed suggestions on the authenticity of the American slang. He accepted Eliot's advice in one case, not in the other: Elijah says, "Say, I am operating all this trunk line" (507), but "You call me up by sunphone any old time" (508).

But two weeks before dispatching this letter to Joyce (May 9), Eliot had written one to John Quinn which is of the highest importance in indicating what was going on in his mind at this time. While admitting that Joyce was "a handful," he stoutly maintained that he had something to be fanatical about, for "the latter part of 'Ulysses,' which I have been reading in manuscript, is truly magnificent." In the same letter he said, "I have a long poem in mind and partly on paper which I am wishful to finish." *The Waste Land,* at least in part, was already being set down as Eliot pored over "Circe."[90]

If Eliot had not read the revised *Ulysses* in its entirety by the end of 1921, we at least have conclusive proof that by the late spring of that year he had carefully read "Circe" in its "penultimate" version; the other two of the "three mss" mentioned in his letter were, on the evidence of Joyce's correspondence, "Oxen of the Sun" and "Eumaeus," and it is not likely that Eliot read them less attentively than "Circe."

Establishing Eliot's close familiarity with the verbal texture and imagery of the Circe episode is of great service in maintaining that the Dog of his poem is a literary descendant of the God-dog of *Ulysses,* and in establishing other links with *The Waste Land.* It is in "Circe," if we ignore all of Joyce's other suggestions as to the God-dog palindrome, that it is specifically proclaimed. In the hallucinatory black Mass toward the end of the episode (598–599) we have a carefully executed inversion of the Introit and other parts of the Mass: "*Introibo ad altare diaboli* . . . the devil which hath made glad my young days," and a blood-dripping Host, "*Corpus meum,*" underlining the theme of traditional religious matter upside down or backwards. It is here that the damned hear the voice of Adonai crying "Dooooooooooog," while the blessed hear the word as "Goooooooooood." More specifically, the passage upon which Eliot comments in his letter is immediately followed by one (508–509) in which the three whores tell of their undoing in language of stilted elegance; the ironic contrast between their situation and their diction irresistibly suggests the contrast between the bedraggled Rhine maidens of Eliot, much come down in the world, and the diction, for example, of la Pia: "*Siena mi fè, disfecemi Maremma.*" Lastly, midway between the two phrases for which Eliot suggested improvement, Elijah-Dowie cries: "Book through to eternity junction, the nonstop run. Just one word more. Are you a *god* or a *doggone* [euphemism for "goddamned"] clod? If the second advent came to Coney Island are we ready?" (507; italics mine). Given the verbal texture and the religious feeling both of *Ulysses* and *The Waste Land,* with their frequent insistence that the true ascent to salvation must begin from the nadir of disgust, and their reiteration that blindness, apathy, and the things of this world are fatal impediments to man's rising from his spiritual grave, "If the second advent came to Coney Island are we ready?" is not a bad summary of both these twentieth-century epics.

Although "*Ulysses,* Order, and Myth," with its striking tribute to Joyce, did not appear until nearly two years after the novel's publication date, *Ulysses* did not lack for notice in the pages of the *Dial,* notice all the more remarkable because of the scarcity of American readers who could be expected to have had access to the book. On March 17, 1922, Joyce wrote to Robert McAlmon, who had done a review of *Ulysses* at his request, offering suggestions for placing it: "As regards *Dial* Pound, Eliot and Colum are all doing or have done articles in it so I fancy they are full up . . . a review to be of service to me should appear shortly" (III, 60). And on April 10 he complained to Harriet Weaver: "I expected that at least *The Dial* would have arrived today with Mr. Eliot's article but not even that has come. It must be very disappointing to you that no review of the book has appeared in the English press" (I, 183). In view of Eliot's solicitude for Joyce's book, his agreement to reply to an article which had appeared in April 1921, and Joyce's apparent expectation of a full-dress review by Eliot in the April 1922 *Dial,* the long delay of Eliot's tribute is difficult to understand. Whatever the reason, Joyce should have been pacified by the fact that the *Dial*'s readers were receiving a steady stream of notices of *Ulysses,* or tantalizingly knowing references to it, from Eliot and others. In August 1921, Eliot observed in his "London Letter": ". . . a new world must have a new structure. Mr. Joyce has succeeded, because he has very great constructive ability; and it is the structure which gives his later work its unique and solitary value. . . . The strongest, like Mr. Joyce, make their feeling into an articulate external world. . . ."[91] The February 1922 *Dial* contained, in Pound's "Paris Letter," a reference to Valéry Larbaud's lecture on *Ulysses* of the preceding December in which "the now usual comparisons [!] of Joyce's genius to that of Swift, Sterne, Fielding" were made; the article ended floridly, "Voltaire printed in Holland and the Bourbons deliquesced; Ulysses on the schedule of Paris events."[92] Pound included another flattering reference to *Ulysses* in his "Paris Letter" for the April issue.[93] In May came Eliot's "London Letter," with a passage which may perhaps explain Joyce's disappointed expectations for April: "This should have been a London letter. But Ulysses does not exactly tumble into it; and must certainly be discussed apart; time enough to include it here when we are able to mark its effect upon London. (The London Mercury has already devoted three pages to Mr. Joyce; perhaps London will be revolutionized in three months.)"[94] The reason that Joyce's novel does not tumble in may be that in the next issue is Pound's "Paris Letter," with seven wildly enthusiastic pages of praise for *Ulysses*.[95] "John Eglinton" writes from Dublin also in June, devoting nearly half his letter to *Ulysses*;[96] in the September issue Eliot was saying: ". . . so the intelligent literary aspirant, studying Ulysses, will find it more an encyclopedia of what he is to avoid attempting, than of the things he may try for himself. It is at once the exposure and the burlesque of that of which it is the perfection. And Ulysses is not a work which can be compared with any "novel."[97] Eglinton devoted his October 1922 letter to *Ulysses,* mentioned it in February 1923, and had a good deal to say about it in August.[98]

It may well be that Eliot, or the *Dial*'s staff, with whom he would have had to be closely in touch, deliberately postponed the appearance of "*Ulysses,* Order, and Myth" in order to avoid giving their readers a surfeit of notices of this almost (legally) inaccessible work; in any case, not only did the autumn of 1923 bring Eliot's handsome tribute in the *Dial,* but a year before he had included a translation of Valéry Larbaud's lecture in the first issue of his newly founded *Criterion.*[99]

Whenever it was that Eliot actually composed his essay on *Ulysses,* we have further evidence connecting *Ulysses* with *The Waste Land* in his "London Letter" for the *Dial*'s issue of October 1921, just previous to the actual composition of the poem in its next-to-final form during his rest cure. The essay deals partly with the music of Stravinsky and in particular with *Le Sacre du Printemps,* a work which made a particularly strong impression on Eliot, and which has been suggested as an important influence on the formation of his poem.[100] Eliot's criticism and his poetry often went hand in hand (it has been noted in detail, for example, how his reading of Marvell and the Jacobean dramatists bore fruit simultaneously in critical articles and in *The Waste Land*),[101] and read in the light of this fact the Stravinsky essay seems almost to be a prospectus for the poem shortly to take shape:

The Vegetation Rite [in the ballet] . . . was interesting to any one who had read The Golden Bough and similar works . . . . In art there should be interpenetration and metamorphosis. Even The Golden Bough can be read in two ways: as a collection of entertaining myths, or as a revelation of a vanished mind of which our mind is a continuation. [In all of *Sacre* except Stravinsky's music] one missed the sense of the present. [The music] did seem to transform the rhythm of the steppes into the scream of the motor horn . . . the roar of the underground railway, and other barbaric cries of modern life.[102]

Method, materials, and imagery for *The Waste Land* are clearly present here, and earlier in the essay as well; for two paragraphs previously Eliot, trying to sum up what he felt about Stravinsky's music in its "quality of modernity," used an expression that must have puzzled many readers, but was so vividly present in his mind that he did not trouble to explain it: "The effect was like Ulysses with illustrations by the best contemporary illustrator."[103] Joyce's novel, *The Golden Bough,* and "the sound of horns and motors" seem to have had equal importance and intensity in Eliot's thoughts, if not in the notes to his poem.

In the years that followed the publication of *Ulysses* and of Eliot's *Dial* essay, relations between Joyce and Eliot were uniformly cordial, as Joyce's correspondence indicates. It appears that at Joyce's instance Eliot made several attempts to discuss *Ulysses* in the pages of the London *Times Literary Supplement,* but these were steadily frustrated.[104] Not only Eliot's role in the publication of *Finnegans Wake* and of *Ulysses* in England, but his indignant "Message to the Fish," after Joyce's death, testify to his continuing admiration for Joyce. Yet there is evidence that Joyce believed Eliot had drawn largely upon *Ulysses* for material in *The Waste Land.* Although Eliot once remarked that "The Hippopotamus" was the only one of his poems which he was sure Joyce had read, a letter from Joyce to Harriet Weaver dated August 15, 1925, contains a long and amusing parody of *The Waste Land* which is close enough to the original and clever enough in its distortions to indicate a thorough knowledge of the poem on Joyce's part (I, 231). A recent study of punning allusions in *Finnegans Wake* maintains that in its pages Joyce depicts himself and Eliot among the avatars of Shem and Shaun, referring to Eliot as a "masterbilker" and as "Keepy Kevin," who while wandering on the beach (a reference to Eliot's reading of "Proteus") found matter that he could use.[105] If we may believe this account, Joyce did not censure Eliot for borrowing material, but for using it in a way which Joyce thought unduly negative and pessimistic; he also felt resentment that while he languished in what he considered obscurity and neglect, Eliot's use of the same material had brought him fame and fortune (the *Dial* award). Cryptic references to Harriet Weaver, the *Little Review,* and Eliot's proof-reading of *Ulysses* are found; and Joyce seems to have believed that "Proteus" and "Hades" gave Eliot his treatment of the themes of water and dryness, death by water, the figures of Tiresias, the drowned man, the rat, and the dog, and the "carious teeth" (Stephen's badly decayed teeth).[106]

Putting these facts and inferences together we find Eliot, from early 1917 through 1922, an assiduous reader of Joyce's work published and in progress as he and Pound received manuscript instalments; an enthusiastic and frequent commentator in influential periodicals on a book which only a handful of his readers could have known; untiring in his efforts to get *Ulysses* printed and reviewed; at least an occasional visitor to Joyce in Paris; and most importantly we have evidence that in 1919 and 1921 he had subjected "Nestor," "Proteus," "Hades," "Scylla and Charybdis," "The Wandering Rocks," "Oxen of the Sun," "Circe," and "Eumaeus" to the most careful and painstaking scrutiny as editor, adviser, proofreader, future reviewer, and (on the evidence of his letter to Quinn and his Stravinsky essay) as a poet already turning over in his mind the materials of *The Waste Land.* Even if we were to accept the unlikely assumption that Eliot knew the remaining episodes only superficially, it is in the eight episodes which Eliot can be proved to have known most intimately that the submerged metaphor or chain of images which we have been examining appears most prominently and is longest sustained.

VII

If we are to establish that *Ulysses* exerted a significant influence on *The Waste Land,* and in fact furnished matter for it in the form of figures, themes, and images, we must counter four objections. These are:

1. That Eliot did not know *Ulysses* early enough, or well enough, for it to have been influential.

2. That Eliot did not refer to *Ulysses* as a source in the notes to *The Waste Land* or elsewhere.
3. That we cannot clearly identify extended phrases or lines in *The Waste Land* as being identical in wording with passages from *Ulysses.*
4. That, even granting the similarity of figures, motifs, situations, and images in the two works, these might have been derived from other sources as well as from *Ulysses,* since the presumed derivations do not fit into a pattern, but seem random and therefore perhaps coincidental.

We have seen that Eliot knew *Ulysses* very well indeed at the time when his poem was growing on paper and in his mind; and therefore its absence from *The Waste Land* notes is of little importance, for a number of reasons. The notes appeared only with the poem's first printing in book form in December 1922, after it had been twice printed in periodicals and months after its writing and revision; according to Eliot himself they were written partly to fill up pages, partly to forestall the fatuous charges of plagiarism from ignorant critics which had already annoyed him, and (perhaps with tongue in cheek) partly to "elucidate" the poem. Even if they were expansions of jottings made earlier for the second of these purposes, they were decidedly *ex post facto.*[107] Eliot made no pretense of identifying every source, and there is no way of telling which of those later identified by scholars he consciously remembered. For example, the Thames scene in "The Fire Sermon" (ll. 266–276) clearly owes details to Conrad's *Heart of Darkness,* and the correspondence between Eliot and Pound when the latter was editing *The Waste Land* indicates Eliot's original intention to employ Kurtz's "The horror! The horror!" as the poem's epigraph;[108] in 1920 Eliot had evinced his intense interest in Conrad (and Joyce) with the observation in an essay that "the language which is more important to us is that which is struggling to digest and express new objects, new groups of objects, new feelings, new aspects, as, for instance, the prose of Mr. James Joyce or the earlier Conrad."[109] Yet Conrad is not mentioned in the notes. We are obliged to conclude either that the evidence for Eliot's use of Conrad proves nothing at all; or that Eliot consciously borrowed these details from Conrad, deliberately concealing his indebtedness; or simply that Eliot did not record a borrowing from Conrad which he did not remember because he was not conscious of it, or because it had slipped from his memory in the intervening months. Indeed, it would be more surprising than otherwise to find *Ulysses* mentioned in the notes. Most of Eliot's references to particular source passages are documented precisely, with line or page references to guide the reader; and Eliot could hardly have directed his readers to a work which was not generally (or legally) obtainable in the United States or England.

The third and fourth objections mentioned above require more extended discussion, since both involve judgments on the validity of certain critical methods. To what extent must "parallel passages" be identical in wording before we may properly conclude that "borrowing" has taken place? What other criteria may be legitimately used to validate the reader's subjective impression that influence exists? The answer may perhaps be reached through Eliot's own discussions of the poetic process, especially as they apply to his practice.

Much of the critical writing on Eliot's poetry has failed to make the crucial distinction between two processes of composition which he himself saw as highly significant yet clearly different. The first is the conscious borrowing of a distinctive line, phrase, or sentence and inlaying it with or without modification, substitution, or rearrangement of words into the fabric of one's poem, to function with a new meaning because of its new context. This method is typical of Eliot, though he shares it with poets as diverse as Pope and Marianne Moore; and he often though not always gives his source, either directly, as in *The Waste Land* notes, or indirectly, as in the epigraphs of *The Hollow Men*. The notes function partly as an acknowledgment that Eliot recognized this mosaic work as a distinctive feature of his poetic idiom. On the second process he laid much stress as fundamental to great poetry—the perpetual saturation of the poet's mind with images from reading at any artistic level ("from picture papers and cheap novels, indeed, as well as serious books")[110] and from the experiences of life, followed by the intuitive fusing and transmuting of these images under the pressure of emotion during composition. For our purposes the great difference is that in one case the borrowing is conscious, clearly recognized, and remembered—we might compare it to the use of *objets trouvés* in collage—and in the other the mind's work is unperceived, recalled only by an effort of memory or not at all. An example of conscious and acknowledged borrowing with some alteration is the line "But at my back [in a cold blast / from time to time] I hear," which is used twice in *The Waste Land,* with its source in Marvell given in the note to its second appearance. The second process is seen in the conclusion to *The Use of Poetry and the Use of Criticism.* "Why," Eliot asks, "do certain images recur, charged with emotion, rather than others?" He gives as an instance "six ruffians seen through an open window playing cards at night in a small French railway junction where there was a water-mill."[111] He does not say whether he used this image, but we may find it, dispersed and much altered, in "Journey of the Magi":

> Then at dawn we came down to a temperate valley,
> Wet, below the snow line, smelling of vegetation,
> With a running stream and a water-mill beating the darkness,
> . . . .
> Then we came to a tavern with vine-leaves over the lintel,
> Six hands at an open door dicing for pieces of silver,
> And feet kicking the empty wine-skins.

As we find the scenes in Eliot's published writings the only elements they have in common are the water mill and six gamblers, yet few readers would contend that there can have been no connection between the details in Eliot's poem of 1927 and those in the scene recollected in 1932.

Again, coming somewhat closer to the relationship between Joyce and Eliot, Hugh Kenner has traced Eliot's lines in *Gerontion,* "Vacant shuttles / Weave the wind," to passages in *Ulysses* where Stephen Dedalus speaks of weaving the wind.[112] (We should remember that *Gerontion* was to have formed part of *The Waste Land* until Pound persuaded Eliot otherwise.)[113] Despite our willingness to admit that "weave the wind" is a startlingly original image, not likely to have been found elsewhere than in *Ulysses,* we might dismiss the similarity as mere coincidence were it not that the phrase occurs twice in *Ulysses,* a few pages apart (21, 25) and that Joyce's and Eliot's contexts clinch the connection. In the first instance Stephen is thinking of heretics, idle mockers, and his actual words are, "The void awaits surely all them that weave the wind." It is precisely the void that awaits the frivolous, empty people of Gerontion's vision, with a repetition of "wind":

> . . . De Bailhache, Fresca, Mrs. Cammel, whirled
> Beyond the circuit of the shuddering Bear
> In fractured atoms. Gull against the wind, in the windy straits . . .

In the second occurrence of the phrase Stephen, in the classroom, thinking of the meanings and possibilities inherent in history, muses despairingly, "Weave, weaver of the wind." And three lines after his own use of the words Eliot has

> Think now
> History has many cunning passages, contrived corridors
> And issues, deceives with whispering ambitions,
> Guides us by vanities.

It is difficult to deny the influence of *Ulysses* here, where context appears to have generated phrase, or phrase context.

Another instructive example is furnished by the opening phrase of Eliot's "Triumphal March" in *Coriolan*: "Stone, bronze, stone, steel, oakleaves horses' heels / Over the paving." These words echo and must, whether consciously or not, have been derived from Joyce's opening line in "The Sirens": "Bronze by gold heard the hoofirons, steelyringing."[114] Both are opening lines, both combine bronze, horsehoofs, and steel; but more importantly, Joyce repeats his terms again and again in the musical construction of the chapter, and with both Joyce and Eliot the procession introduced is that of an insolent conqueror. But we could not suppose Eliot's line to have been influenced by Joyce's unless we knew (as we do) that Eliot knew "The Sirens." We cannot produce a letter of Eliot's acknowledging the use of the line, and we have no note to the poem giving it as a source, but the three elements that should suffice to prove influence are there—Eliot's knowledge of *Ulysses*, the presence of several connected elements condensed from many scattered repetitions in Joyce into one phrase, and most important, the use of the words or phrases in question to suggest or orchestrate clearly parallel situations or ideas. There is no question of plagiarism, nor any need for an explicit admission by Eliot that he remembered the passage; doubtless he did not retain it consciously. But anyone denying that Joyce's chapter provided material to be catalyzed by Eliot's mind would also have to deny flatly that Eliot had read it, or that he could have stored it in memory if he did read it; or else he would have to produce another passage from Eliot's reading or document an experience from his life which even more clearly combined the words Eliot used with the precise evocative context in which he used them.

VIII

If these three criteria—Eliot's proven knowledge of an episode, verbal similarity to phrases, images, or passages repeatedly used by Joyce, and clear parallelism of contexts—are granted sufficient for our purposes, we may proceed with more confidence to examine *The Waste Land* in the light of the material from *Ulysses* already surveyed. It seems impossible to do more than hesitantly suggest the possibility of influence for such very general parallels as London-Dublin, the Liffey-the Thames, the characters of Tiresias–Bloom–Stephen, or on the other hand for such farfetched similarities as "the Lady of the Rocks" and Molly's exclamation "O rocks" or the fact that both Molly and Madame Sosostris practice cartomancy.[115] (The last parallel is particularly unwise to see as derived from *Ulysses,* since Eliot himself admitted that both name and situation came from a scene in Aldous Huxley's *Crome Yellow,* where Mr. Scogan, disguised as a gypsy woman called "Sesostris," tells fortunes at a charity bazaar.)[116] But if we restrict ourselves to passages which can reasonably be seen as re-arrangements or condensations of thematic material often repeated in *Ulysses,* we discover that these are not scattered loosely about *The Waste Land,* but occur in definite clusters; that they all are related to the images we have already observed surrounding Macintosh and the dog in Joyce's rebirth metaphor or image chain; and that they occur in situations or contexts which closely parallel those of Joyce.

The materials—figures or groups of images—in *The Waste Land* which appear to bear the closest relationship with the matter of *Ulysses* may be summarized as follows:

I. "THE BURIAL OF THE DEAD"

1. Death by water, the drowned sailor, 47, 55
2. Ariel's song, 48
3. The dog, 74–75

II. "A GAME OF CHESS"

4. "Rats' alley," dead men, bones, 115–116
5. Ariel's song, 125
6. HURRY UP PLEASE ITS TIME, 141, 152, 165, 168, 169

III. "THE FIRE SERMON"

7. "Rat," "rattle," "bones," 186–187, 193–194
8. Ferdinand (Ariel's song), 189–192
9. The Thames-daughters' narratives, 292–305

IV. "DEATH BY WATER"

10. "Picked his bones;" "Gentile or Jew," 316, 319

V. "WHAT THE THUNDER SAID"

11. Thunder, mountains, rain, "he is dead," 326–343
12. The hooded figure, 360–366
13. Cock, bones, thunder, rain, 391–400
14. The happy boat, 419–423
15. Ferdinand, 424–425

These figures and passages are related, just as in Joyce, by repetition and juxtaposition (though Eliot had arrived at this method long before he knew *Ulysses*); but their associations with Joyce's novel are of three kinds.

1. More or less isolated from the remainder are Nos. 6 and 9. Eliot does not connect them by verbal linkage with the rest; each, as we have seen, is strikingly parallel both in wording and in context to a particular passage in *Ulysses* which Eliot knew well. They might be properly seen as "imitations" in the sense in which Pope used the term for his Horatian poems. The Thames-daughters are closer in speech to Florry, Kitty, and Zoe than to Wellgunde, Woglinde, and Flosshilde; and the parallelism of the situations in which "Time" is called in "A Game of Chess" and "Oxen of the Sun" is reinforced by the fact that both episodes embody hostile criticism of the Waste Land practice of contraception.

2. The Dog and hooded figure (Nos. 3 and 12) occur but once. However, they are connected to the remaining images common to Joyce and Eliot by a multitude of associational threads. They may be regarded as extreme concentrations by Eliot of material widely dispersed through *Ulysses*; they will be discussed in greater detail below.

3. The remaining images—Ferdinand and Ariel, drowned and buried bodies, bones, rats, thunder, rain, and so on—run like a loose skein through the organization of both works. But in addition to their sporadic occurrence in *Ulysses,* as indicated above, they occur in con-

centrated juxtaposition in the parallel and simultaneous meditations of Stephen and Bloom upon the resurrection of the dead in "Hades" and "Proteus" (each in the last page or two of its chapter; 50–51, 114–115), most of them being found in both passages. We know that Eliot had given both episodes professional scrutiny; and the similarity of wording and imagery in both suggests that Joyce was consciously trying to indicate the identity of the two trains of thought by their remarkable number of parallels: both corpses, for example, are "salt-white" (50, 114). It is even harder to believe that Eliot could have escaped having this assemblage of repeated thematic material driven into his mind, to be resurrected in *The Waste Land* with a similar artistic end in view (especially since all the relevant images are clustered together) than it is to suppose that they came at random from other possible sources and happened to coalesce in the manner in which they occur both in his poem and Joyce's novel. Further, in translating "Death by Water" from the French of "Dans le Restaurant" Eliot made cuts, but only five significant changes—"dead" for "noyé," "whirlpool," "picked his bones," "Gentile or Jew," and a final line to rhyme with "Jew." "Picked his bones" may certainly be taken as an echo of Joyce; and it is hardly farfetched, in the light of the other evidence, to regard the new combination "Gentile or Jew" both as a reminiscence of Stephen and Bloom and a memory of Joyce's emphasis on their spiritual identity when facing the deadness of the dead.

The closeness of wording and context between Eliot and Joyce with regard to the first and third categories of material discussed here may reasonably convince us that Eliot derived them from *Ulysses*; but the Dog and the hooded figure require more extended consideration. If they are derived from Joyce they are not mere echoes, but radical condensations, amounting to metamorphoses, of the figures in Joyce's submerged metaphor; and the context in which they operate is not a mere scene or situation, but rather the entire stratum of gropingly religious thought in both works. We must show that Eliot's creative poetizing produced them as central to a vision of modern man which he perceived in *Ulysses* and to which he developed a parallel in *The Waste Land.* To do this we must perforce adopt a method of "mental detection" analogous to that employed by Lowes in *The Road to Xanadu.* It may be objected that from this method conclusive proof by modern scholarly standards is impossible. Yet Eliot himself, in *On Poetry and Poets* and *The Use of Poetry and the Use of Criticism,* repeatedly stressed the high significance of such a method (specifically referring to Lowes's book) and the important role of the unconscious in poetic creation—perhaps because he recognized an affinity between what Lowes had revealed and the results of introspection on the working of his own poetic imagination.[117] Here and elsewhere he placed unusual emphasis upon the role of memory in storing the materials from which a poem's images might be constructed, but he was repeatedly careful to point out that these memories are *transmuted* or *fused* to become the material of the poem in creation, using the famous simile of gases in a chamber which react to form a new compound in the presence of a catalytic filament of platinum, to which he compares the poet's mind. Eliot himself saw the essential function of the poet's creative mind as the ability to combine, or more properly to fuse under intense pressure (of emotion) many disparate images. A recent critic has observed how strongly Eliot "emphasizes the associative power of the imagination (or what he designates as the mind's 'saturation' in images, which are unified by a basic emotion), arguing that Coleridge undervalues the function of memory, the power to recall images."[118]

Eliot is vaguer about the nature of the "basic emotion" that may unify disparate images. In *The Use of Poetry and the Use of Criticism* he implicitly makes the distinction we have noted above between the use of another's word or phrase to "give a new meaning or extract a latent one," which is found in Shakespeare, and the situation in "much good poetry" where "the organization will not reach so rational a level." He gives as an example of the latter the "circuit of the shuddering Bear" from *Gerontion,* which he recognizes as borrowed from the "chariot of the snowy Bear" in the *Bussy D'Ambois* of Chapman, who in turn borrowed it from "sub cardine glacialis ursae" in Seneca's *Hercules Furens* and "sub plaustro patiuntur ursae" in his *Hercules Oetaeus.* Eliot goes on to say:

> There is first the probability that this imagery had some personal saturation value, so to speak, for Seneca; another for Chapman, and another for myself. . . . I suggest that what gives it such intensity as it has in each case is its saturation—I will not say with "associations" . . . but with feelings too obscure for the authors even to know quite what they were.[119]

We cannot trace feelings too obscure for their possessors to define; but we can note a unifying similarity of *context* in Seneca, Chapman, and Eliot, for in each case the Bear is made a concrete indication of farthest

North, and each case it is opposed to the tropics—"sub ortu solis," "quique ferventi quatiuntur axe," "fly where men feel / The burning axletree," and "the Gulf . . . the Trades." We may suspect that the "associations" to which Eliot prefers the term "feelings" may yet be a reliable index to the degree of relationship between an image of his and a suspected source, and that the "less rational" mode of organization in borrowing consists of developing a roughly similar set of images to be the formula of a very similar underlying idea. But we should also note that Eliot's description of the poet's creative act lays great stress both on the *store* of images and on the passive, involuntary, unconscious nature of the process.[120] It is the reverse of the idea which many critics tacitly allow to dominate their thinking—that of the poet carefully and consciously deciding which words should go where. Eliot's declared mode of poetic action is far closer to Pope's "compose with fury, but correct with phlegm."

IX

This being the case, can we demonstrate a clear similarity of context between *Ulysses* and *The Waste Land,* pervasive in both, perceivable by Eliot, and such that if it were perceived in Joyce's novel it could generate a similarity of poetic meaning and symbolic function between Joyce's dog and man and those of Eliot? Are the two pairs of figures the formula of the same idea? The answer would seem to lie in Eliot's specific opinions on the achievement of *Ulysses,* in particular as to its ultimate meaning, its moral force.

Eliot's admiration for Joyce and for *Ulysses* was made clear in his letters and by his efforts in behalf of book and author; his understanding of the enormous significance of Joyce's innovation in the use of myth and of language was proclaimed in his periodical essays. Further opinions he did not commit to paper, and these did not transpire until the publication of Virginia Woolf's diary. To her he made several significant comments: he was "for the first time in [her] knowledge rapt, enthusiastic," and thought *Ulysses* "on a par with *War and Peace.*" "How could anyone write again after achieving the immense prodigy of the last chapter?" Eliot apparently praised the book to Mrs. Woolf on several occasions; but something was to be said on the other side. Joyce had "left out many things that were important." *Ulysses* had "no great conception; that was not Joyce's intention. . . .

[Eliot] did not think that he gave a new insight into human nature—said nothing new like Tolstoy. Bloom told one nothing . . . this new method of giving the psychology . . . doesn't tell as much as some casual glance from the outside often tells."[121]

What are we to make of these elusive fragments of criticism? If Eliot's thinking about *Ulysses* was reasoned and consistent, they must be of central importance, must fit into the frame of mind which he dramatized in *The Waste Land.* What had Joyce left out? In what sense did Bloom tell one nothing? The answer is not difficult to give, especially in view of the significant reference to Tolstoy and Eliot's complaint at the lack of a "great conception." The writer who a decade later was to voice his conviction that Joyce's work was "penetrated with Christian feeling," "with orthodoxy of sensibility and with the sense of tradition," and that Joyce was "the most ethically orthodox of the more eminent writers" of his time,[122] may by then have changed his view of institutional Christianity; but had he changed his view of Joyce? The two sets of statements are not incompatible if we assume that Eliot was at once acutely conscious of the enormous amount of Christian matter in *Ulysses,* of its Christian ethical tone and its "orthodox" sensibility, and acutely pained at the book's failure to point this material in a clearly and explicitly religious direction by dramatizing a "great [and therefore ultimately religious] conception," as Tolstoy surely would have done. A quest—man seeking—is as basic to the movement of *Ulysses* as it is to *The Waste Land,* but the Grail of Bloom and Stephen remains forever obscured in the novel's labyrinthine thickets. Further, we know that specifically religious thought and symbols had ceased to mean to Joyce what they meant then and later to Eliot. Long past the stage of mocking at or rebelling against the Church, Joyce, like Stephen Dedalus, was making perpetual and ingenious use (ingenious as only the "cursed jesuit strain injected backwards" could make it) of the intricate matter of formalized Catholic thought and ritual to body forth his secular religion of art and the physical world.[123] Eliot sought religion out (or was seeking out a means of belief) in 1921; he must have seen in *Ulysses* something of what younger poets, such as Kathleen Raine, saw in his own work:

[Eliot's] stern vision of the hell that lies about us in modern London [had] a quality of grave consolation. . . . The shallow progressive philosophies both religious and secular of our parents' generation sought to eliminate evil from the world. Mr. Eliot's vision of hell restored a necessary dimension to our universe. . . . All those who have lived in the Waste Land of London can, I suppose, remember the particular occasion on which, reading T. S. Eliot's poems for the first time, an experience of the contemporary world that had been nameless and formless, suddenly received its apotheosis.[124]

Most critics, perhaps misled by the panoply of references to fertility rites and primitive cults in *The Waste Land,* have emphasized the way in which the poem subsumes all religion, and have made the Golden Bough outdazzle the Cross. There is no question that Eliot's aims were as large as possible, but a full account of the poem should not deny that it is organized around a quest for *Christian* truth, and around the central mysteries of Christianity—incarnation, crucifixion, death with resurrection. Through the symbolic structure of *The Waste Land* runs an ironically twisted, encoded progression from Good Friday to Easter and Whitsun, by way of Emmaus. Eliot, despite his admiration—perhaps, and pardonably, envious—for Joyce's prodigious technique, must have regarded *Ulysses* as an enormous *tour de force* representing the barren City without God. With his bent for allusion and symbolic pattern and his religious orientation, he would have found in Joyce's all-encompassing day in Dublin an incomparably rich and detailed literary realization of just the sterility, futility, and chaos that his poem would depict; he would have found in Stephen and Bloom two characters by no means distantly approximating the opposite types he had created in Prufrock, paralyzed by intellect, and Sweeney, imprisoned in the body; he would certainly have found an abundance of Christian symbolism parodied, masked, and misconstrued in just the way that his own symbols would be veiled from the inhabitants of the "Unreal City" though discoverable by the perceptive reader. In particular he could have observed that the figures of the dog and the man in the macintosh are repeatedly perceived and misunderstood by Stephen and Bloom.

It is important here to make a distinction between the parallels, subtleties, and symbols of Joyce as we see them with the help of five decades of analysis and explication, and the first impressions which *Ulysses* would have made in the postwar years on a mind such as Eliot's, however perceptive and symbol-oriented. We know that many highly sophisticated literary men were decidedly puzzled by their first experience of *Ulysses* and found clarification only gradually as they read the explanations of others; the climate of opinion was ill prepared for the complexity of reading that Joyce invites.[125] Simple Christian symbols, traditional and familiar, surrounded Joyce's dog and man in abundance, however; and these would have been no more puzzling to Eliot than the emblems of efficacy or allegorical animals in a religious painting of the Renaissance. These symbols could be read to indicate that in *Ulysses,* beginning between eleven and noon (the Roman "ninth hour" of the Crucifixion), simultaneously in Glasnevin Cemetery and on Sandymount strand, Christ "was crucified, dead, and buried; he descended into Hell" and then arose and thereafter walked among men unknown and offering his message in vain; but that these sacred events were lost on Stephen and Bloom, before whose eyes they took place.

Reading by hindsight and using as guides the images and ideas of *The Waste Land* and Eliot's earlier work, it is not difficult to see Bloom and Stephen as Wastelanders. Bloom, far less brutal than Sweeney, is a relatively simple, good-hearted *homme moyen sensuel;* he is impotent both with his wife and in what is nowadays called "life fulfillment." He seems never destined for more than a modest getting-by. He is trapped by the flesh and by the City's necessities; his goals are secular. An avid inquirer after worldly knowledge, he is hopelessly desultory in its pursuit and muddled in what he makes of it. Rootless—a Jew by birth, a Christian by baptism merely (Protestant, Catholic, and now Freemason)—he behaves in an exemplarily Christian manner throughout the novel, yet it is Bloom who according to Eliot "told one nothing"; certainly, though he may be a model for those who lead lives of quiet desperation and though he is a pattern of human, secular love and charity, he is a prisoner of the world, hardly likely to have represented for Eliot an ideal of anything more than living "with a little patience." Indeed, Joyce himself may have conceived Bloom as being able to "tell one nothing" in the religious sense: Lionel Trilling, in a recent investigation of Joyce's thought based upon his novels and *Exiles* as well as his correspondence, comes to the following striking conclusion regarding Bloom's insulation from the struggles, sorrows, and glories of the religious life:

> [Bloom's] innocence, it would appear, is part of Joyce's conception of Jews in general, who, he seems to have felt, through some natural grace were exempt from the complexities of the moral life as it was sustained by Christians. . . . Christian kindness would result from the making of a choice between doing the good deed and not doing it, and would therefore, by

> the Aristotelian definition, be moral; but a Jewish good deed was a matter of instinct, natural rather than moral. It is in natural goodness rather than morality that Mr. Bloom has his being. . . .[126]

Whatever the agnostic may think, the Christian or would-be Christian is obliged to regard Bloom's works without faith, strictly considered, as no more than sounding brass or a tinkling cymbal.

Stephen likewise fits well into the Wastelander pattern, though his defects of love are not Bloom's. Having rejected the Church in the wilful pride of intellect, he remains dominated by its modes of thought and lacerated by his guilt. His defiant *non serviam* characterizes him, at least for the time, as an Antichrist; his religion of art has as yet resulted in nothing. He too is impotent—as an artist—frustrated as a man; he has not even achieved Bloom's modest ability to cope with the secular City. However, the forms and shows of religion obsess and torment him. He is the opposite of Bloom in this respect, as in most others; in Eliot's terms the union of the two, galvanized by a revelation of religious truth, might result in a whole, reintegrated man. The two are united in "Ithaca" in whatever sense one chooses, but the revelation is consistently denied. Bloom and Stephen are made to go through their quests just askew of religious truth, and for the Eliot of the *Waste Land* period their tantalizing nearness to what might have saved them would have been constantly indicated by ironic, symbolic encounters—most often, as with his own characters, by but not in the waters of Babylon-Dublin, as hydrophobe and waterlover wander aimlessly.

X

Our examination of the clusters of imagery involved throughout *Ulysses* with the dog figure and the man in the macintosh has necessarily been lengthy, and has resorted at times to seemingly frivolous means of interpretation. These characteristics have been dictated by the copiousness of material with which Joyce surrounds these figures, the frequency with which they occur, and the very evident fact that Joyce, far from being solemn in working out his epic, was prone to be jocoserious. The sheer abundance of material, however, lends weight to the contention that Joyce saw these enigmatic beings as highly important, and as showings-forth of God, particularly as manifested in the Messianic functions of raising the dead and appearing at the Last Judgment. The very ridiculousness of one figure and the perverse elusiveness of the other make them particularly relevant to Joyce's idea of the miraculous epiphanizing powers of the artist's eye. For Joyce to choose a dog, the Hebrew symbol of filth and his own constant aversion, as an epiphany of the Deity was a triumphant commentary on his theory. Stephen, however, is not yet an artist in *Ulysses*, and it is altogether fitting that he should at first echo Joyce's actual feelings,[127] going beyond them only in the "Circe" episode when his artisthood has at last been totally asserted. But to perceive God through the artist's eye and through the Christian's are far different matters, and there is no reason to suppose, as some critics have, that Joyce was or had again become a Christian when he wrote *Ulysses*.[128] The fact remains that the images which surround the dog and man are for the most part (with the notable exception of the esoteric "K 11") not those of any recondite or private symbolism, but rather those familiar in Christian symbol and iconography as pertaining to the enactment in the life of Christ and in the Church's ritual of the central Christian mysteries. Joyce never says that the man in the macintosh is the particular embodiment of the risen Christ whom one could see in Dublin on Bloomsday, yet the one common denominator of all the facts we learn about him comes to precisely that. Joyce says only once with unmistakable clarity that God is God to the blessed and Dog to the damned, yet again the one common denominator of all that he does say about the dog in *Ulysses* is that the dog brings the dead out of the earth, that he is a friend, and that his attributes, though seen only and never interpreted, are not those of a real dog but of a supernatural being. Dog and man are perpetual puzzles to Dubliners as to Wastelanders. And it is precisely these essential facts which Eliot epiphanizes in his two figures.

If the dog and the man were God as the risen Christ for Joyce, or at any rate that among other things, what is their significance for understanding Eliot's Dog and "hooded figure"? The Dog in the first section of *The Waste Land* has many levels of meaning, the most obvious having been explained by Eliot in his note to line 74. But in developing complex images in this poem to their fullest implications it is prudent to remember two facts: a note of Eliot's is often not a complete explanation of a line—indeed it may serve (either by a deliberate attempt of Eliot's or from our natural tendency to rest in the printed word) to lead us off the track—and that everything a Wastelander says is apt to be a distorted, misunderstood version of the truth, or the truth expressed in a code which our blind guides can no longer understand (as with Madame Sosostris' "*Fear* death by water" and the fact that she is forbidden to see what the Man with Three Staves carries on his back). Eliot's Dog, still an enigma, has provoked a remarkable variety of speculations and disagreements among commentators. It has been dealt with as a projection of the "gros chien" of "Dans le Restaurant" (the poem of death by drowning, part of which was incorporated with important changes into *The Waste Land*), as the interrupter of sensual pleasure, and as the exhumer of buried disgraces; it has been seen as an allusion to Stephen's fox riddle.[129] Coming somewhat closer to the tenor of our discussion, one commentator has envisaged it as the Hound of Heaven, and three have very briefly considered the possibilities of the Dog-God palindrome.[130] It is of course clear that Eliot's two lines about the Dog (74–75) are a parody of Webster's about the wolf. The corpse concerning which Tiresias asks Stetson as they meet on the way to the office is apparently that of a fellow-Wastelander, a sort of bulb, "feeding / A little life with dried tubers," for Tiresias wishes to know if the spring has made it sprout or if an untimely frost has nipped it. He hopes that no dog has interrupted its normal process of growth by digging it up before its time. It would seem that like Bloom and Stephen, Tiresias prefers to think of the dead as thoroughly buried, due to "bloom" (an unconscious reference to Bloom?) at some happily indefinite time in the future, but best left entirely to the tender mercies of the earth. The arrival of new life is for the Wastelander a disturbing notion rather than a hope; if new life comes it will shatter his complacency, raising all sorts of disquieting questions to break up the status quo. In any case the metamorphosis should not be hastened, and any intervention from above the earth (resurrection is an "unnatural," not to say miraculous, process) should be avoided at all costs. Eliot's equation of corpses and spring bulbs serves to enclose and thus define an idea that is not stated. At the same time Tiresias, like Bloom, recognizes that the Dog, whatever he is, is "friend to men," even though he should be prevented from digging tubers up with his well-meaning nails. The unchristian horror with which Stephen (until "Circe") and Bloom (in "Hades") view the idea of "digging up" their dead is perfectly paralleled here. We also remember that in Bloom's thoughts the dog is often associated with "nails," the nails of the Crucifixion. Webster's tone here gives a key to Eliot's associative process; it is a fine Jacobean or baroque pun ("God's nails" was no uncommon oath) to say that Christ is the Dog who with his "nails" performed in a supreme demonstration of "friendship," the sacrifice that enables him to "dig up" or resurrect both himself and mankind. We should also remember that Stephen's dog is often a wolf, and that in Christian symbolism the paradox that the tamed wolf becomes a dog, which is then the ally of man against his wolfish enemy, was often stressed.[131] Eliot's lines, if we see them through *Ulysses,* are a very complex pun upon Christian doctrine, expressed in the manner of Joyce's characters, false prophets who in spite of themselves proclaim through imagery that dog is God. The capitalization of Eliot's "Dog" is a final clue to the statement of truth that Tiresias says but cannot see, for it is hard to discover why else the honorific capital should be bestowed.[132] We have here not a word-for-word borrowing with re-alignment, as in the verbal echoes discussed above, but rather the result of a sorting and condensing process—Eliot's perception that a single meaning inhered in a great many of Joyce's scattered references to the same figure, and his own rendering of this figure, transmuted, with such vivid accidents "fused" into it from yet another source as to sum up what he must have perceived in Joyce's tracing of the dog through the novel's elaborate fabric. Thus if we consciously reconstruct what the poet's mind intuitively accomplished, we can say that in poetic shorthand Dog, nails, digging up the dead, "friend to men," and the necessity of keeping the animal at a distance were sufficient clues in Eliot's parallel context of blinded men in the secular city to evoke all the associations with which Joyce constantly surrounded his figure—Dog as God, Dog as digger, Dog as a thing to be feared—but the "formula of the emotion" was ready to hand in Webster's couplet. Tiresias and Stetson in their tiny but significant scene are a distillation of Bloom and Stephen, and through them of all Wastelanders who to their everlasting loss prefer to let sleeping dogs lie.[133]

The figure "Gliding wrapt in a brown mantle, hooded" of Part V of *The Waste Land* has been identified by Eliot with the journey to Emmaus, and its source with an account of one of the Antarctic expeditions. Clearly Eliot's figure represents the risen Christ, denied by those slow to believe; but an examination of the source Eliot lists produces interesting results. When Eliot wrote his note, his memory was evidently vague; he was not sure which account had struck him, but believed that it was Shackleton's. Eliot was in fact remembering a passage from Shackleton's *South.* It is worth quoting, for what it did not furnish him is as interesting and significant as what it did.

[Worsley, a member of the expedition, after a rest at base camp, was sent back to relieve three others.] Curiously enough, they did not recognize Worsley, who had left them a hairy, dirty ruffian and had returned his spruce and shaven self. They thought he was one of the whalers. . . . Then it suddenly dawned upon them that they were talking to the man who had been their close companion for a year and a half. . . . When I [Shackleton] look back . . . I have no doubt that Providence guided us. . . . I know that during the long and racking march . . . it seemed to me often that we were four, not three. . . . Worsley said to me, "Boss, I had a curious feeling on the march that there was another person with us." Crean confessed to the same idea. One feels "the dearth of human words, the roughness of mortal speech" in trying to describe things intangible, but a record of our journeys would be incomplete without a reference to a subject very near to our hearts.[134]

Here we have the return of a companion changed in appearance who is at first not recognized, providential guidance, the feeling that there is an extra person; but we do not have a *brown* mantle, ambiguous sex, or the repeated question, "Who is that?" It is plausible, in view of Eliot's reading, that *Ulysses* was the source of two of these details, as we have seen from Bloom's constant self-questioning about Macintosh's identity, Stephen's vague perceptions of an unseen presence, the mysterious stranger's often-mentioned *brown* garment, and Joyce's elaborate association of him with the risen Christ. The sexual ambiguity is of course proper to Tiresias and the all-inclusive nature of Eliot's characters, but Bloom too makes the sexual transference while wondering about Macintosh's identity in "The Sirens" (290). The Shackleton passage is indeed imbued with religious feeling, but Eliot could not have found in Shackleton the continual symbolic reference to Christ with which Joyce surrounded Macintosh. Certainly Joyce's figure amplifies the resonances of Eliot's far more than does Eliot's acknowledged source.

If Eliot perceived, with his remarkable literary acuteness, the aura of intricately woven, jumbled, and distorted Christian symbolism which has been indicated here, how did he relate it to his poetic symbols and condense it into the few lines which he gave to his Dog and hooded figure? We cannot suppose that he recognized more than a fraction of it; but even this would have been enough to make him realize that God was hidden behind Joyce's dog and man. The few indications he gave are the crucial ones; such an image as the Dog's nails, for example, though consciously recalled later as belonging to Webster's wolf, can be equally related to many recurring juxtapositions of dog, nails, and digging up the dead in *Ulysses*. The method of Eliot's poetry is in one way opposite to that of Joyce's prose; repetition must give way to the single sharp essential image. To indicate that Joyce said many times what Eliot said once is to sum up both the method and the relationship of their two epics.

Barring the unlikely discovery of a Gutch Memorandum Book for *The Waste Land*, a follower of Lowes cannot demonstrate on a scale commensurate with its subject the process by which Eliot incorporated Joyce's images, phrases, and characters by three of his distinctive poetic methods into parts of his poem. The parallels are there; and Eliot's figures take on new and larger dimensions and clearer meanings if traced to Joyce's. Eliot stressed more and understood better than perhaps any other critic the importance of the unconscious storing and saturation of a poet's mind with images from reading and from life. When he wrote to Joyce "I wish for my own sake that I had not read it," he may have been lamenting a suspected invasion of his storehouse of poetic material;[135] but the invasion is not to be regretted. It was an enrichment for Eliot. For us it is a key to the meaning of *The Waste Land* and *Ulysses*, a means to enlarge our understanding of each by viewing it through the illumination of the other. The multileveled dog and man offer clues to the discovery that the connection between these seminal modernist epics is far closer and more intricate than has been suspected. To borrow Eliot's own words from one of his notes, "The collocation of these two . . . is not an accident."

Acknowledgments

I wish to acknowledge the valuable assistance of Mr. Milton Malkin; Professor Bernard Benstock, Kent State University; Mr. Herbert Cahoon, The Pierpoint Morgan Library; Professors Phyllis Bartlett and Leo Walsh, Queens College; and Professor Robert Scholes, University of Iowa. In particular I wish to express my appreciation of the courtesy of Dr. Lola Szladits, Curator of the Berg Collection in the New York Public Library, in whose care the Eliot manuscripts are now preserved, and who facilitated my access to them.

APPENDIX

THE ELIOT MANUSCRIPTS

The hypothetical nature of much of the foregoing study will have been apparent to the reader; but further and more solid evidence is now in hand. Some months after I had set down my conjectures, one of the most tantalizing literary mysteries of modern times—the whereabouts of Eliot's manuscripts which had been in the possession of John Quinn—was cleared up by the announcement that they had been acquired by the Berg Collection of the New York Public Library. Donald Gallup's bibliographical description of these manuscripts, which appeared in the London *Times Literary Supplement* for November 7, 1968, and was reprinted with some revisions in the *Bulletin of the New York Public Library, LXXII* (December, 1968), 641–652, with its reproductions of three pages of the manuscript of *The Waste Land,* furnishes an admirably precise and detailed guide to the nature and contents of the collection and I shall refer to it (using the later version, which has clearer photographic reproductions) in the discussion that follows.

The manuscript of *The Waste Land* will keep scholars busy for decades, for aside from the question of Ezra Pound's function as "il miglior fabbro" in giving the poem its final form, the lines and phrases, to say nothing of the sections, which Eliot did not choose to print furnish abundant, important clues to his original and intermediate intentions. But our concern is with the relation of the manuscripts to *Ulysses;* and on this point there is significant evidence.

A properly detailed study of the manuscript, and any direct quotation from its contents, must await its publication in facsimile, in an edition by Mrs. Valerie Eliot. But through Mrs. Eliot's kind permission the Berg manuscripts have now been made available for examination by scholars, and I have been granted the opportunity to study their contents.

What Eliot's "lost" manuscripts reveal concerning the relation between *The Waste Land* and *Ulysses* falls into two categories, the general (similarities in ideas, themes, images) and the specific (the handling of individual words and phrases). A discussion of the former must in any case be somewhat conjectural, and cannot be presented in detailed form until the whole manuscript is available in reproduction so that the reader may judge for himself. The following notes, therefore, must carry varying degrees of conviction.

THE DOG

It has long been noted as significant that a "gros chien" appeared to disturb the reminiscing waiter's childish amours in that portion of "Dans le Restaurant" which Eliot did not use in translation for *The Waste Land,* and this dog has been speculatively connected with the Dog "that's friend to men" of line 74. An even closer connection is observable in the manuscript (Gallup, p. 650, [18]) for here the big dog is a *friendly* one.

The long section in Popean couplets describing the lady Fresca, which was intended for "The Fire Sermon" but remained unpublished (Gallup, pp. 643–44), contains at one point speculations on the various roles which the lady might have filled had Fate so decreed, women being adaptable and various. One of these is that of a strumpet, who is vividly presented with details that strikingly recall Stephen's gypsy strumpet in "Proteus," "calling under her brown shawl from an archway where dogs have mired" (47).

Lastly, in line 74 Eliot had originally given the Dog the same epithet as Webster's Wolf (Gallup, p. 643), but canceled this prenominal adjective and substituted the published reading in pencil.

"PROTEUS"

We have seen that "Proteus," especially the concluding passage, had been firmly impressed on Eliot's mind, and that Joyce believed him to have made use of it. It is likely, however, that the force with which this last passage impressed Eliot was due not only to its poetic power but also to the fact that its imagery was closely related to an image cluster which seems to have been almost obsessive with Eliot—the picture of a drowned man moved to and fro with the currents, his flesh dissolving amid beautiful or grotesque undersea fauna and flora. *Prufrock,* the Phlebas passage, and "Mr. Apollinax" furnish the most notable examples. Two poems among the miscellaneous leaves which accompany the *Waste Land* manuscript—"Dirge" and an untitled poem (Gallup, p. 646, [11], [12])—were apparently intended by Eliot for possible inclusion in *The Waste Land*; they are certainly, as Gallup suggests, mentioned by Pound in his correspondence (see D. D. Paige, ed., *The Letters of Ezra Pound, 1907–1941* [New York, 1950], pp. 169–170 and especially lines 13–15 of the poem on p. 170). Both describe a drowned man (who incidentally, suggesting Bloom, is a Jew in one), and Ariel's song is introduced, in part grotesquely parodied. The imagery is remarkably similar in detail to Stephen's fancies about the appearance of the drowned man (50).

Joyce's suspicion about the origin of the "carious teeth" in line 339 of *The Waste Land* is perhaps reinforced by the fact that in the manuscript the adjective modifying "teeth" is a homelier one, appropriate to the badly decayed teeth which Stephen refers to (50), and used by Buck Mulligan

(14) in reference to the deplorable state of Irish teeth. It has been canceled by Eliot; the published reading replaces it.

Line 423, which now reads "I sat upon the shore," gave Eliot a good deal of trouble, and three versions were tried. One of the two canceled lines is in the second, not the third person (as in much of Stephen's "Proteus" soliloquy), and the personage on the shore is not stationary but evidently walking, at least a possible reminiscence of Stephen's wanderings.

The handwritten page photographically reproduced in Gallup's article contains three elements which are at least of hypothetical interest. The section, as Gallup notes (p. 644, n.), is a description of a shipwreck, inspired by the Ulysses canto of Dante's *Inferno*; it also contains echoes of Tennyson's "Ulysses." Joyce's *Ulysses* may or may not have been in Eliot's mind when he composed it; but it will be noted that the ladies singing in the rigging are unmistakably Sirens, and their perch (the final word of the seventh line from the bottom) corresponds to the unorthodox equipment of Joyce's three-master at the conclusion of "Proteus," insisted on by Joyce as an emblem of the Crucifixion.

POUND'S ANNOTATIONS

Pound's marginal notes are mostly of three kinds—exclamations of approval, sarcastic extrapolations, and notes justifying cuts on the grounds of insufficient impact, lack of logic, or unsuitable associations for the context. But two of them seem to indicate that Pound believed Joyce to be lurking in the background of Eliot's work.

At line 64 Eliot has tried two possibilities for the final verb, each twice, before settling on the published "exhaled." Pound has penciled Joyce's initials in the margin. It may be argued that the two letters could stand for something else; but they occur elsewhere with an unmistakable addition. At line 125, after the concluding words of the published version from Ariel's song, Pound has canceled the final word (an exclamation) to give the present reading. The canceled word is also the last word of *Ulysses*, or so Pound must have thought, for in the margin he has written, underlined, the title of the novel's last episode, with the two initials repeated. Pound must therefore have known that Eliot had seen "Penelope" in its final manuscript form, since he expected him to understand what was meant; and the fact that his association of a very common word with "Penelope" was made at all is an argument for the strength of his conviction that Joyce was involved here.

"I AM THE RESURRECTION AND THE LIFE"

One of the fragments among the miscellaneous *Waste Land* leaves is a short untitled poem (Gallup, p. 646, [8]). Like the rest, it may have been tentatively intended as part of *The Waste Land*. In content and imagery it is not unlike Emerson's "Brahma," involving the ubiquity of God. But it is also remarkably like a passage in "Scylla and Charybdis," which Eliot wrote Quinn he had been "living on" ever since he read it. This passage

(185) is part of Stephen's soliloquy, echoed elsewhere in *Ulysses* (301, 510), the second repetition being immediately after the mournful narratives of the three whores in "Circe." It satirizes "AE" (George Russell) and theosophy, but it also echoes the *Bhagavad Gita*—"I am the fire upon the altar. I am the sacrificial butter"—and the reader must decide for himself whether Eliot was drawing his inspiration from Hindu or Irish scripture.

To discuss the implications of these notes in relation to *Ulysses* would require a tedious and space-consuming recapitulation of many points made in the preceding pages. Individually, these pieces of evidence would demonstrate little; taken together, and in the light of our knowledge of what *Ulysses* had come to mean to Eliot, they further establish the importance of the novel's rebirth metaphor, "Proteus," and the dog, to Eliot's poetic process; more (and this is a subject which awaits future investigation), they illustrate how intimately these figures were related to metaphors which were already an organic and central part of Eliot's poetic thinking. The importance of Pound's excisions will long be debated; that he perceived the significance of the role of *Ulysses* in generating Eliot's poem seems now to be incontestable.

REFERENCE MATTER

McCanles: Mythos and Dianoia

1 Northrop Frye, *Anatomy of Criticism* (Princeton, N.J., 1957), pp. 77–78, 83.
2 R. S. Crane, "The Concept of Plot and the Plot of *Tom Jones*," in *Critics and Criticism*, ed. R. S. Crane (Phoenix Books; Chicago, 1957), p. 64.
3 Frye, *Anatomy of Criticism*, pp. 244–245.
4 Aristotle, *Poetics*, trans. Ingram Bywater, in *The Basic Works of Aristotle*, ed. Richard McKeon (New York, 1941), p. 1461.
5 *A Grammar of Motives* (New York, 1954), p. 38.
6 *Poetics*, p. 1462.
7 Ibid., pp. 1463, 1465, 1467.
8 Frye, *Anatomy of Criticism*, p. 214.
9 F. M. Cornford, *Plato's Theory of Knowledge* (London, 1960), *Theaetetus*, 115D, p. 43; Aristotle, *Metaphysics*, 982B: "For it is owing to their wonder that men both now begin and at first began to philosophize," *The Basic Works of Aristotle*, p. 692.
10 Martin Heidegger, *Being and Time*, trans. John Macquarrie and Edward Robinson (New York and Evanston, 1962), p. 51; the italics are Heidegger's.
11 Ibid., pp. 52–53; the italics are Heidegger's.
12 Kenneth Burke, *The Rhetoric of Religion: Studies in Logology* (Boston, 1961), p. 195.
13 Ibid., p. 174.
14 Kenneth Burke, *The Philosophy of Literary Form* (Vintage Books; New York, 1957), pp. 63–64.
15 Immanuel Kant, *Critique of Judgment*, trans. J. H. Bernard (New York, 1951), p. 222.
16 John Donne, *Selected Prose*, chosen by Evelyn M. Simpson, eds. Helen Gardner and Timothy Healy (Oxford, 1967), p. 111.
17 I am indebted to A. E. Malloch, "The Technique and Function of the Renaissance Paradox," *SP*, LIII (1956), 191–203.
18 Donne, *Selected Prose*, pp. 5, 6.
19 John Donne, *The Elegies and the Songs and Sonnets*, ed. Helen Gardner (Oxford, 1965), p. 53.
20 Malloch, *SP*, LIII, p. 195.
21 Some of this analysis has appeared previously in my article "Paradox in Donne," *Studies in the Renaissance*, XIII (1966), 266–287.

22 Robert Ellrodt, *Les Poètes Métaphysiques Anglais,* Première Partie, Tome I: "John Donne et Les Poètes de la Tradition Chrétienne" (Paris, 1960), p. 92.
23 Herbert J. C. Grierson, ed., *The Poems of John Donne,* 2 vols. (Oxford, 1912), I, 273–274; II, 81–100.
24 Ellrodt, *Poètes Métaphysiques,* p. 86.
25 Ibid., pp. 86–87.
26 Burke, *The Philosophy of Literary Form,* p. 28.
27 Donne, *Elegies and the Songs,* pp. 77–78.
28 Leonard Unger, *Donne's Poetry and Modern Criticism* (Chicago, 1950), p. 75.
29 Aron Gurwitsch, "Intentionality, Constitution, and Intentional Analysis," *Phenomenology,* ed. Joseph J. Kockelmans (Anchor Books; Garden City, N. Y., 1967), pp. 128–129.
30 John Donne, *The Divine Poems,* ed. Helen Gardner (Oxford, 1952), p. 2.
31 *The Poems of Sir Walter Ralegh,* ed. Agnes C. Latham (London, 1951); pp. 16–17; I have regularized the spelling.
32 Wayne C. Booth, *The Rhetoric of Fiction* (Phoenix Books; Chicago, 1967).
33 Analyses of *Paradise Lost* to which I am particularly indebted are the following: D. C. Allen, "Milton and the Descent to Light," *JEGP,* LX (1961), pp. 614–630; Jackson I. Cope, *The Metaphoric Structure of "Paradise Lost"* (Baltimore, 1962); Anne Davidson Ferry, *Milton's Epic Voice* (Cambridge, Mass., 1963); Stanley Eugene Fish, *Surprised by Sin: The Reader in "Paradise Lost"* (New York, 1967); C. S. Lewis, *A Preface to "Paradise Lost"* (Oxford, 1942); Isabel Gambel MacCaffrey, *Paradise Lost as "Myth"* (Cambridge, Mass., 1959); William G. Madsen, "Earth the Shadow of Heaven: Typological Symbolism in *Paradise Lost,*" *PMLA,* LXXV (1960), pp. 519–526; Arnold Stein, *Answerable Style* (Minneapolis, 1953); Harold E. Toliver, "Complicity of Voice in *Paradise Lost,*" *MLQ,* XXV (1964), pp. 153–170; George Williamson, "The Education of Adam," *MP,* LXI (1963), pp. 96–109.
34 All citations of *Paradise Lost* are from John Milton, *Complete Poems and Major Prose,* ed. Merritt Y. Hughes (New York, 1957).
35 Cf. A. O. Lovejoy, "Milton and the Paradox of the Fortunate Fall," *Essays in the History of Ideas* (New York, 1955), pp. 277–295.
36 Cf. the description of the "mystical dance" of the angels before God's throne after He manifests the Son (v.615ff.), which in being compared to the movements of the planets is mirrored in the description of the patterns of creation in Book VII, where there is continual emphasis on creation as a pattern of division and separation under the sign of harmony.
37 Milton, *Complete Poems,* p. 993.
38 Fish, *Surprised by Sin,* p. 38.
39 Henri Bergson, *Laughter,* in *Comedy,* ed. Wylie Sypher (Anchor Books; Garden City, N. Y. 1956), pp. 72–73.
40 Frye, *Anatomy of Criticism,* p. 169.
41 Ibid., p. 170.
42 Ben Jonson, *Volpone,* ed. Alvin B. Kernan (New Haven and London, 1962). All references to the play are to this Yale Edition.

43 All citations to *Macbeth* are from *The Complete Plays and Poems of William Shakespeare,* ed. William Allan Neilson and Charles Jarvis Hill (Cambridge, Mass., 1942).
44 I am indebted to G. Wilson Knight, *The Wheel of Fire* (London, 1968), pp. 140ff., for some of the germs of this interpretation.
45 Cf. The Arden Shakespeare *Macbeth,* ed. Kenneth Muir (New York, 1964), pp. xxxiii ff.
46 This critical metaphor is borrowed from Burke, *The Philosophy of Literary Form,* pp. 49–50.
47 Murray Krieger, *A Window to Criticism: Shakespeare's Sonnets and Modern Poetics* (Princeton, N. J., 1964), pp. 202–207.
48 Frye, *Anatomy of Criticism,* p. 122.

Walton: The Romance of Gentility

1 Henry Fielding, *Tom Jones,* New American Library (New York, 1963), p. 364.
2 Henry James, "Preface to 'The Princess Casamassima,'" in *The Art of the Novel: Critical Prefaces,* ed. Richard P. Blackmur (New York, 1937), p. 68.
3 *Tom Jones,* pp. 215–219.
4 Charles Dickens, *Oliver Twist,* Rinehart edition, ed. J. Hillis Miller (New York, 1962), p. 3. For my remarks on *Oliver Twist,* I am indebted to Miller's introduction to this edition and to Joseph M. Duffy, Jr., "Another Version of Pastoral: *Oliver Twist,*" *ELH, A Journal of English Literary History,* XXXV (1968), 403–421.
5 Ibid., p. 59.
6 Ibid., p. 236.
7 Joseph Conrad, *Lord Jim,* Riverside edition, ed. Morton Dauwen Zabel (Boston, 1958), p. 95.
8 Ibid., p. 6.
9 Ibid., p. 7.
10 James Joyce, *Finnegans Wake* (New York, 1958), pp. 3, 628.
11 Daniel Defoe, *The Life, Adventures and Piracies of the Famous Captain Singleton,* ed., James Sutherland, Everyman's Library (New York, 1963), p. 1. Subsequent page references to this edition will appear in parentheses following the quotes.
12 Michael Shinagel, *Daniel Defoe and Middle-Class Gentility* (Cambridge, Mass., 1968), pp. 170–176.
13 Ibid., pp. 137–141.
14 Daniel Defoe, *The Life and Adventures of Robinson Crusoe,* ed. James Sutherland, Riverside edition (Boston, 1968), p. 82.
15 Daniel Defoe, *The History and Remarkable Life of the Truly Honourable Col. Jacque . . . ,* ed., Samuel Holt Monk, Oxford English Novels (London, 1965), p. 1. Subsequent page references to this edition will appear in parentheses following the quotes.
16 The theme of gratitude, a prominent one in Defoe, does not in general lend itself to the interpretation given here. See Maximillian E. Novak, *Defoe and the Nature of Man* (London, 1963), pp. 113–128.
17 *Col. Jacque,* pp. xv–xvi.

18 On the broader significance of this romantic motif, see Walter R. Davis, *Idea and Act in Elizabethan Fiction* (Princeton, 1969), pp. 25–27.
19 Daniel Defoe, *Moll Flanders,* ed. James Sutherland, Riverside edition (Boston, 1959), p. 13. Subsequent page references to this edition will appear in parentheses following the quotes.
20 G. A. Starr, *Defoe and Spiritual Autobiography* (Princeton, 1965), p. 132.
21 Ibid., p. 162.
22 Lionel Trilling, "Introduction," *Emma,* Riverside edition (Boston, 1957), p. x.
23 Robert R. Columbus, "Conscious Artistry in *Moll Flanders,*" *Studies in English Literature,* III (1963), 420–422.
24 Ian Watt, *The Rise of the Novel: Studies in Defoe, Richardson, and Fielding* (Berkeley and Los Angeles, 1959), p. 70. My debt to Watt should be apparent throughout this study.
25 Mary Manley, *Secret Memoirs and Manners of Several Persons of Quality of Both Sexes From the New Atalantis, an Island in the Mediterranean* (London, 1736), Vol. I, 74.
26 Ibid., pp. 76–77.
27 Ibid., p. 82.
28 Daniel Defoe, *Roxana . . .* , ed. Jane Jack, Oxford English Novels (London, 1964), p. 5. Subsequent page references to this edition will appear in parentheses following the quotes.
29 Steven Marcus, *The Other Victorians: A Study of Sexuality and Pornography in Mid-Nineteenth Century England* (New York, 1966), pp. 268–277.
30 The notation of time in this passage and the subsequent details (deleted here) about the origin, fabric, design, and value of the costume lend concreteness to a scene otherwise defined by its dreamlike quality.
31 Northrop Frye, *The Anatomy of Criticism: Four Essays* (New York, 1966), p. 197.
32 W. J. Harvey, "The Human Context," in *The Theory of the Novel,* ed. Philip Stevick (New York, 1967), p. 235.
33 Ibid.
34 C. G. Jung, "The Psychology of the Child Archetype," in Jung and C. Kerenyi, *Introduction to a Science of Mythology,* trans. R. F. C. Hull (London, 1951), p. 109.

Day: Joyce's Waste Land

1 F. O. Matthiessen, *The Achievement of T. S. Eliot*, rev. ed. (New York, 1947), p. 53.

2 Thomas M. Lorch, "The Relationship between *Ulysses* and *The Waste Land*," *Texas Studies in Literature and Language*, VI (1964), 132. For an earlier and more general discussion of the subject, see Claude-Edmonde Magny, "A Double Note on James Joyce and T. S. Eliot," in *T. S. Eliot: A Symposium*, ed. Richard March and Tambimuttu (Chicago, 1949), pp. 208–217.

3 Lorch, *TSLL*, VI, 131–132.

4 Conrad Aiken records that when he read *The Waste Land* for review in 1923, he recognized certain passages with which he "had long been familiar . . . as poems, or part-poems." ("An Anatomy of Melancholy," in *T. S. Eliot: The Man and His Work*, ed. Alan Tate [New York: Delta, 1966], p. 196.)

5 The importance of this point for *Ulysses* was perceived and emphasized as early as 1932 by no less a figure than C. G. Jung, whose essay on the novel earned Joyce's "grateful appreciation." Jung dwells particularly on some of the most important passages discussed in the present study. See "*Ulysses:* A Monologue," *The Collected Works of C. G. Jung*, XV (New York, 1966), 128–130, 132–134.

6 Frank O'Conner, "James Joyce," *American Scholar*, XXXVI (1967), 476.

7 Robert M. Adams, *Surface and Symbol* (New York, 1962), pp. 146–147.

8 A. Walton Litz, *The Art of James Joyce* (New York, 1961), pp. 8–27.

9 Adams, *Surface and Symbol*, p. 113.

10 It is worth noting that *Hamlet* must have exerted a particular influence on Joyce's mind just at the time when his "ragbag" method of composition was flowering; he delivered a series of twelve lectures on *Hamlet* in Trieste in November 1912. See Richard Ellmann, ed., *Giacomo Joyce* (New York, 1968), p. xi. Ellmann's introduction and the text (pp. xii, xvi–xvii, 3, 7, 10) show materials from *Hamlet* intertwined with images which will appear in *Ulysses.* See also Ellmann's *James Joyce* (New York, 1959), pp. 353–359, for additional discussion of Joyce's relations with Signorina Amalia Popper and the writing of *Giacomo Joyce*; notably for our purposes Ellmann cites the idea of God as an "eater of carrion" (p. 356). The text of *Hamlet* used here is found in *Sixteen Plays of Shakespeare*, ed. George Lyman Kittredge (Boston, 1946).

11 See Maurice Beebe, "James Joyce: Barnacle Goose and Lapwing," *PMLA,* LXXI (1956), 317; William M. Schutte, *Joyce and Shakespeare* (New Haven, 1957), pp. 95–120, *passim.*
12 Harry Blamires (*The Bloomsday Book* [London, 1966], pp. 83–84, 185), argues that a reference to God is clearly intended here.
13 See Schutte, *Joyce and Shakespeare,* p. 92.
14 In this connection, if Macintosh is considered as a ghost, it is pertinent to recall that Joyce is said to have maintained that the true "hero" of *Hamlet,* the character which controls and dominates everything in the action, is not Hamlet, but the Ghost. (See Louis Gillet, *Claybook for James Joyce,* trans. G. Markow-Totevy [London and New York, 1958], p. 104.) The relationships of the themes of Shakespeare, ghosts, paternity, and Sabellianism are elaborately analyzed in William T. Noon, S.J., *Joyce and Aquinas* (New Haven, 1957), pp. 114–125.
15 See Beebe, *PMLA,* LXXI, 318.
16 For the importance of this cluster in *Hamlet* and Joyce's work, see Ellmann, *James Joyce,* p. 356.
17 H. K. Russell, "The Incarnation in *Ulysses,*" *Modern Fiction Studies,* IV (1958), 53.
18 Richard Ellmann, "Ulysses, the Divine Nobody," in *Twelve Original Essays on Great English Novels,* ed. Charles Shapiro (Detroit, 1960), p. 236.
19 Ibid., p. 241.
20 This passage from *Ulysses* perhaps throws light on one of the few but significant changes made by Eliot in translating the second part of "Dans le Restaurant" (1916–17) into Part IV of *The Waste Land.* "Un courant de sous-mer l'emporta très loin" became "A current under sea / *Picked his bones* in whispers" (italics mine).
21 John O. Lyons, "The Man in the Macintosh," *A James Joyce Miscellany: Second Series,* ed. Marvin Magalaner (Carbondale, Ill., 1959), pp. 133–138; John Henry Raleigh, " 'Who Was M'Intosh?'," *James Joyce Review,* III (1959), 59–62; John J. Duffy, "The Painful Case of M'Intosh," *Studies in Short Fiction,* II (1964–65), 183–185. Robert Crosman ("Who Was M'Intosh?" *James Joyce Quarterly,* VI [1968], 128–136) accepts the identification with Duffy on the literal level, but sees Macintosh as a ghostly "double" of Bloom.
22 Ellmann, *James Joyce,* p. 530.
23 William York Tindall, *A Reader's Guide to James Joyce* (New York: Noonday, 1959), p. 161.
24 In the notesheets for *Ulysses,* Joyce comments on the character by calling him "Mockintosh"; see Adams, *Surface and Symbol,* p. 145.
25 Matt. 28:9,10; Mark 16:12–14; Luke 24:13–43; John 20:14–29; 21:1–14. All the Biblical references in this study are to the King James version.
26 The ass appears to have been a late addition to the MS; see A. Walton Litz, "Joyce's Notes for the Last Episodes of *Ulysses,*" *Modern Fiction Studies* IV (1958), 8.
27 Hans Leisegang, "The Mystery of the Serpent," *Pagan and Christian Mysteries: Papers from the Eranos Yearbooks,* ed. Joseph Campbell (New York: Harper Torchbooks, 1963), p. 56.

28 Since the above was originally written, the significance of many of the symbols discussed at this point as indicating God, absent from Bloom's existence, and as continuing pervasively into the fabric of *Finnegans Wake,* has been pointed out by Bernard Benstock, "L. Boom as Dreamer in *Finnegans Wake,*" *PMLA,* LXXII (1967), 91–97.

29 Matt. 20:1–16.

30 A detailed and interesting account of the Dublin-London theosophical societies and the books, rituals, and symbols they chiefly used is given by Kathleen Raine, "Yeats, the Tarot, and the Golden Dawn," *Sewanee Review* (Winter, 1969), pp. 112–148. The extent, depth, and accuracy of Joyce's knowledge of his contemporaries' theosophical dabblings are difficult to assess; but the fact that he satirized them (as in "Scylla and Charybdis," "Cyclops," "Oxen of the Sun," and "Circe") does not mean that the symbols and doctrines could not have been grist to his mill. Much was made of *theriomorphic* gods (p. 114), including the donkey and the "Great Cackler," and one would like to know whether Joyce knew that Yeats's name in the Brotherhood, which he acquired in 1887 (p. 116), was *Demon est Deus Inversus*—the title of the *eleventh* chapter, Book II, of Blavatsky's *Secret Doctrine.*

31 See Walter M. Adams, *The House of the Hidden Places* (London, 1895), pp. 200–201 (Joyce's copy, dated 1902 on the flyleaf, is in the Slocum Collection of the Yale University Library); and Éliphas Lévi, *Transcendental Magic,* trans. and ed. Arthur E. Waite (London, 1962), pp. 104n., 386, 390, 428.

32 See Denis Saurat, *Literature and the Occult Tradition* (New York, 1966), pp. 67–77. For an extended discussion of Hermetism-Kabbalism, see Frances A. Yates, *Giordano Bruno and the Hermetic Tradition* (London, 1964); William York Tindall, "James Joyce and the Hermetic Tradition," *Journal of the History of Ideas,* XV (1954), 23–29.

33 See Richard Cavendish, *The Black Arts* (New York, 1967), pp. 53, 79.

34 See Joseph Campbell and Henry Morton Robinson, *A Skeleton Key to "Finnegans Wake"* (New York, 1944), pp. 165–167, 171–172, 178, n. 28, 193–195; and Tindall, *Reader's Guide to James Joyce,* pp. 142, 162, 171, on the significance of "eleven" in *Ulysses.* An example of the length to which Joyce carried this semiprivate symbolism in the *Wake* is "Tutankhamen," a resurrection symbol; the name, with eleven letters, appears eleven times (James S. Atherton, *The Books at the Wake* [London, 1959], p. 195, n. 1).

35 Evert Sprinchorn ("A Portrait of the Artist as Achilles," in *Approaches to the Twentieth-Century Novel,* ed. John E. Unterecker [New York, 1965], pp. 33–34) discusses this passage and identifies the consumptive as Pilate, the hour of eleven as Stephen's "ascension."

36 We should remember that Joyce insisted on retaining the inaccurate "crosstrees" in this passage in order to emphasize the idea of the Crucifixion (Frank Budgen, *James Joyce and the Making of "Ulysses"* [London, 1937], p. 57).

37 Since this essay was written, Joseph Campbell, in *The Masks of God: Creative Mythology* (New York, 1968), pp. 259–260, has made a more ambitious claim for the number eleven. It is the number of restoration, and in conjunction with Mr. Bloom's thirty-two (the rate

of acceleration of falling bodies) forms 1132, a "number clue" to the leading theme of *Finnegans Wake* and a number that recurs throughout Joyce's work in many forms. It symbolizes Fall with Redemption, Death with Resurrection, Tree of Eden and Tree of Calvary, *felix culpa*. Its moral theology is given in the verse "For God has consigned all men to disobedience that he may have mercy upon all," which happily occurs in Rom. 11:32. (One might add that the Gospel of John is also significant in Christian numerology. John is the only Evangelist to relate the raising of Lazarus from the dead, and this story is given in his *eleventh* chapter.)

38 Luke 24:30; John 21:13.

39 John 21:1–14.

40 See Lorch, *TSLL*, VI, p. 125.

41 The most detailed reconstruction of the action in this confusing scene is that of S. Foster Damon, "The Odyssey in Dublin," *Joyce: Two Decades of Criticism*, ed. Seon Givens (New York, 1948), pp. 220–221; see also Daniel Weiss, "The End of the 'Oxen of the Sun': An Analysis of the Boosing Scene in James Joyce's *Ulysses*," *The Analyst*, no. IX (December 1955), pp. 1–16.

42 Matt. 8:20.

43 *St. Andrew Daily Missal* (Bruges, 1953), pp. 942–943.

44 Budgen, *Making of "Ulysses,"* p. 172.

45 Iona and Peter Opie, eds., *The Oxford Dictionary of Nursery Rhymes* (Oxford, 1952), pp. 229–232. A fuller discussion of the Hebrew chant and its implications in *Ulysses* is found in Arnold Goldman, *The Joyce Paradox* (London, 1966), pp. 130–132.

46 For the sources of the fox riddle and the lines which Stephen alters and inserts, see Weldon Thornton, *Allusions in "Ulysses"* (Chapel Hill, 1968), pp. 30–31.

47 Prudentius, "Hymnus ad galli cantum." For a detailed historical account of the tradition, see Don Cameron Allen, *Image and Meaning* (Baltimore, 1968), pp. 231–240.

48 Ellmann, *James Joyce*, p. 794.

49 See Exod. 2:3–10.

50 Eliot's view of history in these poems is explored in Harvey Gross, "*Gerontion* and the Meaning of History," *PMLA*, LXXIII (1958), 299–304, though the similarity with Joyce's hero is not pointed out.

51 It is interesting to note that in the Buffalo manuscript of "Proteus" the passages concerning the bulrushes, "You will not be my master," "Dog of my enemy," "Dogskull, dogsniff . . . dogsbody's body," and "his grandmother" were all inserted in the margin, indicating that in Joyce's mind they probably formed part of the same thematic overlay. There seems to be no exact source for Mr. Deasy's phrase, but it suggests the closing lines of *In Memoriam*, or Arnold's "flux of mortal things . . . moving inly to one far-set goal" from "Westminster Abbey."

52 See Budgen, *Making of "Ulysses,"* pp. 53–54; T. H. White, *The Bestiary* (New York: Capricorn, 1960), pp. 15–17.

53 This calumny, apparently of Hebrew origin, is ancient enough to appear in Origen's *Contra Celsum*; see Joseph Klausner, *Jesus of Nazareth* (New York, 1927), pp. 23–24.

54 Joan Evans and Mary S. Serjeantson, *English Medieval Lapidaries* (New York, 1960), p. 23.
55 See Jung, "*Ulysses:* A Monologue," p. 129.
56 This was Joyce's own feeling in childhood, not easily discarded (Ellmann, *James Joyce,* p. 25). He may, however, have been familiar with the bestiary tradition (White, *The Bestiary,* p. 50) that wolves are born during spring thunderstorms and that this phenomenon symbolizes the fall of Lucifer, since Stephen, just after his meeting with the "wolfdog" associates thunder with himself as Lucifer falling (50). Both Joyce and Eliot ("There is not even silence in the mountains / But dry sterile thunder without rain") may have observed or known of the Alpine folk custom which continues to this day, of marking Easter or the coming of spring with artificial thunder. (See Ellmann, *James Joyce,* p. 423; "Easter Thunderclaps–Fatal Celebration," *New York Herald Tribune,* 11 April 1966, p. 2, col. 4; Fritz Senn, "Some Zurich Allusions in *Finnegans Wake,*" *The Analyst,* XIX (1960), 2–12. Alternatively, one of Eliot's probable sources (Countess Marie Larisch, *My Past* [London, 1913], p. 67), tells of how the Empress Elizabeth took shelter during a storm at the hut of a demented old woman who said that her dead son, who had been lying drowned at the bottom of a nearby lake for seven years, would return during a thunderstorm.
57 See Lorch, *TSLL,* p. 127.
58 Tindall remarks of this passage (*Reader's Guide to James Joyce,* p. 190) that "dog chases god."
59 Helen Gardner, *The Art of T. S. Eliot* (New York, 1950), p. 92.
60 See E. A. Wallis Budge, *Osiris: The Egyptian Religion of Resurrection* (New York, 1961), frontispiece plates and illustrations on pp. 50, 329.
61 Isidore of Seville, like Augustine, takes twenty-two to be a symbol of completion, of all that exists, since "God made twenty-two things." See Cavendish, *Black Arts,* p. 80; Vincent F. Hopper, *Medieval Number Symbolism* (New York, 1938), pp. 87, 101, 111.
62 Of this passage Robert M. Adams remarks with irony (*Surface and Symbol,* p. 111), "Of course, the very indifference of the crowd and ineffectuality of the dog may be read, if one wishes, as a pathetic picture of God in the modern world, where truth cries out in the streets and no man regards it." Such a reading is without doubt farfetched for this passage alone, but is far from inapplicable to the entire dog-God motif of *Ulysses.* Cleanth Brooks, in a recently published essay ("Joyce's *Ulysses:* Symbolic Poem, Biography, or Novel?" in *Imagined Worlds: Essays on Some English Novels and Novelists in Honour of John Butt,* ed. Maynard Mack and Ian Gregor [London, 1968], pp. 419–440), takes issue with Adams on this specific point and on the thematic value of the dog-God material in general. Brooks examines in some detail, as parts of a definite structure of imagery, many of the related images with which the present study is concerned; his conclusion, however, is that while the dog in *Ulysses* is "not a mechanical counter," its chief function is as "one of several symbols of the beastly" (p. 431).
63 See Benstock, *PMLA,* LXXII, 97, for an ingenious commentary on this passage, in which Macintosh is seen as representing God, lost, absent, or unknown to Bloom.

64 Heb. 4:14; 13:1–2. There is no "first" Epistle to the Hebrews, and the presence of the "first/farced" modification in both *Ulysses* and the *Wake* would seem to indicate a thematic connection in Joyce's mind.
65 Schutte, *Joyce and Shakespeare*, pp. 148–152; Beebe, *PMLA*, LXXI, 317–318.
66 Douglas Knight, "The Reading of *Ulysses*," *English Literary History*, XIX (1952) 71, 79, 80.
67 C. M. Bowra, "T. S. Eliot," *The Creative Experiment* (London, 1949), pp. 166, 180–181.
68 Lorch, *TSLL*, VI, 129–130. For a full chronology of the serial publications of *Ulysses*, see Litz, *The Art of James Joyce*, Appendix C.
69 *The Letters of James Joyce*, ed. Stuart Gilbert and Richard Ellmann (New York, 1966); Forrest Read, ed., *Pound/Joyce* (New York, 1966); B. L. Reid, *The Man from New York: John Quinn and His Friends* (New York, 1968).
70 Read, *Pound/Joyce*, pp. 59, 60.
71 Ibid., pp. 96, 103.
72 Ibid., pp. 125–126.
73 Ibid., p. 128.
74 Ibid., p. 131.
75 Leonard Woolf, *Beginning Again* (New York, 1964), pp. 245–247. It was through Eliot that Miss Weaver approached the Woolfs; they decided to publish *Ulysses*, but after several efforts found that no English printer would risk prosecution, and so abandoned the project; see Michael Holroyd, *Lytton Strachey* (London, 1968), II, 368.
76 Read, *Pound / Joyce*, pp. 143, 158, 160.
77 *The Egoist*, V (1918), 87.
78 See Reid, *Man from New York*, p. 406.
79 Ibid., p. 405
80 Ibid., p. 407.
81 T. S. Eliot, "Contemporanea," *The Egoist*, V (1918), 84–85.
82 T. S. Eliot, "A Foreign Mind," *Athenaeum*, no. 5643 (4 July 1919), p. 553.
83 See Patricia Hutchins, *James Joyce's World* (London, 1957), pp. 106, 239.
84 Ibid., p. 240.
85 See Read, *Pound / Joyce*, pp. 165, 166. Pound also urged Joyce to write to Eliot, to insure his presence.
86 This is described at some length by Wyndham Lewis, *Blasting and Bombardiering* (London, 1937), pp. 272–294.
87 T. S. Eliot, "*Ulysses*, Order, and Myth," *Dial*, LXXV (1923), 480–483.
88 Richard Aldington, "The Influence of Mr. James Joyce," *English Review*, XXXII (1921), 333–341.
89 Quoted in Hutchins, *James Joyce's World*, p. 128.
90 Reid, *Man from New York*, pp. 488–489.
91 *Dial*, LXXI (1921), 216.
92 Ibid., LXXII (1922), 189, 192.
93 Ibid., p. 403.
94 Ibid., p. 513.
95 Ibid., pp. 623–629.

96 Ibid., pp. 621–622.
97 Ibid., LXXIII (1922), 329.
98 Ibid., pp. 434–437; LXXIV (1923), 188; LXXV (1923), 180–181.
99 *Dial,* LXXV (1923), 480–483; *Criterion,* I (October, 1922), 94–103.
100 Grover Smith, Jr., *T. S. Eliot's Poetry and Plays* (Chicago, 1956), p. 71.
101 David E. Ward, "The Cult of Impersonality: Eliot, St. Augustine, and Flaubert," *Essays in Criticism,* XVII (1967), 175.
102 *Dial,* LXXI (October, 1921), 453.
103 Ibid., p. 452.
104 Ellmann, *James Joyce,* p. 546. See also *Letters,* III, 292–300.
105 Nathan Halper, "Joyce and Eliot: A Tale of Shem and Shaun," *Nation,* CC (1965), 590–595.
106 Tindall, in *A Reader's Guide to Finnegans Wake* (New York, 1969), goes into yet greater detail. He finds in the *Wake* no less than seventeen references to *The Waste Land* and other poems of Eliot, usually as parodies of specific lines (see esp. pp. 85, 94, 106, 126–127, 155, 160, 181, 204, 227, 229, 261, 262, 329), and eight passages in which Eliot is represented as a rival, as having taken and used material from *Ulysses,* and sometimes less charitably as a plagiarist (pp. 33, 60, 78, 102, 118, 142, 181, 233). However, it is probable that Joyce's annoyance arose solely from what he regarded as an inequitable distribution of fame and fortune, and that he completely understood and sympathized with Eliot's absorption and use of material from *Ulysses,* for as Ellmann has pointed out (Introduction to Stanislaus Joyce, *My Brother's Keeper* [New York, 1958] p. xv), "inspired cribbing was always part of Joyce's talent. His gift was for transforming material, not originating it."
107 Eliot's letters to John Quinn during 1922 furnish information on the progress of the notes. On June 25 he speaks of "notes that I am adding" (Reid, *Man from New York,* p. 534), but whether this means that he is working on the notes or is about to start is uncertain. On July 19 he says, "I shall rush forward the notes to go at the end" (p. 535), but this again is ambiguous. On the whole it seems safe to assign the composition of the notes to the late summer or fall of 1922. Eliot's account of writing the notes is in *On Poetry and Poets* (New York, 1967), p. 121. See also the comments of Eliot and Pound quoted in Hugh Kenner, *The Invisible Poet: T. S. Eliot* (New York, 1959), pp. 151–152.
108 The title page of *The Waste Land* manuscript, exhibited at the New York Public Library in the winter of 1968–69, not only bears this exclamation but the sentences which immediately precede it in Conrad, giving a valuable clue to Eliot's intentions in the conduct of the poem.
109 See D. D. Paige, ed., *The Letters of Ezra Pound, 1907–1941* (New York, 1950), pp. 169–172; T. S. Eliot, "Swinburne as Poet," *The Sacred Wood,* rev. ed. (New York, 1927), p. 150; Robert A. Day, "The 'City Man' in *The Waste Land:* The Geography of Reminiscence," *PMLA,* LXXX (1965), 288–289. For further clearly demonstrated echoes not acknowledged by Eliot, see Giorgio Melchiori, *The Tightrope Walkers* (New York, 1956), pp. 63–71; George W. Nitchie, "A Note on Eliot's Borrowings," *Massachusetts Review* VI (1965), 405.

110 T. S. Eliot, *The Use of Poetry and the Use of Criticism* (London, 1933), p. 70.
111 Ibid., p. 141.
112 Kenner, *The Invisible Poet,* p. 130.
113 See Paige, *Letters of Ezra Pound,* p 171.
114 See Melchiori, *Tightrope Walkers,* p. 87.
115 These are suggested by Lorch, "*Ulysses* and *The Waste Land,*" pp. 124–125.
116 Smith, *Eliot's Poetry and Plays,* p. 76.
117 See Eliot's *On Poetry and Poets,* p. 119, and *Use of Poetry,* pp. 69–70, 138–141.
118 Allen Austin, "T. S. Eliot's Theory of Personal Expression," *PMLA,* LXXXI (1966), 303, n. 5.
119 Eliot, *Use of Poetry,* pp. 139–141.
120 In this connection Eliot cites Housman's description of his own poetic passivity in composition with approval as a confirmation of his experience (ibid., p. 138, n. 1).
121 Leonard Woolf, ed., *A Writer's Diary* (New York, 1954), pp. 349, 46, 49.
122 T. S. Eliot, *After Strange Gods* (New York, 1934), pp. 52, 40, 41.
123 For discussions of the place of religion in Joyce's thought at this period see Ellmann, "*Ulysses,* the Divine Nobody," pp. 234–239; S. L. Goldberg, *The Classical Temper* (London, 1961), pp. 306–311.
124 Kathleen Raine, "The Poet of our Time," *T. S. Eliot: A Symposium,* pp. 78–79.
125 See Marvin Magalaner and Richard M. Kain, *Joyce: The Man, The Work, The Reputation* (New York, 1956), pp. 162–192.
126 Lionel Trilling, "James Joyce in His Letters," *Commentary,* XLV (1968), 64.
127 See Ellmann, *James Joyce,* pp. 25, 629.
128 The difference is put clearly and forcefully by Joseph Campbell (*Masks of God,* pp. 260–261): ". . . the artist reads [Christian symbols] in the universally known old Greco-Roman, Celto-Germanic, Hindu-Buddhist-Taoist, Neoplatonic way, as referring to an experience of the mystery behind theology that is immanent in all things, including gods, demons, and flies. The priests, on the other hand, are insisting on the absolute finality of their Old Testament concept of a personal creator God 'out there,' who, though omnipresent, omniscient . . . is ontologically distinct from the living substance of his world." On the latter point see William T. Noon, S.J., "James Joyce: Unfacts, Fiction, and Facts," *PMLA,* LXXVI (1961), 262–263.
129 George Williamson, *A Reader's Guide to T. S. Eliot* (New York, 1953), pp. 134–135; Smith, *Eliot's Poetry and Plays,* pp. 78–79; Melchiori, *Tightrope Walkers,* pp. 74–76, 79–80, 84.
130 Nathan A. Scott, Jr., "T. S. Eliot: A Contemporary Synthesis," *Rehearsals of Discomposure* (New York, 1952), pp. 215–217; A. D., "Some Notes on *The Waste Land,*" *Notes and Queries,* CXCV (1950), 367; James D. Merritt, "Eliot's *The Waste Land,* 74–75," *Explicator,* XXII (1964), Item 31; Herbert Knust, "Eliot's *The Waste Land,* 74," *Explicator,* XXIII (1965), Item 74.

131 A notable example, particularly in view of Joyce's and Eliot's knowledge of Dante, is the passage at the end of Canto I of the *Inferno* (lines 101–106) in which the She-Wolf, symbolizing incontinence (though the wolf was also a common symbol of the Devil; see White, *Bestiary*, pp. 59–60), is to be vanquished by the "Veltro" or Greyhound, which will bring *salute* or salvation. On the iconology of this paradox, see R. E. Kaske, "Dante's 'DXV' and 'Veltro,'" *Traditio*, XVII (1961), 227–252.

132 The point is made by Merritt; see note 130.

133 In his elaborate investigation of comparative mythology, *The Masks of God*, pp. 273–277) Joseph Campbell reaches an analogous conclusion by another route—since "it is of the essence of this philosophy that divinity inheres in the lowest as well as the noblest things, one of the most striking traits of its literature is the frequent representation of its arcana in coarse and even revolting symbols," one of these being the dog. In this connection Campbell sees the fairy dog of the Tristram legend, Stephen's dog on the beach, Eliot's dog, and their associated images as arising from the same basic mythmaking impulse. A medieval diagram of the music of the spheres (p. 100) with a three-headed Cerberus at the bottom linked by a snake to a God-figure at the top, explains why Joyce reveals dog to be God in reverse and why Eliot capitalizes "Dog." Ariel's song, the seeress, and the Hanged Man blend into the myth. For further detailed illustrations of the importance of this doctrine in the poetic thought of both Joyce and Eliot, and of its influence on their symbolism, see Jackson I. Cope, "*Ulysses*: Joyce's Kabbalah," *James Joyce Quarterly*, VII (1970), 93–113; John Senior, *The Way Down and Out: The Occult in Symbolist Literature* (Ithaca, N.Y., 1959), pp. 170–198.

134 Sir Ernest H. Shackleton, *South* (London, 1919), pp. 208–209.

135 Herbert Howarth (*Notes on Some Figures Behind T. S. Eliot* [Boston, 1964], p. 243) says unequivocally regarding this statement that Eliot "feared that Joyce's work, overpowering in its immensity, would color his own for the immediate future." Eliot's letters to Joyce and Quinn amply reinforce this statement.